On Human Fl

M000233978

On Human Flourishing

A Poetry Anthology

Edited by
D.J. MOORES,
JAMES O. PAWELSKI,
ADAM POTKAY,
EMMA MASON,
SUSAN J. WOLFSON *and*
JAMES ENGELL

McFarland & Company, Inc., Publishers
Jefferson, North Carolina

ALSO OF INTEREST: D.J. Moores, *The Ecstatic Poetic Tradition: A Critical Study from the Ancients through Rumi, Wordsworth, Whitman, Dickinson and Tagore* (McFarland, 2014)

LIBRARY OF CONGRESS CATALOGUING-IN-PUBLICATION DATA

On human flourishing : a poetry anthology / edited by D.J. Moores, James O. Pawelski, Adam Potkay, Emma Mason, Susan J. Wolfson and James Engell.
    p.   cm.
    Includes bibliographical references and index.

    ISBN 978-0-7864-9580-1 (softcover : acid free paper) ∞
    ISBN 978-1-4766-2135-7 (ebook)

    1. Happiness—Poetry.   2. Well-being—Poetry.   3. Quality of life—Poetry.   I. Moores, D. J.   II. Pawelski, James O., 1967–   III. Potkay, Adam, 1961–   IV. Mason, Emma.   V. Wolfson, Susan J., 1948–   VI. Engell, James, 1951–

PN6110.H14O5 2015
808.81'9353—dc23   2015028880

BRITISH LIBRARY CATALOGUING DATA ARE AVAILABLE

© 2015 D.J. Moores, James Pawelski, Adam Potkay, Emma Mason, Susan Wolfson and James Engell. All rights reserved

No part of this book may be reproduced or transmitted in any form or by any means, electronic or mechanical, including photocopying or recording, or by any information storage and retrieval system, without permission in writing from the publisher.

Front cover images © 2015 Thinkstock

Printed in the United States of America

McFarland & Company, Inc., Publishers
  Box 611, Jefferson, North Carolina 28640
    www.mcfarlandpub.com

For Buddy
(December 3, 2006–February 24, 2015)

Acknowledgments

We, the editors, wish to thank the following people and institutions for their generous assistance with this project: Aaron Boczkowski, Amanda Foster, Nekeisha Hatch, Anthony Melillo, and James Cowen. Other contributors to this project include the Library at Ocean County College and the Positive Psychology Center at the University of Pennsylvania. We also wish to thank Joseph Pupuri and Susanna Anaker for their diligent work as editorial assistants. Last, and perhaps most of all, we wish to extend a hearty thanks to the following associate editors whose input and devoted labor shaped this work in beautiful and meaningful ways: Gabriella Basile, Kelly Johnson, Meggan McGuire, David Torosian and Jamie Wasco.

Gabriella Basile teaches literature at the Performing Arts Academy, a prestigious high school for precocious, talented students in Lakehurst, New Jersey. Fluent in Italian, she contributed a number of fine translations to this anthology.

Kelly Johnson is a specialist in both literature and special education who currently works as an in-class support and reading teacher at Pinelands Regional High School in Tuckerton, New Jersey.

Meggan McGuire is finishing her master's degree in English at Rutgers University, where she teaches writing and serves as a graduate assistant in the English Literature Department.

David Torosian is the associate editor of the award-winning entertainment magazine *Closer Weekly*. When not chasing down celebrities, he continues to pursue his passion for travel and music.

Jamie Wasco teaches high school English at Perth Amboy Vocational and Technical High School. A gifted educator, she won the prestigious Governor's Teacher Recognition Program Award in 2013.

Table of Contents

About the Editors

James Engell is the Gurney Professor of English and a professor of comparative literature at Harvard University. He has authored or edited the following books: *Saving Higher Education in the Age of Money*; *The Committed Word: Literature and Public Values*; *Coleridge: The Early Family Letters* (editor); *Forming the CriticalMind*; *The Creative Imagination*; and *Coleridge's Biographia Literaria* (co-editor).

Emma Mason is a professor of English and comparative literary studies at the University of Warwick. A specialist in poetry and poetics, she examines in her work intersections of religion, emotion, and literature. Her published books include *Reading the Abrahamic Faiths*, *Women Poets of the Nineteenth Century*, *The Cambridge Introduction to Wordsworth*, and (with Mark Knight) *Nineteenth Century Religion and Literature*.

D.J. Moores is an associate professor of literature at National University in San Diego. He is the author of numerous scholarly articles and conference papers, as well as three critical books: *Mystical Discourse in Wordsworth and Whitman* (2006), *The Dark Enlightenment* (2010), and *The Ecstatic Poetic Tradition* (2014). In addition to compiling and editing *Wild Poets of Ecstasy: An Anthology of Ecstatic Verse* (2011), he is also the co-editor (with James Pawelski) of *The Eudaimonic Turn* (2012).

James O. Pawelski is a senior scholar at the University of Pennsylvania, where he serves as the founding director of the Master of Applied Positive Psychology (MAPP) Program and as a special advisor to the Positive Psychology Steering Committee. He is the founding executive director of the International Positive Psychology Association (IPPA) and a charter member of the board of directors of that organization.

Adam Potkay is a professor of English and a William R. Kenan Professor of Humanities at the College of William and Mary. Among other books, he wrote *The Story of Joy: From the Bible to Late Romanticism*, which won the Harry Levin Prize, the American Comparative Literature Association's award for the best book in literary history and literary criticism.

Susan J. Wolfson is a professor of English at Princeton University and the author of several critical essays and books involving the study of poetry. She has also edited and produced several editions, most recently for Harvard University Press's "Annotated" series. She has been the recipient of awards from the National Endowment for the Humanities, the Guggenheim Foundation, and the American Council of Learned Societies.

Introduction

D.J. MOORES

Can serious literature be about happiness, or what scholars today prefer to call human flourishing? The arbiters of literary taste, at least as narratives are considered, seem to have sided with unhappiness, ill-being, suffering, and tragedy. To be sure, there are notable exceptions, such as classical and Elizabethan comedies and well done but light-hearted novels and plays. The general point, however, is undeniable. William Faulkner likely would not have won the Nobel Prize if he only wrote happy stories about his fictional southern county. According to longstanding ideas, narrative, regardless of its genre, by necessity needs to be rooted in conflict, tension, and struggle because such elements rather effectively capture reader interest. Well-done narratives can surely be inspiring, but the nature of story-telling says characters in stories must be confronted with challenges, strife, loss, or grief, even if the reader is ultimately uplifted. In other words narratives need complication, or some thickening agent, to be interesting. To my knowledge, there are no interesting or critically acclaimed *narratives*, either classical or contemporary, that do not also integrally feature conflict, struggle and suffering. There simply is no such thing as an artistically complex story about someone who is happy and lives with other joyous people in pure felicity. As ideal and preferable as such a utopia may be, it is just not interesting *as a story*.

But what about non-narrative poetry, particularly the lyric? Here we find a genre rich in ideas about human well-being, not simply in a negative form as the condemnation of its opposite—ill-being—but in its many positive manifestations. The arbiters of literary taste, regardless of whether they consciously accept such an idea, must finally admit that the lyric is the one genre in which a serious writer can be excused and even applauded for reveling in happiness and human well-being. As this anthology shows, even our greatest poets seem to be more than casually interested in human flourishing. For some of these bards, well-being is even a principal concern—a preoccupation.

Great poets indeed often sing felicitously of felicity, capturing in verse the myriad complexities of what it means to be well in the fullest sense and

1

live a good, full human life. William Wordsworth, for instance, taught his readers to reconnect with the natural world and to be self-fulfilled through the cultivation of ethical engagement, self-emptying, and "wise passiveness." Walt Whitman, the nineteenth century's greatest and thus most problematic optimist, claimed that what was he was trying to convey in "Song of Myself" "is form, union, plan—it is eternal life—it is Happiness" (1318).[1] In the verse attributed to her, the medieval Indian poet Mirabai valiantly defied patriarchal and caste prejudices, finding inner peace by turning within herself and cultivating a sacred relationship with her god, Krishna. Throughout much of his poetry, E.E. Cummings waxed rhapsodic over the glories of spring, love, "Isness," and being "alive," all of which are related to his implied conception of the good life. Even contemporary poets, such as Mary Oliver, Sharon Olds, Wendell Berry, Galway Kinnell, Jane Hirshfield, Maya Angelou, and many others, seem to have devoted a central space in their verse to positive experience in its myriad manifestations as clarity, strength, growth, wisdom, peace, belongingness, forgiveness, gratitude, and so much else implied by the concept of human flourishing. Countless poets in the world's literary traditions have similarly used verse to capture the "soul at the white heat," to use Emily Dickinson's image. The literary canons plentifully offer poems about anguish, suffering, and despair, but they also contain a treasure trove of verse about the good life, variously conceived. The global poetic tradition thus represents a rich source of wisdom on the subject of well-being.

The world has finally caught up with such poetic wisdom in the recognition that well-being is neither literary rhetoric, the "honied lies of rhyme" and dreamy-eyed poets whose beautiful words belie the hard realities, as Byron famously wrote in *Childe Harold's Pilgrimage* (I.3.8)[2]; nor is it dismissible on the grounds that it is reducible to a naïve defense mechanism against such realities. To the contrary, well-being is quite real and rather substantial, as thinkers in several disciplines over the last decade have shown in various sustained inquires. The subject of being well now has an undeniable cachet.

The turn of the twenty-first century ushered in this new focus on well-being. Since then, psychologists have augmented a century-long focus on psychopathology, the study of psychological disease, with thousands of studies of the positive aspects of the healthy psyche. Medical researchers have paid close attention to the role of levels of happiness, hope, and optimism in their patients, exploring how these impact mortality rates and recovery time from surgery or illness. The spread of naturopathy has challenged the paradigm of medicine conceived as the mere treatment of disease, and wellness centers have sprouted across the West. Neurologists have mapped and even probed the brains of experienced meditation practitioners and other people who claim high levels of happiness, positive emotion, and life satisfaction. Economists have engaged in copious research in order to determine ways to measure the happiness of whole nations. Philosophers and ethicists have reignited the fires of ancient discussions about what it means to be well. Influential business leaders have taken a deep interest in what makes people succeed and organizations thrive. Many educators have embraced the notion that happiness should be a factor in the classroom, initiating ways to effect such an outcome. Some historians have moved away from examining human life solely in terms of war and political clashes, writing interesting histories of happiness. Architects have factored well-being into the aesthetics and functionality of their designs. Joy, ecstasy, wonder, and other forms of positive affect have emerged as highly credible subjects in literary discussions. Rumi's poetry, which configures well-being in complex ways, has outsold (by millions) even the best verse by Pulitzer Prize-winning poets. Well-being has come to occupy center stage in the collective consciousness and has indeed become an important subject of academic and popular inquiry.

In one sense it is possible to account for *how* the new millennium ushered in this focus on being well. An immediate source of the collective turn is the work of Martin Seligman, an influential psychologist who used his tenure as the APA president in 1998 to catalyze a radical transformation in psychology. With the help of several other top psychologists, Seligman significantly changed his discipline by inspiring a whole generation of researchers with the idea that the study of disease is only half of psychology's potential. The other "positive" half, his work compellingly shows, had been largely neglected until the end of the twentieth century. Positive psychology, as it is called, thus represents a deep concern with human well-being. One of the foundational principles in this branch of the psychological tree is that the study of the positive aspects of human experience, conceived first as happiness but then more recently as well-being, is as important as the study of disease. The findings in positive psychology seem to have overgrown disciplinary lines, creeping into several other fields of study, as well as popular culture, business, sports, and government.

However, the question remains: *Why* has positive psychology proven to be so fecund? What, in other words, were the conditions that enabled it to blossom? And why has it found such rich, receptive soil outside of its own domain in the past decade? These are complex questions. One way to answer them is look to *The Story of Joy* by Adam Potkay, one of the co-editors of this anthology. In his concluding chapter, Potkay clearly shows that the twentieth century was plagued by a negativity bias, the result of the widespread embrace of pessimism and despair that characterized the West after World War I. At such a point, concepts such as joy, happiness, and well-being came to be looked upon, given the collective disillusionment the war caused, as being soft, or worse, as symptoms of neurotic denial.[3] By the end of the century, however, many people inside and outside of academe became conscious of such a negativity bias. It is as if we awoke from a strange, collective nightmare in which the most important aspect in human life, human well-being, appeared as a symptom of psychopathology. Happiness was a disease, a naïve illusion we would do well to dispel. Those who have made the turn towards well-being heartily reject such a nightmare as nonsense, pointing to the metaphysical groundlessness of assuming that life warrants a response of pessimism and despair to its essentially negative realities. To the contrary, just as human life is characterized by suffering, tragedy, and other negatives, so is it deeply informed by love, connection, fulfillment, and a host of other forms of positivity, so many of which the twentieth century, at least until its end, deemed irrelevant and even construed as symptoms of psychopathology or objectionable politics.

Another factor in the answer to the question of why positive psychology has exerted such an enormous influence is to consider its widespread embrace as a response to the threat of species extinction. At the end of the twentieth century, no doubt in part because of millennia-old millennial fears, we seem to have become collectively conscious of several significant threats, such as global warming, nuclear proliferation, overpopulation, dwindling energy resources, and the like, all of which carry the potential of our species' complete demise. In some ways the recent turn towards well-being may be a reaction to the possibility that our species faces the all-too-real prospect of ultimately rendering itself extinct—the fate, incidentally, of 99.999% of all of the other species that have ever existed on the planet. Implied in such a statement is the idea that we think most fully and deeply about happiness and being well when we are staring their opposites in the face. In one sense, then, "the eudaimonic turn," as James Pawelski and I call it in an eponymous collection,[4] is the culmination of a century of negativity bias coupled with distressing challenges that carry with them the threat of ill-being, or worse.

It is important to note, nevertheless, that the central topic in the fruitful discussions about well-being now taking place is not merely *surviving*, which implies the minimal changes necessary for the perpetuation of human life, even if such changes entail living in conditions that, while deplorable, prove preferable to human extinction; the new discourse, rather, is about *thriving* in the fullest sense. What has re-emerged in the recent discourse on well-being is the concept of eudaimonia, an ancient Greek term best translated as "flourishing," a metaphor suggesting the full flowering of human life. According to such an image, surviving is not the same as thriving, a point Seligman has made in several of his writings. To be well in the fullest sense, then, one must do more than meet basic needs in a minimal way. One must grow, cultivate potentials, realize goals, relate to others, love, play, work, dream, and do so much else.

The poems in this anthology rest on such a premise. They suggest a twofold truth: (1) human beings are capable of not only enduring hardship, injustice, cruelty, illness, and tyranny but also doing so in a way that enables us to *triumph* over such adversity; and (2) there is a positive range of complex emotions, experiences, character traits, and states of being sometimes related to but not necessarily bound to discord, pain, and struggle. The poems selected here thus signify the human spirit at its apex, a complex juncture at which several complexities intersect: wisdom, virtue, strength, agency, intimacy, friendship, sociability, growth through overcoming hardship, and positive transformation through positive affect, as well as peak experiences, ecstasies, self-awareness, and love. This anthology represents the best aspects of human experience, the splendors of being fully alive.

No doubt, this last statement will be off-putting to many individuals, particularly some of those in academe. We do not typically use such grandiloquent language in common speech. When asked how we are doing, seldom do we say, "I am glorious," or worse, "I have fully flowered." To use such terms, in fact, would likely elicit suspicion in our interlocutor, who might surmise that we are cracked in the head, operating from some kind of neurotic defense mechanism that enables us to avoid the unpleasant aspects of life by over-identifying with the pleasantries of a saccharine existence. Regardless, sometimes life is glorious, and many human beings do, perhaps more than one realizes, fully flower. Although this life is often harsh and brutal, it also carries with it the potential for fulfillment and well-being. To be human is no doubt to suffer, but to be *fully* human, one might argue, is to experience the full range of eudaimonic possibilities that exist as potentials in nearly every lifespan. It is possible to soar in this life.

The Life Well Lived

So what does it mean to be well, or to live the good, full life implied by the concept of eudaimonia, not merely in the sense of surviving and minimally meeting basic needs but in the sense of thriving, or living in a manner that brings a sense of total fulfillment and completion? This is a difficult question to answer. The term *eudaimonia* was in use among the ancient Greeks for centuries before Aristotle, and, as one might expect, there was considerable disagreement over what constituted human fulfillment. For Homer, the good life involved honoring the gods, taking revenge, fully enjoying the pleasures and sensations of physicality, reveling in the glories of stealing cattle and women from rivals, and ultimately going back home to one's family. For Hesiod, to be well entailed doing one's work properly and not offending the gods. For other Greeks, particularly the dramatists, eudaimonia was a matter of luck or fate, existing beyond one's conscious control.

For still others, it signified the enjoyment of pleasures, the attainment of honor, or the acquisition of wealth. For Aristotle, to experience eudaimonia involved obeying, through the proper exercise of reason, one's *daimon*, or good spirit—*eudaimon* as a noun etymologically means good (*eu*) spirit (*daimon*)—whose dictates, if followed, enabled one to cultivate the highest virtues and thus live a blessed life. Even Aristotle, however, acknowledged the problem of so defining what constitutes a life well lived.

Later thinkers, particularly the Greek and Roman Stoics and Epicureans, as well as countless Jewish and Christian theologians, philosophers, poets, and others, continued the debate about the good, blessed life. Because I do not have the necessary space here in order to do justice to such intellectual history, I refer readers to part one of the introduction to the aforementioned work, *The Eudaimonic Turn: Well-being in Literary Studies*, in which my erudite colleague, James Pawelski, more thoroughly discusses the subject. Darrin McMahon's influential study, *Happiness: A History*, is another thorough treatment of the construct from antiquity all the way through the modern science of happiness.[5] The matter is complex, and there simply is not enough space to do it full justice here.

It is necessary to attempt some kind of an answer to the question, nevertheless, even if this means entering a centuries-long debate that will probably in some ways never be fully resolved. So let me explore the question by engaging six perspectives on eudaimonia: (1) Martha Nussbau's functional capabilities; (2) Seligman's PERMA, an acronym used to designate statistically measurable elements of well-being; (3) Christopher Peterson and Seligman's identification of virtues and strengths of character that seem to be universally valued; (4) several ideas on the ecstatic experience, the effects of which result in significant eudaimonic transformation; (5) concepts from depth psychology related to self-awareness and psychic wholeness through an engagement with the unconscious; and (6) poetic, religious, and philosophical wisdom on the power and centrality of love. Let us now deal with each of these perspectives in more detail.

Functional Capabilities

In her rejection of the paralyzing position that anti-essentialism[6] creates, philosopher Martha Nussbaum cites the existence of ten "universals" that do indeed transcend cultures and thus function as a common link in the human chain, serving as a kind of "soft essence." Nearly all human lives, she argues, are organized around conceptions of mortality, corporeality, cognition, early infant development, practical reason, affiliation with other human beings, relatedness to other species and to nature, humor and play, separateness, and strong separateness.[7] She is careful to avoid returning to the essentialism of old, however, by acknowledging that such universals "never turn up in ... [such a] vague and general form ... but always in some specific and historically rich cultural realization." Accompanying such universals is the idea that to live well it is necessary to exercise what Nussbaum calls "functional capabilities" in each of the aforementioned domains. These include (1) living a full life span; (2) having good health, proper nourishment, shelter, sexual satisfaction, and mobility; (3) being able to avoid non-beneficial pain and enjoying pleasure; (4) using the five senses and the mind; (5) having other-directed attachments to things and people beyond ourselves, the result of which is grief, love, longing, and gratitude; (6) being able to form a conception of the good and planning one's life around such a concept; (7) engaging in familial and social interaction; (8) having concern for and relatedness to animals, plants, and the natural world; (9) laughing, playing, and enjoying recreational activities; (10) living one's own life and nobody else's; and (10a) living one's life in one's own surroundings and context. Nussbaum argues that to be fully human and to live a good full life, it is necessary to actualize potentials through exercising functional capabilities. Implied in such an idea is the fulfillment of needs and the exercise of agency. To be well in this sense involves having one's physical, psychological, and social needs gratified and also exercising agency, that is, having the freedom to make decisions for oneself and to live according to one's conception of a satisfying life.[8]

In her discussion of capabilities, Nussbaum also offers a helpful definition of what it means to flourish. She argues that such human functional capabilities can be judged according to whether they fall above one of two possible thresholds: (1) "a threshold of capability to function, beneath which a life will be so impoverished that it will not be human at all"; and (2) "a somewhat higher threshold, beneath which those characteristic functions are available in such a reduced way that, though we may judge the form of life a human one, we will not think it a *good* human life."[9] To state the idea in positive form—living a good human life above the second threshold implies flourishing—well-being conceived in terms of needs gratification and the actualization of potentials through exercising functional capabilities.

Nussbaum's universals, capabilities, and thresholds strongly imply the necessity of appropriate *external* conditions necessary for human flourishing, such as strong familial and social networks, sufficient economic opportunities, political freedom, as well as possibilities for recreation, sexual gratification, and self-expression or self-realization. One cannot flourish if there is little food available and copious nuclear fallout in the air. As philosopher Sisela Bok points out in her work *Exploring Happiness: From Aristotle to Brain Science*, it is both sentimental and wrong to imagine that "happiness has nothing to do with standards of living, that it can be achieved equally well by all persons in spite of poverty, ill health, or denials of basic human rights; or that levels of happiness alone should count regardless of concern for such rights."[10] It is important, however, not to misconstrue what Bok is arguing by overstating the case. Human well-being, to an arguable extent, is dependent upon external conditions, but it is never reducible to them. Some people achieve a high level of happiness in spite of deplorable external conditions, while others never flourish, even though all of the external determinants seem to offer the possibility of doing so. It is necessary, therefore, to stress the role of the internal conditions that bear on well-being. Nussbaum's ideas do imply the need for such conditions, particularly biological and psychological factors. One cannot live a rich life, according to her benchmarks, with a body wracked by pain or a mind plagued by psychosis. For all of the important insight suggested in her approach, however, Nussbaum deliberately leaves her capabilities vague because she articulates them in the context of refuting anti-essentialism and offering a universal standard by which we might define humanness. To be too specific, at least in the context in which she writes, is to run the risk of undermining the notion of a universal standard of what it means to live well. For more specificity, then, it is necessary to look to psychology.

PERMA

In his most recent book *Flourish*, Seligman challenges his own earlier conception of happiness, which he articulated in *Authentic Happiness*, *Learned Optimism*, and other writings. In his newer work he admits his previous definition of happiness was based too much on the concept of life satisfaction, which is problematic for a number of reasons, foremost among which is that the mood people are in when they are asked to rate their level of happiness significantly informs the level of satisfaction they claim. When people are in a good mood, they report higher levels of happiness than they do when foul-tempered. Life satisfaction, he thus concludes, "is not entitled to a central place in any theory that aims to be more than a happiology."[11] A better construct, then, is well-being, which, Seligman claims, contains several measurable elements, each contributing to human flourishing but none wholly defining it. To designate the construct, he uses the acronym PERMA, which consists of positive emotion, engagement or flow, positive relationships, a sense of meaning and purpose, and the pride of accomplishment. Let us explore these more fully.

Positive Emotion. Until the end of the twentieth century, all emotions were understood according to a model that really only applies to negative emotions, that is, they were understood as "specific action tendencies," which seem to have served an evolutionary advantage by constricting or focusing consciousness and prompting a specific behavioral action tied to survival. Anger, for instance, causes us to fight, disgust to spit, fear to run, etc.... Such a conceptual model surely applies to negative emotions, but by no means does it work effectively in the domain of positive affect.

Barbara Fredrickson's pioneering work in psychology, however, has changed all of this. According to Fredrickson, positive emotions such as gratitude, serenity, interest, hope, pride, amusement, inspiration, awe, joy, elevation, and love often do not prompt an immediate behavioral response. Still, such emotions are highly complex, and they are also of central importance in well-being, as they broaden and build resources for later use. While negative emotions are useful in the immediate moment, often prompting immediate behavioral action, positive emotions typically exert downstream effects, such as fostering creativity, mindfulness, and receptivity, as well as altering values, enhancing relationships, and undoing negative emotions and pessimism. While negative emotions draw us away from circumstances, positive emotions compel us towards them.

Fredrickson's research surprisingly shows that most people experience, in a ratio of 2:1, twice as many positive emotions as they do negative ones. Despite Thoreau's famous statement, most people do not lead lives of "quiet desperation." Even people in undeveloped nations typically regard themselves as being moderately to very happy and thus regularly experience positive affect. The people who report the highest levels of well-being, nevertheless, experience positive to negative emotions in a ratio of approximately 3:1. Those who flourish, according to Fredrickson, feel positive emotions almost three times more frequently than they do negative ones.[12]

Positive affect is a central component in well-being, but it alone, according to Seligman, does not constitute the totality of eudaimonia. However debatable it may be, he calls positive emotion merely the "pleasant life," claiming that on its own such affect cannot lead to eudaimonia. It is possible, in other words, to experience and express positive affect regularly and still be ultimately unsatisfied with one's life. The converse is also true. It is possible not to experience positive affect on any kind of regular basis but still have a very strong sense of well-being. Positive affect is important in well-being, but it is not the *summum bonum* of human existence.

Engagement. For Seligman, therefore, another aspect of well-being is engagement, or what Mihalyi Csikszentmihalyi has called "flow," an optimal state of being in which one immerses oneself in an activity, at once goal directed and bounded by rules, one "that require[s] the investment of psychic energy, and that could not be done without the appropriate skills."[13] In states of flow people muster their greatest effort, call upon their greatest strengths, and lose consciousness of themselves, at least temporarily, in the pursuit of accomplishing some goal, whether it be in sports, business, government, video games, or any other kind of activity that requires the significant cultivation of one's resources. People typically emerge from states of flow, according to Csikszentmihalyi, with a more complex sense of self. While such states are usually not accompanied by affect, positive emotions often follow after the state ends. Flow, according to Csikszentmihalyi, is characterized by eight elements: (1) a chance of completing the task; (2) intense concentration; (3) clearly defined goals; (4) immediate feedback; (5) deep but effortless involvement that removes from awareness the worries and frustration of everyday life; (6) exercise of control over actions; (7) loss of a sense of self, which nevertheless emerges more strongly after the experience is over; and (8) alteration of time (that is, time is either lengthened or shortened).[14]

As an element of well-being, flow implies an engagement in various activities that challenge us and call upon us to develop skills and actualize potentials. In some ways it is a call to be our best in whatever we do. By itself, however, flow cannot lead us to the good life, for it is possible to enter states of flow, as people often do, in solitary moments. And in the end the construct of PERMA says that to be well we also need other people in our lives.

Positive Relationships. It is possible to experience high levels of positive emotion and deep states of flow but be thoroughly self-absorbed and miss one of the most important elements in well-being—the sustaining and life-enhancing power of healthy, positive relationships. Despite Sartre's famous line, "hell is other people," an idea not without some measure of truth, most human beings, with notable exceptions, need engagement with other human beings. For most of us, the absence of other people is actually a horrible thing. Hell, for many of us, is surely a solitary life with no human contact. The Greeks and Romans who frequently used banishment or exile as a form of punishment knew this all too well, as do prisoners locked in solitary confinement for extended periods. Along with oversized brains and a sex drive not bound by a season or period of estrus, complex social relations surely played a significant role in human evolution. Given our oversized limbic systems and their neuromodulator oxytocin, which plays a major role in sexuality, mother/infant bonding, pair-bonding, friendship, hugging, and other forms of human connection, there is hard-wired in the body and brain of most people a deep-seated need to connect with other people. To be sure, malignant narcissists, psychopaths, and others who are born with congenital defects likely have a different wiring, but by and large, most people, even introverts, need other people.

We may meet our people-needs in a minimal, perhaps even degraded, way and still not really be well. In other words we may have significant human contact but still not derive a sense of fulfillment from such engagement. The necessary ingredient in relationships, according to the construct of PERMA, is that they be conducive to our well-being. When I first entered college, I remember my philosophy professor once saying in passing that if we can surround ourselves with three or four people who support us unconditionally, we can achieve whatever we set out to do. While there may be limitations to the idea, the statement has stayed with me for many years, and I often repeat it to my own students. While it is sometimes necessary to sacrifice one's well-being for another, a positive relationship is, generally speaking, mutually beneficial and conducive to the growth and well-being of both people. To be sure, this does not mean relationships should be free of conflicts and pose no challenges. It is likely that such conflicts and challenges are something like an emperor moth's struggle inside of its cocoon. If given an early egress and thus denied the opportunity for struggle inside of the cocoon, the moth will never be able to develop the short body and beautiful, powerful wings that enable it to soar. A relationship free of conflict and challenges, according to this analogy at least, is not a positive relationship. By no means, however, is a positive relationship characterized by struggle alone. To the contrary, as Seligman points out, the better moments in such relationships represent the high points of our lives. In the last couple of years I have had the honor of doing life reviews with dying people for a local hospice, and the greatest joys people typically recall during the interviews are so often centered around their closest loved ones. The people in their lives, the dying so often say in retrospect, are what made it a life worth living. Positive relationships make life meaningful.

Meaning and Purpose. It is next to impossible to excise positive relationships from the fourth category in the PERMA construct: having a sense of meaning and purpose in life. One's deepest sense of meaning might simply be located in being a great parent, a loyal husband, or an excellent, supportive friend. But it is also possible to derive a sense of meaning from spirituality, from support of a noble cause such as tending to the poor, as Theresa of Calcutta famously and admirably did, or, like Gandhi, from helping a nation to overthrow the yoke of tyranny. The common link here is a sense of "belonging to and serving something that you believe is bigger than the self," as Seligman puts it.[15] Despite the school of absurdism—which rose, not coincidentally, to its apogee in the twentieth century—the new discourse on eudaimonia says having a sense of meaning and purpose is a central ingredient in well-being. Sometimes the drive for or commitment to such meaning results in ill-being, particularly when the person, cause, or organization we have dedicated our lives to calls for our own literal or figurative self-sacrifice. By and large, however, devoting oneself to a cause outside of the self, whether spiritual, organizational, familial, or other, richly enhances one's sense of well-being by rendering life meaningful and purposeful. Offering up oneself to the other makes it all seem valuable and worthwhile. "Are you willing to be sponged out, erased, cancelled, made nothing?" asks D.H. Lawrence in his poem, "Phoenix." "If not, you will never really change" (1, 3).[16] However paradoxical it may be, the best way to enrich the self is through self-transcendence achieved by engagement with something beyond one's confines.

Accomplishment. For all of this self-effacement, well-being conceived as PERMA calls for the validation of self through the pride of accomplishment. Although pride is often looked upon as a character flaw—it is one of the seven deadly sins and can indeed manifest in toxic ways—there is nothing intrinsically wrong with being proud of oneself and deriving a deep sense of satisfaction from one's actions and accomplishments. In fact, it is quite healthy to do so. When a child finally learns to balance a bicycle without training wheels, the appropriate response, if we are good parents and teachers, is to applaud, to lavish praise, and to instill a sense of pride of accomplishment. Such applause is beneficial and will likely contribute greatly to the child's overall sense of well-being. For adults, too, there is nothing wrong with deriving a sense of satisfaction from and taking great pride in one's achievements. To state it more positively—it is quite right to do so and will likely enrich one's sense of feeling and being well.

The category of accomplishment in the PERMA construct represents a transformation in Seligman's thinking, for it enabled him to account for intrinsic motivation. Sometimes people pursue goals and engage in activities for no other reason than to pursue the goal or partake in the activity for the sake of excellence. Intrinsic motivation accounts for why *some* CEOs will remain at the helm long after they no longer financially need to do so; why successful people in many walks of life remain working long after retirement age; and why some people sacrifice high salaries to engage in more spiritually rewarding careers. In such cases the motivating factor is often merely the satisfaction derived from achievement itself. Seligman acknowledges that the pride of achievement is in many ways inextricable from the other constituents of PERMA. People who pursue goals and engage in activities for intrinsic reasons often experience positive emotions, states of flow, enriched relationships, and an enhanced sense of meaning. Such benefits, however, are typically incidental and must be so if intrinsic motivation, by its definition, is the motivating factor. Accomplishment for accomplishment's sake best characterizes this last category of PERMA. To be well in this sense is to do something, or perhaps even several things, well simply for the sake of excellence.

Virtue, or Strength

To achieve for its own sake is to embody such universally valued character strengths as perseverance, industriousness, integrity, and perhaps others. All of the elements PERMA comprises, in fact, are similarly undergirded by one or more virtues, or to be more precise, character strengths. For several ancient and contemporary thinkers, the cultivation of character is intimately tied to the question of the good life. In such lines of thinking, it is not possible to have true eudaimonia and a bad or deficient character. This may sound a bit morally heavy-handed, and in one sense it is, since the virtues are qualities that moral philosophers and theologians highly favor. Recent ideas that have emerged in eudaimonic discourse, nevertheless, point to the universally recognized value of cultivating the character strengths that also seem to coincide with those honored by various philosophical and religious systems.

The late Christopher Peterson, another influential psychologist, co-authored (with Seligman) a massive tome of compiled research on the subject. In *Character Strengths and Virtues: A Handbook and Classification*, Peterson and Seligman make a compelling case for the cultivation of character in a detailed discussion of twenty four strengths, each of which they locate in a family related to one of six traditionally conceived virtues: wisdom, courage, humanity, justice, temperance, and transcendence.[17] *Character Strengths and Virtues* is an answer to the prevalence in psychology of a disease focus, which can be seen in the *Diagnostic and Statistical Manual of Mental Disorders* (*DSM*), published by the American Psychiatric Association in several editions from 1952 to the present. As a system of classification with supporting research, *Character Strengths and Virtues* is intended to serve as a counterbalance to the various symptoms, disorders, and diseases found in the *DSM*. In so much of their work Peterson and Seligman have argued that psychopathology is only half of the story of human psychology. The other positive half involves identifying and studying, as they have inspired a whole generation of psychologists to do, character strengths and other subjects associated with well-being in its fullest sense.

In consulting a vast array of ancient and contemporary literature on the topic, Peterson and Seligman conclude that there are twenty four, nearly universal character traits valued across the globe by past and present cultures: creativity, curiosity, open-mindedness, love of learning, perspective or wisdom, bravery, persistence, integrity, vitality, love, kindness, social intelligence, citizenship, fairness, leadership, forgiveness and mercy, humility and modesty, prudence, self-regulation, appreciation of beauty and excellence, gratitude, hope, humor, and spirituality. Absent from this list is righteous anger, which is arguably indicative of character strength. To be sure, such a form of anger can represent a defense mechanism and manifest in other toxic ways, but it can also signify the strength necessary to rectify perceived injustice and to signal to others that one will not tolerate being wronged. In so many contexts, this trait is indeed a virtue. Martin Luther King was brimming with it, as were Ghandi, Nelson Mandela, and so many others. Righteous anger compelled Frances Harper, a former slave, to write, "All that my yearning spirit craves, / Is bury me not in a land of slaves" ("Bury Me in a Free Land" 31–32).[18] Righteous anger calls upon us to muster the necessary psychological resources to deal with political injustice, oppression, corruption, inequality, wrongful violence, and other perceived negatives. It is a valuable character strength.

The strengths Peterson and Seligman identify are at once indicators and facilitators of well-being. We typically say that so-and-so is a remarkable person because he or she has pronounced character strengths or "good qualities." In such a sense the strengths are *signs* of well-being; they are characteristics that indicate the existence of a commonly valued trait. In some cases such traits might even be heritable. Many people are born with kind dispositions and thus inherit through their genes the virtues of kindness and its close cousins, love and social intelligence. In another sense, however, character strengths are acquired, or to be more precise, developed through experience, and thus serve to *facilitate* well-being. In other words we do have a say in the matter. The influence of genetics notwithstanding, we are in many ways the sum total of our thoughts, actions, and experiences. A passage from the Upanishads speaks to the point: "As a man acts and walks in the path of life, so he becomes."[19] Just as we are capable of downward spirals into depression and anguish, so are we capable, as Positive psychologists have shown, of upward spirals of well-being. In some ways the choice is ours, a significant determining factor being how we choose to cultivate our signature strengths. To be well in the fullest sense, then, entails character growth through the acquisition and utilization of the rich resources implied in the strengths Peterson and Seligman classify in their study.

Engagement with the Unconscious

Regardless of their value, there are limitations in cultivating virtues. It is possible to exhibit admirable character traits that other people observe and even to identify with them in our conscious minds while also embodying their opposites. Carl Jung, the great depth psychologist who spent his career analyzing and theorizing about the unconscious, noted such contradictions. He observed that the dreams of his overly pious, Christian clients, who typically identified with and embodied traditionally conceived virtues, were often of the most sordid variety, consisting of incest, murder, dishonesty, selfishness, and the like. Jung's conclusion was that such dreams were a form of compensation for an imbalance in the psyches of people whose value system could only allow for the presentation, both to the world and to themselves, of virtues and goodness, the expression and consciousness of which forced the repression of their opposites. Repressed energies, however, never really go away. They are always with us in one way or another, lying in unconscious obscurity and reappearing in dreams and momentary losses of self-control. Modern priming studies clearly speak to the point, supporting the idea that we are sometimes, perhaps even often, not who we think we are. Although the subjects in such studies claim not to be racist (and by implication embody the virtues of humanity and justice), they often unwittingly exhibit a reaction of fear, unbeknownst to themselves, when shown pictures of black people at a rate of speed their conscious minds cannot detect but which clearly register at the unconscious level.[20] The human psyche, these studies indicate, is not all of a piece. The brain itself, according to neurologists, is a loose confederation of modules sometimes operating in unison but at other times working at cross purposes. The result is a multidimensional self, or rather a band of selves, each of which represents some aspect of a highly diverse psyche. Although Jonathan Haidt discusses the unconscious in his brilliant book, *Happiness: A Hypothesis,*[21] the idea does not play a significant role in Positive psychology largely because the two principal theorists of the unconscious, Freud and Jung, did not use statistics and employed highly questionable methods that, according to contemporary psychologists, call depth psychology into question.

For all of their excesses, nevertheless, both pioneering psychologists were brilliant and have something valuable to contribute to the new discourse of eudaimonia. Despite his crude reduction of all human experience to libido, Freud gave us the important insight that consciousness is only the tip of the iceberg, an image implying that the psyche contains energies, and rather powerful ones at that, lying outside of conscious awareness. Jung, one of the first "positive" psychologists, rejected his mentor's focus on psychopathology and developed, in twenty volumes of prolific writing, a theory of psychic wholeness, an idea suggesting that there is an innate drive in all of us to integrate the myriad components of a diverse psyche. The theory of individuation, as Jung calls it, is ultimately about being well in the fullest sense through an honest engagement with unconscious energies and their ultimate retrieval and balancing. To be whole, in this sense, involves making room in consciousness for the repressed other, or what Matthew Arnold calls the "buried life" in his eponymous poem. Jung believed this life consisted not only of Freud's personal unconscious, or all of the disagreeable things in us that society deems unacceptable, but also our potential, the strengths we have yet to actualize, the positive emotions we sometimes do not allow ourselves to feel. The Jungian unconscious is where our psychic gold is located. Jung's ideas about the multiplicity of the self decenter the primacy of the ego and call for one to make room in consciousness for other psychic energies. The endpoint is something like polyphony, a type of music in which multiple melodic voices function independently but also contribute to an overall whole.[22]

An engagement with the unconscious is deep inner work and requires one to plumb the sometimes frightening depths of the multidimensional self.[23] There are no doubt dangers involved in such work. Jung himself said there is little difference between the mystic and the madman, as they both plunge into the same ocean (the unconscious). The mystic survives and thrives, however, because he knows how to swim back to shore, while the madman drowns. Having engaged in his own personal confrontation with the unconscious, Jung knew how psychologically destabilizing such work can be. One needs a lifeguard in the form of a therapist, a guru, a life coach, a spiritual path, a dream analyst, or some other means by which we can learn how to integrate unconscious energies slowly over a long period of consciousness expansion to achieve a balancing of the psyche. This is necessary work, according to Jung. All visitors to the ancient oracle of Delphi were greeted with the maxim, "Man, know thyself." How can we possibly do so without first exploring our psychic totalities? The endpoint, as Jung and the post–Jungians claim, is a high degree of expanded self-awareness and a rarified level of psychological development.

Ecstatic Experience

Such an engagement with the unconscious is a form of *ekstasis*, the ancient Greek word for standing outside of oneself. *Ekstasis* is not necessarily a positive experience, and it can manifest in many varieties—negative, neutral, and positive. We can be *beside* ourselves with grief, anger, jealousy, love, bliss, awe, or even in strange moments of perception in which we feel uncannily as though we are not our normal selves but experience no accompanying affect. The famous mystery schools of ancient Greece, particularly those of Pythagoras and the Greater and Lesser Eleusinian Mysteries, taught people how to cultivate a positive form of ego-transcendence, which the Greeks highly valued. This was in spite of the negative perspective Euripides took on the subject in his famous play *The Bacchae*, as well as Plato's reservations about being ecstatically enraptured because it interferes with reason. Because initiates of the mysteries were required to take an oath of silence, little is known about the nature of their experiences. Several oblique references to them do exist, however, and suggest that the ecstatic experience they facilitated resulted in a highly beneficial, eudaimonic transformation.

In his seminal work *Varieties of Religious Experience*, William James saw immense value in ecstatic religious experiences, regardless of the question of the metaphysical groundlessness of the dogmas and doctrines associated with them.[24] Marghanita Laski, one of the first social scientists to study ecstasies, saw such experiences, particular their secular variety, as representing the highest state of being and suggested people should try to cultivate them.[25] Abraham Maslow, a forerunner of the current eudaimonic turn who also called what he was doing "positive psychology," claimed that among the super healthy "self-actualizers" he spent his career studying, there was a strikingly high incidence of peak experiences, or what he also referred to as ecstasies.[26]

So what precisely is ecstasy? The term has come to be used synonymously with intense bliss or joy, but such usage is erroneous and flattens a multidimensional state of being by reducing it down to one plane: positive emotion. Ecstasy, however, is not reducible to the bliss or joy that accompany it, and it should not be confused with such emotions. To be sure, most ecstasies induce a high degree of such positive emotions in those who are blessed to experience them, but there are also other emotions that can accompany ecstatic moments. Just as any strong emotion can cause *ekstasis*, so can any positive emotion cause an ecstasy. An experience of one of the associate editors of this anthology speaks to the point. Once, while in a supermarket, she experienced a bizarre moment of defamiliarization in which "the walls of the enormous store seemed to stretch away," and, as she puts it, "I felt as though I could see everything contained within them all at once."[27] The result was that she felt completely overwhelmed with profound feelings of wonder and gratitude for the sheer abundance of food available for purchase. She felt neither joy nor bliss per se, but her sense of self was powerfully transformed in a moment of overpowering positive affect—in this case not joy but wonder and then gratitude. Her ecstasy also exerted downstream transformation, as she claims the experience caused her to become more of an optimist, to realize that she has a choice in how she reacts to mundane moments like shopping and doing other chores, and to be empowered with a greater ability to overcome ingratitude, self-pity, and irritation. Therefore, *any* kind of positive affect, such as awe, wonder, gratitude, love, elevation, inspiration, and the like, can catalyze an ecstatic experience. In this sense ecstasies are something like an emotional orgasm, and, like sexual climaxes, they are highly gratifying. Or, to use another simile, they are like the cresting of an affective wave that knocks us out of self and also exerts highly beneficial effects once we make it back to shore. Ecstasies are thus characterized by three important elements—the climax of any positive emotion, its resulting self-transcendence, and beneficial downstream effects that facilitate a values-shift, an increase in self-awareness, a more integrated perspective, and no doubt other aspects of well-being.

Ecstasy should thus not be confused with or reduced to the pleasant life of positive emotions. It is not, in fact, an emotion at all, but an unusually deep state of consciousness in which we become larger and better, both in the immediate moment and later on as the echoes of the experience reverberate through the labyrinthine halls of the psyche. Maslow paid close attention to such transformations in his self-actualizers, particularly in the values-shifts that occurred after they experienced an ecstasy. In interviews with over one hundred such people, he noticed a common thread of core values that resulted from peak experiences. These include: truth, beauty, wholeness, dichotomy-transcendence, aliveness-process, uniqueness, perfection, necessity, completion, justice, order, simplicity, richness, effortlessness, playfulness, and self-sufficiency.[28] Ecstasy is neither simply a moment of heightened bliss, nor is it some minor aspect of eudaimonia. To the contrary, it is a valuable state of being that represents the highpoint of positive emotion in a deep state of engagement, the result of which is often the embrace of more humane values; deeper relationships; an enhanced sense of meaning and purpose; and the cultivation of character strengths, including not only those underpinning intrinsically motivated accomplishment but many others.

How does one have an ecstasy? Many people have them, or at least varying degrees of them, several times throughout the course of their lifespans. While there is an element of passivity in ecstatic experiences in that they seem to happen to people, it is also possible that people can make them happen, or at least engage in activities that foster receptivity to them. Laski cites the following most frequently mentioned "triggers" of the ecstatic experience: nature, sex, giving birth, exercise, religion, art, the pursuit of knowledge, creative work, introspection, and observing beauty. She also cites four "anti-triggers" most commonly cited as elements responsible for ending an ecstatic experience: reason, language, commerce, and other people. Despite Laski's use of the words trigger and anti-trigger, it is more accurate to view these as correlates rather than causes. It is possible never to have an ecstasy while hiking in the woods, or having sex, or giving birth, just as it is possible to have an ecstasy despite the presence of what she calls anti-triggers. A student of mine once had something of an ecstatic experience while reading in a bookstore, that is, his ecstasy occurred despite the use of reason, his engagement with the language on the page, and the presence of other people, most of whom were shopping for books.[29]

Laski's triggers and anti-triggers are thus not causative, but if the historical record is any guide, there are means one can take to become receptive to the ecstatic experience. From time immemorial, people in cultures all over the world have engaged in what are called ecstatic techniques to induce profound consciousness transformation. Some of these include chanting, visualizing, drumming, dancing, whirling, fasting, enduring climatic extremes, sleep deprivation, breath manipulation, prolonged gazing, lucid dreaming, ingesting hallucinogens, praying, singing, and other activities. Perhaps the simplest and most effective way of experiencing ecstasy, however, is through meditation. As I briefly noted, neurologists have begun to map the brains of experienced meditants, and the results clearly show a thickening in the left prefrontal cortex, an area of the brain implicated in processing positive affect. These people experience ecstasies on such a regular basis that it transforms their neurological wiring, making their brains larger and significantly enhancing their eudaimonia.

Ecstasy is in some ways relatable to ideas in positive psychology, whose researchers have come close to Maslow's ecstasies in the emotion of "elevation," a hitherto unidentified form of positive affect elicited by witnessing, whether in literature or real life, acts of virtue and moral beauty. In his fascinating research on the subject, Jonathan Haidt has observed that elevation results in an observable physiological response, typically a feeling of warmth and openness in the chest/heart, the result of which is that people are prompted to behave more virtuously and nobly themselves.[30] The likeness to ecstasy here should be apparent. To be elevated is to experience positive affect and to be *ekstatically* lifted up and out of one's normal sense of self, the result of which is a positive downstream effect, particularly a heightened consciousness of morality and virtue. Defined as such, elevation is a form of ecstasy. While elevation might be one of its varieties, however, not all forms of ecstasy manifest as elevation, which is one of the *many* positive emotions that can climax and result in an ecstatic experience. Elevation is ecstasy, then, but ecstasy is not necessarily elevation.

Another positive psychological idea that one might relate to ecstasy is the concept of flow, that is, a state of intense engagement in which one *ekstatically* loses his or her sense of selfhood. Once again, however, *ekstatic* and ecstatic experiences differ in that the latter carry with them both positive affect and downstream eudaimonic effects. States of flow no doubt later result in a more complex sense of self, an aspect of eudaimonia, but they are not characterized by positive affect. States of flow, then, are *ekstatic* but not ecstatic. Ecstasies, moreover, often require no effort whatsoever and sometimes, though not always, spontaneously happen, whereas in flow self-exertion is required. There is common ground between flow and ecstasy, nevertheless, in ecstatic techniques, the resulting states of which seem to be identical with states of flow if no affect is present. When people engage in such techniques as breath manipulation, whirling, contemplation, meditation, and many others, they often enter states of emotionless flow. If their techniques result in a climax of positive emotion and exert eudaimonic downstream effects, they leave flow and enter the realm of ecstatic transformation. Because I deal with this topic more substantially in the introduction to *Wild Poets of Ecstasy: An Anthology of Ecstatic Verse*,[31] and *The Ecstatic Poetic Tradition*[32] I will not belabor the point here other than to stress that while ecstatic techniques are flow inducing, ecstasies are not merely states of flow. They differ in intensity and in the presence of affect.

Ecstasies are synonymous with well-being, and they occupy a central position in the good life. In myriad ways the historical record supports the point that positive *ekstasis* is a highly valuable, eudaimonic experience. Mystics in several traditions, including Christian, Sufi, Jewish, Indian, Buddhist, and others, have for centuries attested to the transformative power of ecstatic experiences. In the tens of thousands of recorded cases of near-death experiences in which one often literally stands outside of the physical body, the majority of people who claim such ecstasies report that their whole value system changes. One previously competitive, individualistic, aggressive, and materialistic man, for instance, had an ecstatic near-death experience, after which he began growing daylilies by the hundreds simply to give them away as gifts to people to symbolize the joys of his transformation.[33] Regardless of the question of their validity, such experiences do seem to be highly beneficial. "Struck by that light," as William Cowper puts it in "The Happy Change," "the human heart, / A barren soil no more" (9–10).[34] Ecstasies in many varieties result in eudaimonic transformation.

Love

Love, too, plays a major role in eudaimonia. Listed as one of the positive emotions researchers are now investigating, love is also implied as a given in the third element of PERMA: close positive relationships. I have treated it here as a separate category, however, for two reasons: (1) My intuitions tell me it deserves, as the most important element in well-being, its own treatment because, unlike the other elements, love is the *summum bonum* of human existence. With love, everything makes sense, and everything has meaning and purpose. Without love, there seems to be no point to anything, and life is all simply an absurd accident. But love is not merely that which makes life bearable; it is also what makes it exquisitely beautiful. To be sure, there are qualifications to this enthusiastic endorsement, but the power of love to enhance well-being is undeniable. (2) Love, like ecstasy, is not reducible to positive emotion, and it is not merely the cement in positive relationships. To be sure, love is generally associated with affect, but simply because it registers in the emotional center by no means indicates it is merely an emotion. It is certainly unlike the other emotions, even the positive ones. Love is a profound experience, a complexity with myriad eudaimonic effects. I do not have statistics to back up this claim, and I speak as a (post) human-ist, not as a social scientist. But I do so while standing on the shoulders of countless poets, ancient philosophers, love-intoxicated mystics, philosoph-ical psychologists, wise sages, shamans, and brilliant artists, so many of whom indicate that love is in many ways an unquantifiable, irreducible mys-tery. To be sure, statistics can shed productive light on love, but our greatest wisdom traditions point to its otherness, its strangeness. We often say love is a many splendored thing, but it is not really a thing at all. It is only an object when we look at it through an objective lens. Love is ultimately an incomprehensible but wondrous mystery, and to view it as such and sur-render to it without trying to understand it intellectually represents living fully and well.

But let me bring the mystery down to earth: human beings need love for survival. We know this from the so-called sterile orphanages of the 1940s and 1950s. Because of mid-twentieth-century ideas about disease, the babies in such nurseries were minimally touched. There were cared for in the strictest sense—that is, they were properly bathed, fed, and clothed, receiving all of the necessary medical attention they required—but they were never tickled, caressed, held, squeezed, or hugged. The tragic result is that most of them died—sterile nurseries reported a 75% to 100% mortality rate—because, in effect, they were not loved.[35] Such stupidity on the part of those who conceived of sterile orphanages seems deplorable to those of us operating from intuition on the matter of love. We instinctively know that love and its physical demonstration—whether through sex, hugging, kissing, hand-shaking, back-rubbing, smiling, and other forms—are critically important components of human well-being. Even Freud, despite his reduction of most aspects of human experience to psychopathology, admitted the power of love. When asked by a friend about the nature of "oceanic" experiences, or ecstasies in which the boundaries of the ego dissolve, Freud appealed to a disease model and located the experience in narcissistic regression to an earlier phase of psychological development before ego had fully dissociated itself from the objects of its perceptions. He did admit, however, that there is at least one type of oceanic experience not reducible to psychopathology—love, which, he claimed, represents a healthy form of ego loss.[36] Love, even for Freud, is a grand mystery, the effects of which are not psychopathology but eudaimonia.

Love comes in many forms. In English there is only one word to designate such a complexity, but in ancient Greek there were at least five: *epithumia* (lust), *eros* (romance), *storge* (family), *philia* (friendship), and *agape* (spiritual love). People who have had near-death experiences and ecstatic mystical epiphanies are often profoundly transformed by this last form of love, claiming it is the cement that binds together not only human life but all of reality. *Agape* represents non-selfish love in its fullest expression. It is what compels us to love all people, even those we do not know and have never met. It is what causes us to love our pets and parks, as well as all flora and fauna on the planet. Agape inspires compassion and instills in us a sense of the sacredness of all existence. In the Christian tradition, in which it is by no means completely confined, *agape* is love of God. In many other traditions it is love of the sacred principle, often love itself.

One way to experience more love is to engage in what Fredrickson calls loving-kindness meditation, which she adopted from ancient Buddhist practices. In such meditation, practitioners focus on sending love and kindness first to themselves—note the implied valuation of self-love, which is not listed among the Greek varieties—and then to ever-widening circles of others, eventually encompassing the whole world. In her studies of those who regularly engage in loving-kindness meditation, which she claims is an alternative to the more cerebral mindfulness meditations of other Buddhist practices, Fredrickson has found that the activity leads to a "wide sweep of benefits." These include "improved abilities to savor and be mindful";

enhanced self-acceptance and abilities to trust others; increased life satis-
faction and a deeper sense of meaning; and physical benefits such as fewer
aches, pains, colds, and flus.[37]

Another, less formal way to experience the transformative nature of
love is simply to place one's attention on it, perhaps on a daily basis. Ask
the following questions: What can I do, great or small, for love today? How
can I serve the people I love and those who are nearest to me? How can my
actions better facilitate love? How would love, if embodied, resolve this con-
flict? Are my words and deeds in the interests of love? One does not need
to donate a kidney to live according to the dictates of love. While giving up
an organ is a highly noble act, there are other ways to experience the eudai-
monic benefits of love. Every little act of love—running an errand for some-
one, smiling at a sad face, giving a compliment, and countless
others—carries the potential of eudaimonic transformation. Just as a but-
terfly flapping its wings somewhere on a Pacific island can alter weather
patterns on the other side of the world, so can a tiny act of love have con-
siderable effects that ripple outward and impact the well-being of oneself
and others in substantial ways.

To recapitulate, then, eudaimonia, according to the perspectives I have
outlined here, consists of several elements, the first of which is exercising
functional capabilities, as Nussbaum calls them, in the following domains:
the body; relationships with other people and with flora and fauna; affect;
cognition; recreation, play, and laughter; individuality enjoyed in one's cho-
sen surrounding and context; and the freedom to form a conception of the
good life and to take actions to actualize it. The second element is Seligman's
PERMA, an acronym designating five markers of well-being: regularly expe-
riencing positive emotion, ideally three times more frequently than one
experiences negative affect; frequently entering states of flow that demand
the cultivation of strengths and resources and result in a more complex
sense of self; close, mutually beneficial, positive relationships that not only
sustain us during times of hardship but provide us with the high points in
life; achieving a sense of meaning and purpose through dedication to some-
thing outside of the self, whether it be an abstract cause, a practical move-
ment, a profession, a religion, and the like; and achievement for its own
intrinsic value, simply because excellence is its own reward. The third ele-
ment is the cultivation of character strengths and virtues, which are both
signs and catalysts of well-being. The fourth element is the expansion of
consciousness through engagement with the unconscious, the result of
which is self-awareness and psychic wholeness. The fifth element is the
ecstatic experience, which cannot be willed but surely can be prepared for,
particularly through meditation and other forms of ecstatic technique. The

last element constituting eudaimonia is love, the grand mysteries of which manifest as physiological, emotional, and perhaps even spiritual needs. When such needs are met maximally, everything falls into place and life takes on an enhanced sense of meaning and purpose. Life is then good.

The Eudaimonic Turn in Literary Studies

How has well-being been received in literary studies? The negativity bias of the twentieth century found significant expression in the discipline, particularly in the final three decades, during which so many scholars adopted what Paul Ricouer famously called a "hermeneutics of suspicion."[38] Such an interpretive framework compelled scholars to look suspiciously upon texts, the result of which was that we read with the intention to deconstruct; to question manifest illusions; to discern latent psychopathological content; and to tease out the various ways in which texts are complicit with any number of undesirable ideologies, such as patriarchy, imperialism, heterosexism, racism, and others. Such a hermeneutics has proven to be invaluable in literary studies, resulting in the rich tradition of critical theory with its complex ideas and the sophisticated methodologies they enable. As a theorist and scholar working in the depth psychology tradition, I am indebted to the hermeneutics of suspicion, having used it quite substantially in my research and my classrooms.

Suspicion, however, has its limitations. Ricouer himself saw it as one among many, possible interpretive strategies. While suspicion can be very productive, it can blind us to other textual dimensions. An analogical equivalent here is the view we might take when we suspect someone of being a thief. Even if the person is innocent, suspicion will compel us to look for signs indicative of a lack of scruples and blind us to his or her other admirable characteristics. Similarly, in literary studies the hermeneutics of suspicion has compelled scholars to look for symptoms of psychopathology or complicity with undesirable ideologies in literature, while often ignoring its eudaimonic value, which can manifest in myriad ways but go unnoticed because of the hermeneutic framework one has adopted. The problem here is not that there is no psychopathology or questionable ideology in literary texts but that there are also other textual dimensions to which scholars are blind if they exclusively focus on neurosis, imperialistic values, and undesirable ideologies.

Influenced by the multidisciplinary eudaimonic turn that has taken place over the last decade, literary scholars have begun to recognize the limitations of suspicion and to seek out ways in which it might be augmented with newer points of focus and even new interpretive models. In one way or another, my brilliant co-editors of this anthology have all challenged the exclusive use of suspicion and adopted alternative reading strategies that enable one to see the eudaimonic value in literary texts, whether ethical, formal, religious, philosophical, psychological, or otherwise. James Pawelski, a philosopher by training and also the Executive Director of the International Positive Psychology Association, is intimately involved in challenging suspicion in an ongoing project that extends across the humanities. An example of his approach can be seen in the fine study, *The Dynamic Individualism of William James*, in which he explores the eudaimonic value of religious experience.[39] In the aforementioned study, *The Story of Joy: From the Bible through Late Romanticism*, Adam Potkay resists the twentieth-century tendency to look upon joy as being without substance, demonstrating in his award-winning and highly influential work that joy and its many social constructions are of central importance in Western literary culture. In other works he has eruditely explored the complexities of ethics and happiness.[40] Emma Mason, a highly influential scholar in the United Kingdom, has employed a number of rich interpretive strategies, including what is called "new prosody" and "eudaimonics" in her critical explorations of religion and affect in literary texts. In her work on nineteenth-century poetry, Mason focuses on the rhythmic expression of emotional experience, using a phenomenological approach to questions of feeling and being. This emphasis on the poetic communication of emotion is repeated in her various publications on the reciprocal relationship between religion and literature, in which she refuses to reduce religious experience to ideology and rejects the hostile reaction dominant in literary studies to questions of "faith" and "devotion." Susan Wolfson, the major figure behind what is sometimes pejoratively called "new formalism,"[41] has, in impressively sophisticated ways, called into question the anti-humanist suspicion of formal reading strategies and its accompanying focus on extra-literary concerns in literary studies, compellingly refocusing attention on the inescapable value of form. In doing so she has inspired a whole new generation of scholars who have themselves become suspicious of late twentieth-century anti-humanism and find richness, vibrancy, and complexity in the formal concerns literary theory has neglected.[42] James Engell has brilliantly analyzed the eudaimonic aspects of the powers of the imagination.[43] In more general terms he has also demonstrated that there is considerable eudaimonic value in literary study, which is important, he argues, because it raises consciousness of ethics, fosters social engagement, and helps us to discern the values, objectionable or otherwise, that underpin our lives.[44] In my own work I have analyzed the eudaimonic value of mystical language,[45] the aspects of well-being implied in the Romantic engagement with the unconscious,[46] the positive psychological benefits of ecstatic experiences,[47] and the importance of adopting alternatives to the hermeneutics of suspicion.[48]

And we are by no means the only scholars in the discipline over the last decade to be suspicious of suspicion, to adopt alternative reading strategies, and to discuss how eudaimonia is a significant factor in literary texts. The multidisciplinary turn toward the investigation of well-being has significantly registered across the field of literary studies. Once again, for a more complete discussion, I refer the reader to *The Eudaimonic Turn: Well-being in Literary Studies.* Suffice it here to say that several influential literary scholars, such as Rita Felski,[49] Heather Love,[50] Stephen Best and Sharon Marcus,[51] Charles Altieri,[52] Philip Fisher,[53] Vivasvan Soni,[54] and others, have helped to transform the discipline in rich ways by rejecting the hermeneutics of suspicion, at least as it was conceived in the last three decades of the twentieth century, casting literary texts and the methodologies and theories scholars use to interpret them in a eudaimonic light. The turn toward well-being has begun to transform and enrich literary studies in productive ways, the result of which is that literary scholars have contributed much to the multidisciplinary discussion of eudaimonia in a productive, circular exchange.

Eudaimonic Poetry and the Present Volume

The present volume represents an intention to support such a turn in literary studies and also in other disciplines by demonstrating to scholars that the literature of well-being can be at once exquisitely beautiful and worthy of academic inquiry in its ability to illuminate the construct of eudaimonia in ways not possible in other perspectives. Eudaimonic verse is thus by no means literature light. To the contrary, it is deeply and richly substantial.

On Human Flourishing is in many ways an outgrowth of the work I previously mentioned—*Wild Poets of Ecstasy: An Anthology of Ecstatic Verse.* After I sent a copy of that book to Martin Seligman and James Pawelski and thus began dialoguing with the former and collaborating with the latter, I realized that the larger question behind ecstatic poetry, as well as all of my work up to that point, was eudaimonia. From the very beginning of my graduate studies through the present moment, I have been fascinated with the question of what it means to be well. In all cases, including tragedy, there are very few texts that do not, whether implicitly or explicitly in negative or positive forms, touch on the matter of what it means to live well. Some forms of literature suggest its absence by foregrounding ill-being, while others, particularly the lyric poetry found in *Wild Poets of Ecstasy* and in the present volume, configure its positive presence in meaningful ways.

The question remains, however, whether the lyric, with its "egotistic" subjectivity and ahistorical character, is worth studying. Plato and other Greek thinkers devalued the lyric on the grounds that it is powerfully affective and interferes with the reasoning process. The judgment persisted throughout several centuries until the lyric emerged as a credible form during the Italian Renaissance in its manifestation as the sonnet. Despite this renewed interest in the form, lyrical expression carried a stigma that was not entirely removed until Wordsworth and the German Romantics elevated the genre to new heights. Since then, the lyric has eclipsed all other poetic genres. To speak of poetry in the present age is almost always to speak of the lyric. Despite this status, the lyric in the last three decades of the twentieth century came under attack by suspicion-minded literary scholars who were concerned less with affect and its formal configurations than they were with (nonetheless important) sociopolitical ideas. Mikhail Bakhtin's view of the lyric, which many twentieth-century critics adopted, captures the spirit of such bias. Bakhtin condemned the lyric because "... it denies history and its heteroglossic superfluity of meaning." In such a perspective, the form is seen as being "in flight from history and the real." The lyric, Bakhtin argued, "is defined by a willful and permanent forgetting, an active refusal to allow the whole to be seen, and that part of the whole which is lost is the interaction of the world and the object over time, which has produced layers of supplementary or contradictory meaning."[55] The genre has also suffered at the hands of poststructuralist critics, who refuse to treat it as affect, reducing it to language and pointing out its myriad contradictions, gaps, and aporias.

In the last decade, however, there has been a return, particularly in the study of poetry, to a recognition of the importance of affect, the foreground of most lyrics. Influential works have brought to light the dismissal of affect in literary studies and emphasized its centrality.[56] Among many others, Charles Altieri in *The Particulars of Rapture: An Aesthetics of the Affects* and Philip Fisher in *Wonder, the Rainbow, and the Aesthetics of Rare Experiences* and in *The Vehement Passions* compellingly demonstrate the complexities and undeniable importance of emotions and their formal configurations. The lyric, with its privileging of affect and affective states, thus finds new support in this new century. A new day has dawned for poetry.

So we offer you the following anthology, the poems of which suggest the many aspects of eudaimonia. The five co-editors who graciously agreed to join me on this project are fine scholars who contributed a number of the selections. Their contributions have greatly enriched this volume. I also cherry-picked five of the brightest English majors from my university, working with them over a period of about three years in order to decide upon suitable selections. In addition to the many poems suggested by my colleagues, I had my excellent students—Gabriella Basile, Kelly Johnson, Meggan McGuire, David Torosian, and Jamie Wasco—offer possibilities for selection. In regular, weekly meetings that often proved magical, leaving us all feeling ecstatic, we met to do nothing but read and discuss eudaimonic poetry in order to select what we felt best represented the genre. We pored over dozens of volumes of verse suggested by our co-editors to determine selections. What we found was that human beings have been writing the poetry of well-being from time immemorial and continue to do so in the twenty-first century across the globe. The selections we offer here are by no means exhaustive, as we found that there was far too much extant material. Still, we have tried to be as comprehensively representative as possible, offering at least some poems in translation from several other languages. Most of the translations were commissioned expressly for this project, and we are indebted to the translators who have done them. The rest of the poems are written in English and extend from the seventeenth to the early twentieth centuries. Copyrights prohibited the reproduction of many twentieth-century poems, although we do include a number of selections from this period.

The criteria we used more or less corresponded to the six perspectives on well-being that I previously discussed. We chose poems that configure (1) the use of functional capabilities in various domains; (2) all of the elements of PERMA; (3) character strengths or virtues; (4) increased self-awareness through an engagement with one's unconscious depths; (5) peak experiences or ecstasies; and (6) the mysteries of love. In all cases we strongly considered formal and aesthetic qualities, favoring poems that offer some measure of sophistication or artistic merit. We also favored pithiness and concision, because short, wisdom-bearing poems quintessentially embody lyrics in their yoking of density with brevity. In some cases we chose poems in which speakers longed for a better state because, although a yearning to be well is not exactly well-being, it functions as "ground zero" and points in the right direction. The final and perhaps most important criterion, however, was whether the poem spoke to us at a deep level, that is, at the level of the whole self, whatever that is. In most cases the lyrics we chose were the ones that immediately evoked a visceral, intuitive "yes," even though we formally selected each poem only after considerable discussion and debate.

Originally starting with 55 different themes covering positive emotions, character strengths, and the like, we finally condensed all of these into the following 14 thematic cycles:

Cycle 1 Wisdom
Cycle 2 Pride, Self-Love and Resilience
Cycle 3 Ecstasy, Elevation and Rapture
Cycle 4 Consciousness Expansion, Growth and Engagement with
         Unconscious Depths
Cycle 5 Romantic Love and Lust
Cycle 6 Language, Inspiration and the Imagination
Cycle 7 Relatedness to the Environment, Flora and Fauna
Cycle 8 Hope, Optimism and Idealism
Cycle 9 Childhood, Innocence, Wonder and Awe
Cycle 10 Sensory Delights, Vitality and Mindfulness

Each cycle is a kind of umbrella covering multiple-but-related ideas about human well-being. We organize the volume in such a way so readers may locate poems in broad categories related to well-being but also have the freedom to interpret them in their own ways. Classifying sophisticated poems too narrowly is exceedingly difficult and problematic not only because poems are not reducible to statement or theme but also because good poems suggest multiple ideas at once. A poem about gratitude, for instance, can also suggest concepts about relatedness to others, love, elevation, ecstasy, nature, and so much else. It is a bit reductive, then, to say "x" poem is a gratitude poem, particularly when it might signify in so many other domains. We felt, nevertheless, the necessity to arrange the poems thematically for the benefit of the reader's understanding. The subject of well-being in the poetic tradition is far too large and complicated to present in a chronological arrangement. Given the wide scope of each cycle, we hope to deflect the criticism that we have put poems in neat little boxes. Surely, we have not done so.

By no means are all of these poems fit for polite conversation at tea parties and political correctness roundtables. Some of them, in fact, contain unmentionables and other "impolite" images that might be construed as offensive in this hyper-sensitive age. Others convey righteous anger over perceived injustices, and still others point to growth through hardship and struggle. We are by no means offering here a yellow smiley face against a blue sky. Well-being is not saccharine. When it is sweet, the sugar is real but never cloying. When it is bittersweet, the bitter combines with sweet to produce a complex flavor for a sophisticated palate. Nevertheless, we are unabashed about endorsing the sweetness and the light. Eudaimonic experience, we contend, is not only real but of the utmost significance.

These poems are a mirror of human potential, and they convey so much of what is meaningful in life. Some of them are about the deep mysteries of love, or empowerment through exercising agency and cultivating character strengths, or peak moments of consciousness dilation resulting in growth and self-awareness. Also bubbling in this heady brew are the exquisite joys and complexities of positive emotion. This is a book of poems about hope, wonder, inspiration, abiding connections to nature and animal life, elevation, and so much else that indicates and catalyzes eudaimonic transformation. It is a book about human beings at full bloom. We hope you enjoy it and find in it, as we have, aesthetic and formal delights as well as important ideas about what it means to be well in the fullest sense.

Cycle 1 : Wisdom

WILLIAM BLAKE 1757–1827

ETERNITY

He who binds to himself a joy
Does the winged life destroy
But he who kisses the joy as it flies
Lives in eternity's sun rise

WILLIAM WORDSWORTH 1770–1850

EXPOSTULATION AND REPLY

"Why, William, on that old grey stone,
Thus for the length of half a day,
Why, William, sit you thus alone,
And dream your time away?

"Where are your books?—that light bequeathed
To Beings else forlorn and blind!
Up! Up! and drink the spirit breathed
From dead men to their kind.

"You look round on your Mother Earth,
As if she for no purpose bore you;
As if you were her first-born birth,
And none had lived before you!"

One morning thus, by Esthwaite lake,
When life was sweet, I knew not why,
To me my good friend Matthew spake,
And thus I made reply:

"The eye—it cannot choose but see;
We cannot bid the ear be still;

Our bodies feel, where'er they be,
Against or with our will.

"Nor less I deem that there are Powers
Which of themselves our minds impress;
That we can feed this mind of ours
In a wise passiveness.

"Think you, 'mid all this mighty sum
Of things for ever speaking,
That nothing of itself will come,
But we must still be seeking?

"—Then ask not wherefore, here, alone,
Conversing as I may,
I sit upon this old grey stone,
And dream my time away."

THE TABLES TURNED
AN EVENING SCENE ON THE SAME SUBJECT

Up! Up! my Friend, and quit your books;
Or surely you'll grow double:
Up! Up! my Friend, and clear your looks;
Why all this toil and trouble?

The sun above the mountain's head,
A freshening lustre mellow
Through all the long green fields has spread,
His first sweet evening yellow.

Books! 'tis a dull and endless strife:
Come, hear the woodland linnet,
How sweet his music! on my life,
There's more of wisdom in it.

And hark! how blithe the throstle sings!
He, too, is no mean preacher:
Come forth into the light of things,
Let Nature be your teacher.

She has a world of ready wealth,
Our minds and hearts to bless—
Spontaneous wisdom breathed by health,
Truth breathed by cheerfulness.

One impulse from a vernal wood
May teach you more of man,

Of moral evil and of good,
Than all the sages can.

Sweet is the lore which Nature brings;
Our meddling intellect
Mis-shapes the beauteous forms of things:—
We murder to dissect.

Enough of Science and of Art;
Close up those barren leaves;
Come forth, and bring with you a heart
That watches and receives.

ALEXANDER S. PUSHKIN 1799–1837

GOD, DON'T LET ME LOSE MY MIND

God, don't let me lose my mind.
No, easier were the staff and bag;
No, easier labor and want.
It is not that I value my reason, not that
I would not gladly part with it:

If I were left alone
At freedom, how with alacrity
I would rush in the dark woods!
How I would sing in a flaming frenzy,
How I would forget myself in a cloud
Of formless wondrous dreams.

And I would listen to the waves for hours,
And I would gaze, bliss filled,
Into the empty skies;
And I would be free and strong,
Like a whirlwind, pillaging the fields,
    breaking down the forests.

But here's the rub: lose your mind,
And you will be frightening like the plague,
You will be locked up straight away,
They will chain and brand you, a fool,
And through the grate will come to tease you
Like some tiny animal.

And in the night I will hear
Not the nightingale's bright voice,

Not the rustling leaves of oak groves,
But the cries of the mates of mine,
And the night watchers' curses,
And shrieks, and the clang of chains.
                        —Trans. Tatsiana DeRosa

WALT WHITMAN 1819–1892

WHEN I READ THE BOOK

When I read the book, the biography famous,
And is this then (said I) what the author calls a man's life?
And so will some one when I am dead and gone write my life?
(As if any man really aught of my life,
Why even I myself I often think know little or nothing of my
    real life,
Only a few hints, a few diffused faint clews and indirections
I seek for my own use to trace out here.)

THAT SHADOW MY LIKENESS

That shadow my likeness that goes to and fro seeking a
    livelihood, chattering, chaffering,
How often I find myself standing and looking at it where it flits,
How often I question and doubt whether that is really me;
But among my lovers and caroling these songs,
O I never doubt whether that is really me.

THE BASE OF ALL METAPHYSICS

And now gentlemen,
A word I give to remain in your memories and minds,
As base and finale too for all metaphysics.
(So to the students the old professor,
    At the close of his crowded course.)

Having studied the new and antique, the Greek and Germanic
    systems,
Kant having studied and stated, Fichte and Schelling and Hegel,
Stated the lore of Plato, and Socrates greater than Plato,
And greater than Socrates sought and stated, Christ divine
    having studied long,
I see reminiscent to-day those Greek and Germanic systems,
See the philosophies al, Christian churches and tenets see,

Yet underneath Socrates clearly see, and underneath Christ
    the divine I see,
The dear love of man for his comrade, the attraction of friend
    to friend,
Of the well-married husband and wife, of children and parents,
Of city for city and land for land.

ME IMPERTURBE

Me imperturbe, standing at ease in Nature,
Master of all or mistress of all, aplomb in the midst of
    irrational things,
Imbued as they, passive, receptive, silent as they,
Finding my occupation, poverty, notoriety, foibles, crimes, less
    important than I thought,
Me toward the Mexican sea, or in the Mannahatta or the
    Tennessee, or fat north or inland,
A river man, or a man of the woods, or of any farm-life of
    these States or of the coast, or the lakes or Kanada,
Me wherever my life is lived, O to be self-balanced for
    contingencies,
To confront night, storms, hunger, ridicule, accidents, rebuffs,
    as the trees and animals do.

EMILY DICKINSON 1830–1886

WATER, IS TAUGHT BY THIRST

Water, is taught by thirst.
Land—by the Oceans passed.
Transport—by throe –
Peace—by its battles told –
Love, by Memorial Mold –
Birds, by the Snow.

A.E. HOUSMAN 1859–1936

XXXVIII

Oh stay at home, my lad, and plough
    The land and not the sea,
And leave the soldiers at their drill,
And all about the idle hill

Shepherd your sheep with me.
Oh stay with company and mirth
    And daylight and the air;
Too full already is the grave
Of fellows that were good and brave
    And died because they were.

Loveliest of Trees, the Cherry Now

Loveliest of trees, the cherry now
Is hung with bloom along the bough,
And stands about the woodland ride
Wearing white for Eastertide.
Now, of my threescore years and ten,
Twenty will not come again,
And take from seventy springs a score,
It only leaves me fifty more.

And since to look at things in bloom
Fifty springs are little room,
About the woodlands I will go
To see the cherry hung with snow.

Stephen Crane 1871–1900

The Impact of a Dollar upon the Heart

The impact of a dollar upon the heart
Smiles warm red light
Sweeping from the hearth rosily upon the white table,
With the hanging cool velvet shadows
Moving softly upon the door.

The impact of a million dollars
Is a crash of flunkeys
And yawning emblems of Persia
Cheeked against oak, France and a sabre,
The outcry of old beauty

Whored by pimping merchants
To submission before wine and chatter.
Silly rich peasants stamp the carpets of men,
Dead men who dreamed fragrance and light
Into their woof, their lives;

The rug of an honest bear
Under the feet of a cryptic slave
Who speaks always of baubles,
Forgetting place, multitude, work and state,
Champing and mouthing of hats
Making ratful squeak of hats,
Hats.

A Man Saw a Ball of Gold in the Sky

A man saw a ball of gold in the sky
He climbed for it,
And eventually he achieved it –
It was clay.

Now this is the strange part:
When the man went to the earth
And looked again,
Lo, there was the ball of gold.
Now this is the strange part:
it was a ball of gold.
Aye, by the heavens, it was a ball of gold.

Once There Came a Man

Once there came a man
Who said:
"Range me all men of the world in rows."
And instantly
There was terrific clamor among the people
Against being ranged in rows.
There was a loud quarrel, world-wide.
It endured for ages;
And blood was shed
By those who would not stand in rows,
And by those who pined to stand in rows.
Eventually, the man went to death, weeping.
And those who stayed in bloody scuffle
Knew not the great simplicity.

E.E. Cummings 1894–1962

XXIX

let it go—the
smashed word broken
open vow or
the oath cracked length
wise—let it go it
was sworn to
        go
let them go—the
truthful liars and
the false fair friends
and the boths and
neithers—you must let them go they
were born
        to go
let all go—the
big small middling
tall bigger really
the biggest and all
things—let all go
dear
      so comes love

Chinmoy Kumar Ghose 1931–2007

The Answer

Wait and see.
The temporary emptiness
Of not discovering
The answers of life
Cannot last,
For the Answer itself
Is blossoming
Petal by petal
For you.

NOT WORD, BUT WORK

Not word, but work:
This sweet message awakens strength
In our heart.
Inside work remains hidden
The fragrance of flowers.
Let work be the language of our heart
And our proclamation.
Our only aim is progress,
Not victory or failure.

JOYCE SNYDER 1945–

CHANGE

Change came to the door and because it knocked, I opened it.
Oh, Change, I said, *No thanks, none today.*
It tried to put its foot inside,
but I was quick.
I blocked it; sent it on its way.

Change came to the door with a bouquet of flowers
and thrust them forward for me to take.
There's no occasion, I smiled, *it's not for me.*
I pushed them back while Change
nodded knowingly.

Change came to the door and I opened it.
Change smiled and I frowned.
I told you before, I said somewhat irritably,
*I have no need for what you bring
I do not wish to change a thing.*

The door burst open with a ferocious blast
and a thunderous crack.
The more I fought the more it blew me back.
It knocked me down, it brought me to my knees.
Change was *so* insistent that I finally agreed

Change came to my door; I heard the knock.
I opened it slightly and peeked out.
Oh Change, I said, *my love.*
I embraced it and took it in,

I held it, I made it mine.
I married it, became its wife.

All of change, I found, is nothing more
than all of life.

ADELE KENNY 1948–

THIS LIVING

It's not destination, but more what silence is when
you enter it deeply—like walking in snow (the hush
and spell). You have fallen your whole life to land
here (your long, exhausted sigh and only a stone
where love has left you: the minor key of it, the

pricked stars). You step back for perspective. Branches
move like voices; and just there, you hear the voice you
haven't heard in years (your own)—a kind of whistling
(what some call song). The leaves are astonished—
no shame in surprise, in anything moving or rooted—

it's what you get when you live long enough. So why
define what opened in your life or disappeared? You did
or didn't. And, yes, you remember how to live. The soul
does that. It's what moves you forward. (God and your
ghosts on the other side.) And here: this wing, this living.

BHIKSHUNI WEISBROT 1953–

SAFETY HARBOR

Years ago, it could have been Tahiti,
we sat together, looked at the stars
watched the night blackened water
lap at our feet.
What we talked then was night philosophy—
whisperings of insight lent by the cosmos,
opening of the intuitive eye.
It was there we pondered gaps of infinitude
riding back like a night horse to
the beginning of time.
On fire the conversation ran its course.

We sparkled incandescent,
two sea nymphs at the water's edge,
flowers in our hair,
the scent of frangipani so rich
it followed us through sleep
like a well thought out trail.

It seems so long ago, the luxury
of unguarded conversation,
freedom's beauty dazzling us with
a siren's façade.
We are no longer so young to pretend
girlish safety or to laugh in late night giddiness
in a hard fight against sleep.
You live somewhere in danger city
in a clean co-op with hip neighbors and
have given up the search for light,
but I am still here—
a faint pulse on this shaky richter scale
of a planet, monitored from above
like a heartbeat on a screen, deciding,
(at least for today), not to face the
cracking cover of a world made sad
by bad decisions.

I shall keep my faith and
I shall build my patience,
not for a brave new world
but for the daily miracle of love.

Cycle 2: Pride, Self-Love and Resilience

THOMAS TRAHERNE 1637–1674

THE RAPTURE

Sweet Infancy!
O Fire of heaven! O sacred Light
    How fair and bright,
    How great am I,
Whom all the world doth magnify!

O Heavenly Joy!
O great and sacred blessedness
    Which I possess!
    So great a joy
Who did into my arms convey?

From God above
Being sent, the Heavens me enflame:
    To praise his Name
    The stars to move!
The burning sun doth show His love.

O how divine
Am I! To all this sacred wealth,
    This life and health,
    Who raised? Who mine
Did make the same? What hand divine?

WALT WHITMAN 1819–1892

ONE'S-SELF I SING

One's-Self I sing, a simple separate person,
Yet utter the word Democratic, the word En-Masse.

Of physiology from top to toe I sing,
Not physiognomy alone nor brain alone is worthy for the
    Muse, I say the Form complete is worthier far,
The Female equally with the Male I sing.

Of Life immense in passion, pulse, and power,
Cheerful, for freest action form'd under the laws divine,
The Modern Man I sing.

LAWS FOR CREATIONS

Laws for creations,
For strong artists and leaders, for fresh broods of teachers and
    perfect literats for America,
For noble savans and coming musicians.

All must have reference to the ensemble of the world, and the
    compact truth of the world,
There shall be no subject too pronounced—all works shall
    illustrate the divine law of indirections.

What do you suppose creation is?
What do you suppose will satisfy the soul, except to walk free
    and own no superior?
What do you suppose I would intimate to you in a hundred
    ways, but that man or woman is as good as God?
And that there is no God any more divine than Yourself?
And that that is what the oldest and newest myths finally
    mean?
And that you or any one must approach creations through
    such laws?

O ME! O LIFE!

O me! O life! of the questions of these recurring,
Of the endless trains of the faithless, of cities fill'd with the
    foolish,
Of myself forever reproaching myself, (for who more foolish
    than I, and who more faithless?)

Of eyes that vainly crave the light, of the objects mean, of the
    struggle ever renew'd,
Of the poor results of all, of the plodding and sordid crowds I
    see around me,
Of the empty and useless years of the rest, with the rest me
    intertwined,
The question, O me! so sad, recurring—What good amid
    these, O me, O life?
                           Answer—
That you are here—that life exists and identity,
That the powerful play goes on, and you may contribute a
    verse.

Sara Teasdale 1884–1933

The Answer

When I go back to earth
And all my joyous body
Puts off the red and white
That once had been so proud,
If men should pass above
With false and feeble pity,
My dust will find a voice
To answer them aloud:
"Be still, I am content,
Take back your poor compassion,
Joy was a flame in me
Too steady to destroy;
Lithe as a bending reed
Loving the storm that sways her—
I found more joy in sorrow
Than you could find in joy."

Langston Hughes 1902–1967

Mother to Son

Well, son, I'll tell you:
Life for me ain't been no crystal stair.
It's had tacks in it,
And splinters,

And boards torn up,
And places with no carpet on the floor—
Bare.
But all the time
I'se been a-climbin' on,
And reachin' landin's,
And turnin' corners,
And sometimes goin' in the dark
Where there ain't been no light.
So boy, don't you turn back.
Don't you set down on the steps
 'Cause you finds it's kinder hard.
Don't you fall now—
For I'se still goin,' honey,
I'se still climbin,'
And life for me ain't been no crystal stair.

THE NEGRO SPEAKS OF RIVERS

I've known rivers:
I've known rivers ancient as the world and older than the flow
 of human blood in human veins.

My soul has grown deep like the rivers.

I bathed in the Euphrates when dawns were young.
I built my hut near the Congo and it lulled me to sleep.
I looked upon the Nile and raised the pyramids above it.
I heard the singing of the Mississippi when Abe Lincoln went
 down to New Orleans, and I've seen its muddy bosom turn
 all golden in the sunset.

I've known rivers:
Ancient, dusky rivers.

My soul has grown deep like the rivers.

NEGRO

I am a Negro:
 Black as the night is black,
 Black like the depths of my Africa.

I've been a slave:
 Caesar told me to keep his door-steps clean.
 I brushed the boots of Washington.

I've been a worker:
    Under my hand the pyramids arose.
    I made mortar for the Woolworth Building.

I've been a singer:
    All the way from Africa to Georgia
    I carried my sorrow songs.
    I made ragtime.

I've been a victim:
    The Belgians cut off my hands in the Congo.
    They lynch me still in Mississippi.

I am a Negro:
    Black as the night is black,
    Black like the depths of my Africa.

CHARLES BUKOWSKI 1920–1994

MIND AND HEART

unaccountably we are alone
forever alone
and it was meant to be
that way,
it was never meant
to be any other way—
and when the death struggle
begins
the last thing I wish to see
is
a ring of human faces
hovering over me—
better just my old friends,
the walls of my self,
let only them be there.

I have been alone but seldom
lonely.
I have satisfied my thirst
at the well
of my self
and that wine was good,
the best I ever had,

and tonight
sitting
staring into the dark
I now finally understand
the dark and the
light and everything
in between.

peace of mind and heart
arrives
when we accept what
is:
having been
born into this
strange life
we must accept
the wasted gamble of our
days
and take some satisfaction in
the pleasure of
leaving it all
behind.

cry not for me.

grieve not for me.

read
what I've written
then
forget it
all.

drink from the well
of your self
and begin
again.

MAYA ANGELOU 1928–2014

WOMAN ME

Your smile, delicate
rumor of peace.
Deafening revolutions nestle in the

cleavage of
your breasts.
Beggar-Kings and red-ringed Priests
seek glory at the meeting
of your thighs.
A grasp of Lions. A lap of Lambs.

> Your tears, jeweled
> strewn a diadem
> caused Pharaohs to ride
> deep in the bosom of the
> Nile. Southern spas lash fast
> their doors upon the night when
> winds of death blow down your name
> A bride of hurricanes. A swarm of summer wind.

Your laughter, pealing tall
above the bells of ruined cathedrals.
Children reach between your teeth
for charts to live their lives.
A stomp of feet. A bevy of swift hands.

Chinmoy Kumar Ghose 1931–2007

Aspiration

Aspiration
Is a very brave step
Into the Unknowable.

Obstructions

Obstructions loom large within and without.
Nevertheless, like a kite I shall rise
Without fail against the wind.

Joyce Snyder 1945–

I Came Here to Fly

Do you think I want to bargain with you over this?
Do you think we can work out a trade?
I give you my Soul; you give me your approval—
Do you think it works like that?

I didn't come here to play your game
or march to your tune.
I came here to fly.

I was here before—crawling.
I walked, I stumbled, I fell.
I was here before, playing in your band;
it was music made in hell.

I came here this time and promised myself
I'd do it or I'd die.
I came with my own song because
this time I came to fly.

Before, in other lifetimes
my heart was like a stone.
Anchored by the weight
it kept me earth-bound, far from home.

Before, I wandered aimlessly
not knowing right from wrong.
Enchanted by false gifts, I sold
my treasures for a song.

But this time things are different,
and I can tell you why.
   It's all in how you see yourself,
   and I came here to fly.

ADELE KENNY 1948–

LIKE I SAID

Okay, so it's Sunday. I didn't
go to church. I'm an Irish Catholic,
I know about sin, but I was tired and
just didn't feel like getting dressed.

On Thursday night, I fell and broke
a slat from the garden fence. My
hip still hurts—the bruise is as big
as my Yorkie's head.

That would have been enough, but
this morning the vacuum coughed up

a hairball and quit. The only food in
the fridge is a bearded yogurt.

The washing machine refuses to spin.
There's no clean underwear left, so
I'm not wearing any. Like I said,
I was tired; I didn't feel like getting

dressed, so I didn't go to church and
abdicated rights to all that grace.
I put on a pair of dirty jeans, a dirty
shirt, and sat outdoors all morning.

I did nothing but talk to my dogs,
watch squirrels, and wonder what it
might be like to nibble Prozac from
Johnny Depp's lower lip.

SURVIVOR

A jay on the fence preaches to a
squirrel. I watch the squirrel quiver,
the way squirrels do—its whole
body flickers. I'm not sure why this
reminds me of when I was five and

something died in our drain spout.
Feather or fur, I watched my father
dig it out, knowing (as a child knows)
how much life matters. I have seen how
easily autumn shakes the yellow leaves,

how winter razes the shoals of heaven.
I have felt love's thunder and moan, and
had my night on the wild river. I have
heard the cancer diagnosis with my name
in it. I know what mercy is and isn't.

Morning breaks from sparrows' wings
(life's breezy business), and I'm still here,
still in love with the sorrows, the joys –
days like this, measured by memory, the
ticking crickets, the pulse in my wrist.

SOMEHOW THE ANGEL

It happens like this: the sudden waking,
your heart skipped and flipped, lungs

strung like pebbles on wire; and that
next breath—you're sure you can't take it,
but you *do* breathe.

You think *sleep*, and not sleep. You think
about pills, about taking *all* the pills –
what that would mean, where you would
be if you weren't here—and you
almost consider it.

Always, then, the old angel wheezes in.
Not quite luminous, never on his knees,
his wings creak, beat at oblique angles
(all that flapping—it's hardly celestial),
but his own

weight escapes him, and he flies toward
you, wrists like bells ringing, a miracle in
each fist. You say you believe (though
you know you talk to yourself) – you
believe in anything

with wings, no cage to hold it, and it's
okay, it's okay—the angel walks you up
the stairs. Over the trash bin. Dumpster.
And, somehow, somehow, you pull
yourself through.

Cycle 3: Ecstasy, Elevation and Rapture

Jalâl al–Din Rumi 1207–1273

Top of the Morning, You're Already Smashed

Top of the morning, you're already smashed
    oh yes you are! you tied your turban crooked.
Today your eyes look shot, all glazed over
    I think you drank a hundred proof last night
Light of our lives and light of our hearts!
    Salutations to you! How are you feeling?
You imbibed and traveled to the heavens
    got yourself sotted and broke all bonds
        The face of reason always freezes hearts.
        The face of love turns all heads giddy
You got sotted, started wrestling lions
    wine-suckled, rode bareback on a lion's neck
Like an old shaykh the aged wine guided you
    Go now, freed from the ancient spinning wheel.

Sâqi,[1] you hold truth and justice on your side
    refusing worship to all things but wine
You've borne away our reason,
but this time carry us away
like we'll never go again

                —Trans. Franklin D. Lewis

With Each New Breath the Sound of Love

With each new breath the sound of love
surrounds us all from right and left
Now up we go, head heavenward
who wants to come and see the sights?

We've been before in heaven's realm,
The angels there our constant friends,
we'll go again
for we were born
all in that town.

We are ourselves above the skies
a greater host than angels there;
why should we not exceed their rank
since our abode is Majesty?
The purest pearl
does not belong
in earthly dust.

What brought you down? What place is this?
Pack up!
By fortune blessed to give our lives,
the caravan will guide our steps:
 Our pride in life, the Chosen One
 By His bright orb the moon was split
 (it would not turn its gaze away)
 And so luck smiled upon the moon
  the lowly moon that begs its light!
 The wind's sweet scent drips from his locks
 His image shines with brilliant rays
 from his bright face, reflecting from
 "And the sun in its zenith"
See how my heart with every beat
reveals the moon cleft clear in two
 Why do you turn your sight down from such a sight?
 Like water birds, man's born within
 the sea of soul
 How could he nest within the mire,
 that ocean bird?
 and we are all pearls in that sea,
 afloat on it,
 or else why wave on wave would surge
 all through our hearts?
 Over our boat just like a wave
 broke "Am I not"
 Our ship's ribs staved the boat will sink
 our time has come for reunion,
 to meet with God.

—Trans. Franklin D. Lewis

Juan de la Cruz 1542–1591

In pursuit of an amorous encounter

In pursuit of an amorous encounter
and not lacking hope
I flew so high so high
that I reached my hunted.

So that I could reach
this divine encounter
much flying brought me convenience
such that I would be lost from sight
and with all in this trance,
I lacked the flying skills
yet love went so high
that I reached my hunted.

As I much higher flew
the sight dazzled me
and the much stronger conquest
fled more into the dark,
as it was a love encounter
I made a blind and dark leap
and I went so high, so high
that I reached my hunted.

As I much higher arrived
of this encounter so raised
so much lower and tired
and defeated I found myself
I said: There is none who can reach.
I prostrated so much so much
thus I went so high so high
that I reached my hunted.

In a strange way
a thousand flights I passed from one
because hope from the sky
so much reaches what is expected
I expected only this encounter
and in expectancies I was not lacking
thus I went so high so high,
that I reached my hunted.

                         —Trans. Sandra Kunanele

HENRY VAUGHAN 1621–1695

THE MORNING WATCH

O joys! infinite sweetness! with what flowers
And shoots of glory, my soul breaks and buds!
    All the long hours
    Of night and rest,
    Through the still shrouds
    Of sleep, and clouds,
  This dew fell on my breast;
    O how it bloods,
And spirits all my earth! hark! in what rings,
And hymning circulations the quick world
    Awakes, and sings!
    The rising winds,
    And falling springs,
    Birds, beasts, all things
  Adore Him in their kinds.
    Thus all is hurled
In sacred hymns and order; the great chime
And symphony of Nature. Prayer is
    The world in tune,
    A spirit-voice,
    And vocal joys,
  Whose echo is heaven's bliss.
    O let me climb
When I lie down! The pious soul by night
Is like a clouded star, whose beams, though said
    To shed their light
    Under some cloud,
    Yet are above,
    And shine and move
  Beyond that misty shroud.
    So in my bed,
That curtained grave, though sleep, like ashes, hide
My lamp and life, both shall in thee abide.

BABA BULLEH SHAH 1680–1757

HE WHO IS STRICKEN BY LOVE

    He who is stricken by Love
    Sings and dances out of tune.

He who wears the garb of Love
Gets blessings from above.

Soon as he drinks from this cup
No questions and no answers remain.

He who is stricken by Love
Sings and dances out of tune.

He who has the Beloved in his heart,
He is fulfilled with his Love.

No need he has for formality,
He just enjoys his ecstasy.

He who is stricken by Love
Sings and dances out of tune.

—Trans. Mahmood Jamal

PERCY BYSSHE SHELLEY 1792–1822

To Constantia

Thy voice, slow rising like a Spirit, lingers
O'ershadowing me with soft and lulling wings;
The blood and life within thy snowy fingers
Teach witchcraft to the instrumental strings.
    My brain is wild, my breath comes quick,
    The blood is listening in my frame,
    And thronging shadows fast and thick
    Fall on my overflowing eyes,
    My heart is quivering like a flame;
As morning dew, that in the sunbeam dies,
I am dissolved in these consuming extacies.

I have no life, Constantia, but in thee;
Whilst, like the world-surrounding air, thy song
Flows on, and fills all things with melody:
Now is thy voice a tempest, swift and strong,
    On which, as one in trance upborne,
    Secure o'er woods and waves I sweep
    Rejoicing, like a cloud of morn:
    Now 'tis the breath of summer's night
    Which, where the starry waters sleep

Round western isles with incense blossoms bright,
Lingering, suspends my soul in its voluptuous flight.

A deep and breathless awe, like the swift change
Of dreams unseen, but felt in youthful slumbers;
Wild, sweet, yet incommunicably strange,
Thou breathest now, in fast ascending numbers:
> The cope of Heaven seems rent and cloven
> By the inchantment of thy strain,
> And o'er my shoulders wings are woven
> To follow its sublime career,
> Beyond the mighty moons that wane
Upon the verge of Nature's utmost sphere,
Till the world's shadowy walls are past, and disappear.

Cease, cease—for such wild lessons madmen learn:
Long thus to sink,—thus to be lost and die
Perhaps is death indeed—Constantia turn!
Yes! in thine eyes a power like light doth lie,
> Even though the sounds, its voice, that were
> Between thy lips are laid to sleep—
> Within thy breath and on thy hair
> Like odour it is lingering yet—
> And from thy touch like fire doth leap:
Even while I write my burning cheeks are wet—
Such things the heart can feel and learn, but not forget!

RALPH WALDO EMERSON 1803–1882

BACCHUS

Bring me wine, but wine which never grew
In the belly of the grape,
Or grew on vine whose tap-roots reaching through
Under the Andes to the Cape,
Suffered no savor of the world to 'scape.

Let its grapes the morn salute
From a nocturnal root
Which feels the acrid juice
Of Styx and Erebus,
And turns the woe of night,
By its own craft, to a more rich delight.

We buy ashes for bread,
We buy diluted wine;
Give me of the true,—
Whose ample leaves and tendrils curled
Among the silver hills of heaven,
Draw everlasting dew;
Wine of wine,
Blood of the world,
Form of forms and mould of statures,
That I intoxicated,
And by the draught assimilated,
May float at pleasure through all natures,
The bird-language rightly spell,
And that which roses say so well.

Wine that is shed
Like the torrents of the sun
Up the horizon walls;
Or like the Atlantic streams which run
When the South Sea calls.

Water and bread,
Food which needs no transmuting,
Rainbow-flowering, wisdom-fruiting;
Wine which is already man,
Food which teach and reason can.

Wine which music is,—
Music and wine are one,—
That I, drinking this,
Shall hear far Chaos talk with me,
Kings unborn shall walk with me,
And the poor grass shall plot and plan
What it will do when it is man:
Quickened so, will I unlock
Every crypt of every rock.
I thank the joyful juice

For all I know;
Winds of remembering
Of the ancient being blow,
And seeming-solid walls of use
Open and flow.

Pour, Bacchus, the remembering wine;
Retrieve the loss of me and mine!

Vine for vine be antidote,
And the grape requite the lote.
Haste to cure the old despair,—
Reason in nature's lotus drenched,
The memory of ages quenched;
Give them again to shine.
Let wine repair what this undid,
And where the infection slid,
And dazzling memory revive;
Refresh the faded tints,
Recut the aged prints,
And write my old adventures, with the pen
Which, on the first day drew,
Upon the tablets blue,
The dancing Pleiads and the eternal men.

WALT WHITMAN 1819–1892

ONE HOUR TO MADNESS AND JOY

One hour to madness and joy! O furious! O confine me not!
(What is this that frees me so in storms?
What do my shouts amid lightnings and raging winds mean?)

O to drink the mystic deliria deeper than any other man!
O savage and tender achings! (I bequeath them to you my
    children,
I tell them to you, for reasons, O bridegroom and bride.)
O to be yielded to you whoever you are, and you to be yielded
    to me in defiance of the world!
O to return to Paradise! O bashful and feminine!
O to draw you to me, to plant on you for the first time the lips
    of a determin'd man.

O the puzzle, the thrice-tied knot, the deep and dark pool, all
    untied and illumin'd
O to speed where there is space enough and air enough at last!
To be absolv'd from previous ties and conventions, I from mine
    and you from yours!
To find a new unthought-of·nonchalance with the best of
    Nature!
To have the gag remov'd from one's mouth!
To have the feeling to-day or any day I am sufficient as I am.

O something unprov'd! something in a trance!
To escape utterly from others' anchors and holds!
To drive free! to love free! to dash reckless and dangerous!
To court destruction with taunts, with invitations!
To ascend, to leap to the heavens of the love indicated to me!
To rise thither with my inebriate soul!
To be lost if it must be so!
To feed the remainder of life with one hour of fulness and
    freedom!
With one brief hour of madness and joy.

ANNE BRONTË 1820–1849

IN A WOOD ON A WINDY DAY

My soul is awakened, my spirit is soaring
And carried aloft on the wings of the breeze;
For above and around me the wild wind is roaring,
Arousing to rapture the earth and the seas.
The long withered grass in the sunshine is glancing,
The bare trees are tossing their branches on high;
The dead leaves beneath them are merrily dancing,
The white clouds are scudding across the blue sky
I wish I could see how the ocean is lashing
The foam of its billows to whirlwinds of spray;
I wish I could see how its proud waves are dashing,
And hear the wild roar of their thunder to-day!

DANTE GABRIEL ROSSETTI 1828–1882

LOVE'S TESTAMENT

O thou who at Love's hour ecstatically
    Upon my heart dost ever more present,
    Clothed with his fire, thy heart his testament;
Whom I have neared and felt thy breath to be
The inmost incense of his sanctuary;
    Who without speech hast owned him, and, intent
    Upon his will, thy life with mine hast blent,
And murmured, "I am thine, thou'rt one with me!"
O what from thee the grace, to me the prize,

And what to Love the glory,—when the whole
Of the deep stair thou tread'st to the dim shoal
And weary water of the place of sighs,
And there dost work deliverance, as thine eyes
Draw up my prisoned spirit to thy soul!

EMILY DICKINSON 1830–1886

EXULTATION IS THE GOING

Exultation is the going
Of an inland soul to sea,
Past the houses past—the headlands –
Into deep Eternity –

Bred as we, among the mountains,
Can the sailor understand
The divine intoxication
Of the first league out from land?

WILD NIGHTS—WILD NIGHTS!

Wild Nights—Wild Nights!
Were I with thee
Wild Nights should be
Our luxury!

Futile—the Winds –
To a Heart in port –
Done with the Compass –
Done with the Chart!

Rowing in Eden –
Ah, the Sea!
Might I but moor—Tonight –
In Thee!

GERARD MANLEY HOPKINS 1844–1889

THE WINDHOVER
To Christ our Lord

I caught this morning morning's minion, king-
    dom of daylight's dauphin, dapple-dawn-drawn Falcon, in his riding

Of the rolling level underneath him steady air, and striding
High there, how he rung upon the rein of a wimpling wing
In his ecstasy! then off, off forth on swing,
    As a skate's heel sweeps smooth on a bow-bend: the hurl and gliding
    Rebuffed the big wind. My heart in hiding
Stirred for a bird, – the achieve of, the mastery of the thing!

Brute beauty and valour and act, oh, air, pride, plume, here
    Buckle! AND the fire that breaks from thee then, a billion
Times told lovelier, more dangerous, O my chevalier!

    No wonder of it: shéer plód makes plough down sillion
Shine, and blue-bleak embers, ah my dear,
    Fall, gall themselves, and gash gold-vermilion.

GEORGE MARION MCCLELLAN 1860–1934

A SEPTEMBER NIGHT

The full September moon sheds floods of light,
And all the bayou's face is gemmed with stars
Save where are dropped fantastic shadows down
From sycamores and moss-hung cypress trees.
With slumberous sound the waters half asleep
Creep on and on their way, twixt rankish reeds,
Through marsh and lowlands stretching to the gulf.
Begirt with cotton fields Anguilla sits
Half bird-like dreaming on her summer nest
Amid her spreading figs, and roses still
In bloom with all their spring and summer hues.
Pomegranates hang with dapple cheeks full ripe,
And over all the town a dreamy haze
Drops down. The great plantations stretching far
Away are plains of cotton downy white.
O, glorious is this night of joyous sounds
Too full for sleep. Aromas wild and sweet,
From muscadine, late blooming jessamine,
And roses, all the heavy air suffuse.
Faint bellows from the alligators come
From swamps afar, where sluggish lagoons give
To them a peaceful home. The katydids[2]
Make ceaseless cries. Ten thousand insects' wings
Stir in the moonlight haze and joyous shouts

Of Negro song and mirth awake hard by
The cabin dance. O, glorious is this night.
The summer sweetness fills my heart with songs
I cannot sing, with loves I cannot speak.

ANDREI BIELY
(BORIS NIKOLAEVICH BUGAEV) 1880–1934

ON THE MOUNTAINS

The mountains wear wedding wreaths.
I am blissful, full of youth.
On my mountains I feel
A cleansing cold.

And just now to my rock
Stumbled a gray-haired hunchback.
He bore a gift with him for me-
Pineapples from an underground dungeon.

He danced in bright raspberry red,
In praise of the azure sky.
With his beard he swept
Whirlwinds of storming silver blizzards.

He roared
In a deep voice
And threw in the sky
The pineapple.

And drawing an arch,
Lighting everything around,
A pineapple fell, casting luminescence,
Into the unknown.

Leaving a golden dew,
As if ducats were falling.
Down below they said:
"It's a disk of a flaming sun ..."

Golden fountains of fire
And dew like crystal,
Flaming red,
Rang out and flew down
Bathing the rocks too.

I poured wine in glasses,
Sneaking aside, and
Drenched the hunchback
With an effulgent foamy flood.

—Trans. Tatsiana DeRosa

WILLIAM CARLOS WILLIAMS 1883–1963

DAWN

Ecstatic bird songs pound
the hollow vastness of the sky
with metallic clinkings—
beating color up into it
at a far edge,—beating it, beating it
with rising, triumphant ardor,—
stirring it into warmth,
quickening in it a spreading change,—
bursting wildly against it as
dividing the horizon, a heavy sun
lifts himself—is lifted—
bit by bit above the edge
of things,—runs free at last
out into the open—! lumbering
glorified in full release upward—
                    songs cease.

SIEGFRIED SASSOON 1886–1967

EVERYONE SANG

Everyone suddenly burst out singing;
And I was filled with such delight
As prisoned birds must find in freedom,
Winging wildly across the white
Orchards and dark-green fields; on—on—and out of sight.
Everyone's voice was suddenly lifted;
And beauty came like the setting sun:
My heart was shaken with tears; and horror
Drifted away ... O, but Everyone
Was a bird; and the song was wordless; the singing will never be done.

EDNA ST. VINCENT MILLAY 1892–1950

GOD'S WORLD

O world, I cannot hold thee close enough!
    Thy winds, thy wide grey skies!
    Thy mists that roll and rise!
Thy woods this autumn day, that ache and sag
And all but cry with color! That gaunt crag
To crush! To lift the lean of that black bluff!
World, World, I cannot get thee close enough!

Long have I known a glory in it all,
    But never knew I this;
    Here such a passion is
As stretcheth me apart,—Lord, I do fear
Thou'st made the world too beautiful this year;
My soul is all but out of me,—let fall
No burning leaf; prithee, let no bird call.

SHARON OLDS 1942–

FULL SUMMER

I paused, and paused, over your body,
to feel the current of desire pull
and pull through me. Our hair was still wet,
mine like knotted wrack, it fell
across you as I paused, a soaked coil
around your glans. When one of your hairs
dried, it lifted like a bare nerve.
On the beach, above us, a cloud had appeared in
the clear air, a clockwise loop coming
in out of nothing, now the skin of your scrotum
moved like a live being, an animal,
I began to lick you, the foreskin lightly
stuck in one spot, like a petal, I love
to free it—just so—in joy,
and to sip from the little crying lips
at the tip. Then there was no more pausing,
nor was this the taker,
some new one came
and sucked, and up from where I had been hiding I was

drawn in a heavy spiral out of matter
over into another world
I had thought I would have to die to reach.

BHIKSHUNI WEISBROT 1953–

DAINTREE[3]

You speak the language of
trees.
I speak the language of
astonishment,
the architecture of your
veins and roots,
the tidiness of your vines,
you are a house of personality.
I will live under the source of
your replication,
under the wooden arches where
your duality is a mirror of symmetry—
I will live inside your
burnished arms, in the
ovals, in the perfect
circles I will place myself.
It is raining—
Jubilation!
If I could possess that dragon lizard's
stillness,
I would affix myself forever
to this day.

J.C. AUGUSTINE WETTA 1971–

RUNNING DOWN STRAIGHT STREET

It was too
Hot.
The air was thick with steam,
Rising like warm breath from rocks and ferns.
But I ran
Like terror
Out of my cool cell
Into the sun

Furious with heat.
A clenched fist at the small of my back.

And my feet steamed in my shoes,
And my breath baked in my chest
And every slap of the pavement rang sweat upon my face.
But I ran on.

Jaded trees scorned my effort. Quiet. Exhausted.
Even the insects received my fury in silence.

And the sweat shook into my face with each stride
And the salt collected in the corners of my eyes.
And the world turned a shade of red.
But I ran on

Pushing through the summer air
So thick, my breath seemed cool by comparison.

Until
A drop
Between
The eyes
Stopped
Me

Like the cool finger of God.
And to be sure
He had my attention,
Another
Tapped the crown of my head
And another
My chin,
My cheek,
My lip.
And another.
Then with a flash and a crack,
I was enveloped
By a thousand cold touches
Like the fingertips of a blind man,
Till there was no taste of salt left.
And I ran on,
My shirt slapping my back like a heavy hand
And my toes pushing water through the seams of my shoes
And all about me, nature stretched its jade leaves
Heavenward.

Rachel Jamison Webster 1974–

Through Hooded Clouds Untranslatable, Once

I ploughed through sky toward it,
then after promise and partial
consummation, shadow purled
with knots of sun, I flew back again,
looking down on cobbles of white,
clods of mist in the heights.
I was flying! I had always been
myself and never more
than gathering and dispersal,
ever motion, ever flux,
burdened by the very water
that will make me real.
And all this time, I've had only one
thing to do: learn to love.
My vaulted mouth splits
as that air enters me.

Cycle 4: Consciousness Expansion, Growth and Engagement with Unconscious Depths

FARIDUDDIN 'ATTAR 1145–1221

I SHALL BE DRUNK TONIGHT

I shall be drunk tonight and
Dance with a cup of wine in my hand!
I shall wander through the streets
Of drunkenness and lose all in a game of chance.
How long shall I be a hypocrite?
How long will I worship my Self?
I want to tear this veil of puritan pride;
I want to break this false vow of abstinence;
Time has come to have some courage
And prepare to be a slave of Love.
Give me such intoxicating wine, O Saqi;
Hurry or the sorrow will pervade my soul!
Pass the wine, yes, pass the wine!
So that we can bring down the skies under our feet,
So Mercury becomes obedient to our wish,
And Venus our adoring lover.
Like Attar we shall cross the bounds
And lose ourselves in boundless Love!
>   —Trans. Mahmood Jamal

KABIR 1440–1518

XVI

Between the poles of the con-
    scious and the unconscious, there
    has the mind made a swing:
Thereon hang all beings and all worlds,
    and that swing never ceases its
    sway.
Millions of beings are there: the sun
    and the moon in their courses are
    there:
Millions of ages pass, and the swing
    goes on.
All swing! the sky and the earth and
    the air and the water; and the
    Lord Himself taking form:
And the sight of this has made Kabir
    a servant.
              —Trans. Rabindranath Tagore

GIACOMO LEOPARDI 1798–1837

THE INFINITE

Always dear to me was this lone hill,
And this hedge, from so grand a part
The last horizon excludes the view.
But sitting and gazing, there is boundless
Space beyond the superhuman
Silence, and profound quiet.
In my thoughts I pretend
that my heart does not fear. And like the wind
I hear rustling through these plants. To that
infinite silence I compare this voice.
And I recollect the eternal, and the dead seasons,
and the present and living, and the sound of her.
This way, between immensity, my thoughts drown.
And the shipwreck is sweet in this sea.
              —Trans. Gabriella Basile

HERE THE WAVES MURMUR

Here the waves murmur,
And the fronds tremble
In the breeze of morning, and the saplings
And over the green branches the wandering birds
Sing gently,
And the East smiles;
Here dawn already appears,
And she reflects herself in the sea,
And reassures the sky,
And the fresh frost impearls the countryside,
And adorns the high mountains in gold:
O beautiful and wandering Aurora,
The breeze is your messenger, and you the breeze's,
Who restores each burned heart.

—Trans. Gabriella Basile

ALEXANDER S. PUSHKIN 1799–1837

TO ...

I remember a miraculous moment:
You appeared in my life,
Like a passing apparition,
Like the genius of striking beauty.

In the tyranny of hopeless sadness
In the troubles of noisy hustling,
I heard your tender voice for so long,
And saw your dear face in my dreams.

Years passed. Violent gusts of storms
Dissolved my former dreams,
And I forgot your tender voice,
Your heavenly face.

In the darkness of restraint,
My days dragged on quietly,
Without faith, without inspiration,
Without tears, without life, without love.

Then my soul awoke:
And you appeared in my life again,

Like a passing apparition,
Like the genius of striking beauty.

And now my heart beats in delight,
And remembers all at once
Faith, and inspiration,
And life, and tears and love.

—Trans. Tatsiana DeRosa

ELIZABETH BARRETT BROWNING 1806–1861

VII

The face of all the world is changed, I think,
Since first I heard the footsteps of thy soul
Move still, oh, still, beside me, as they stole
Betwixt me and the dreadful outer brink
Of obvious death, where I, who thought to sink,
Was caught up into love, and taught the whole
Of life in a new rhythm. The cup of dole
God gave for baptism, I am fain to drink,
And praise its sweetness, Sweet, with thee anear.
The names of country, heaven, are changed away
For where thou art or shalt be, there or here;
And this ... this lute and song ... loved yesterday,
(The singing angels know) are only dear
Because thy name moves right in what they say.

X

Yet, love, mere love, is beautiful indeed
And worthy of acceptation. Fire is bright,
Let temple burn, or flax; an equal light
Leaps in the flame from cedar-plank or weed:
And love is fire. And when I say at need
I love thee ... mark! ... I love thee—in thy sight
I stand transfigured, glorified aright,
With conscience of the new rays that proceed
Out of my face toward thine. There's nothing low
In love, when love the lowest: meanest creatures
Who love God, God accepts while loving so.
And what I *feel*, across the inferior features
Of what I *am*, doth flash itself, and show
How that great work of Love enhances Nature's.

WALT WHITMAN 1819–1892

THAT MUSIC ALWAYS ROUND ME

That music always round me, unceasing, unbeginning, yet long
    untaught I did not hear,
But now the chorus I hear and am elated,
A tenor, strong, ascending with power and health, with glad
    notes of daybreak I hear,
A soprano at intervals sailing buoyantly over the tops of
    immense waves,
A transparent base shuddering lusciously under and through
    the universe,
The triumphant tutti, the funeral wailings with sweet flutes
    and violins, and all these I fill myself with,
I hear not the volumes of sound merely, I am moved by the
    exquisite meanings,
I listen to the different voices winding in and out, striving,
    contending with fiery vehemence to excel each other in
    emotion;
I do not think the performers know themselves—but now I
    think I begin to know them.

TO YOU

Whoever you are, I fear you are walking the walks of dreams,
I fear these supposed realities are to melt from under your feet
    and hands,
Even now your features, joys, speech, house, trade, manners,
    troubles, follies, costume, crimes, dissipate away from you,
Your true soul and body appear before me,
They stand forth out of affairs, out of commerce, shops, work,
    farms, clothes, the house, buying, selling, eating, drinking,
    suffering, dying.

Whoever you are, now I place my hand upon you, that you be
    my poem,
I whisper with my lips close to your ear,
I have loved many women and men, but I love none better
    than you.

O I have been dilatory and dumb,
I should have made my way straight to you long ago,
I should have blabb'd nothing but you, I should have chanted
    nothing but you.

I will leave all and come and make the hymns of you,
None has understood you, but I understand you,
None has done justice to you, you have not done justice to
     yourself,
None but has found you imperfect, I only find no imperfection
     in you,
None but would subordinate you, I only am he who will never
     consent to subordinate you,
I only am he who places over you no master, owner, better,
     God, beyond what waits intrinsically in yourself.

Painters have painted their swarming groups and the centre-
     figure of all,
From the head of the centre-figure spreading a nimbus of gold-
     color'd light,
But I paint myriads of heads, but paint no head without its
     nimbus of gold-color'd light,
From my hand from the brain of every man and woman it
     streams, effulgently flowing forever.

O I could sing such grandeurs and glories about you!
You have not known what you are, you have slumber'd upon
     yourself all your life,
Your eyelids have been the same as closed most of the time,
What you have done returns already in mockeries,
(Your thrift, knowledge, prayers, if they do not return in
     mockeries, what is their return?)

The mockeries are not you,
Underneath them and within them I see you lurk,
I pursue you where none else has pursued you,
Silence, the desk, the flippant expression, the night, the
     accustom'd routine, if these conceal you from others or
     from yourself, they do not conceal you from me,
The shaved face, the unsteady eye, the impure complexion, if
     these balk others they do not balk me,
The pert apparel, the deform'd attitude, drunkenness, greed,
     premature death, all these I part aside.

There is no endowment in man or woman that is not tallied in
     you,
There is no virtue, no beauty in man or woman, but as good is
     in you,
No pluck, no endurance in others, but as good is in you,
No pleasure waiting for others, but an equal pleasure waits for you.

As for me, I give nothing to any one except I give the like
    carefully to you,
I sing the songs of glory of none, not God, sooner than I
    sing the songs of the glory of you.
Whoever you are! claim your own at any hazard!
These shows of the East and West are tame compared to you,
These immense meadows, these interminable rivers, you are
    immense and interminable as they,
These furies, elements, storms, motions of Nature, throes of
    apparent dissolution, you are he or she who is master or
    mistress over them,
Master or mistress in your own right over Nature, elements,
    pain, passion, dissolution.

The hopples fall from your ankles, you find an unfailing
    sufficiency,
Old or young, male or female, rude, low, rejected by the rest,
    whatever you are promulges itself,
Through birth, life, death, burial, the means are provided,
    nothing is scanted,
Through angers, losses, ambition, ignorance, ennui, what you
    are picks its way.

MATTHEW ARNOLD 1822–1888

THE BURIED LIFE

Light flows our war of mocking words, and yet,
Behold, with tears mine eyes are wet!
I feel a nameless sadness o'er me roll.
Yes, yes, we know that we can jest,
We know, we know that we can smile!
But there's a something in this breast,
To which thy light words bring no rest,
And thy gay smiles no anodyne.
Give me thy hand, and hush awhile,
And turn those limpid eyes on mine,
And let me read there, love! thy inmost soul.

Alas! is even love too weak
To unlock the heart, and let it speak?
Are even lovers powerless to reveal
To one another what indeed they feel?

I knew the mass of men concealed
Their thoughts, for fear that if revealed
They would by other men be met
With blank indifference, or with blame reproved;
I knew they lived and moved
Tricked in disguises, alien to the rest
Of men, and alien to themselves—and yet
The same heart beats in every human breast!

But we, my love!—doth a like spell benumb
Our hearts, our voices?—must we too be dumb?

Ah! well for us, if even we,
Even for a moment, can get free
Our heart, and have our lips unchained;
For that which seals them hath been deep-ordained!

Fate, which foresaw
How frivolous a baby man would be—
By what distractions he would be possessed,
How he would pour himself in every strife,
And well-nigh change his own identity—
That it might keep from his capricious play
His genuine self, and force him to obey
Even in his own despite his being's law,
Bade through the deep recesses of our breast
The unregarded river of our life
Pursue with indiscernible flow its way;
And that we should not see
The buried stream, and seem to be
Eddying at large in blind uncertainty,
Though driving on with it eternally.

But often, in the world's most crowded streets,
But often, in the din of strife,
There rises an unspeakable desire
After the knowledge of our buried life;
A thirst to spend our fire and restless force
In tracking out our true, original course;
A longing to inquire
Into the mystery of this heart which beats
So wild, so deep in us—to know
Whence our lives come and where they go.
And many a man in his own breast then delves,
But deep enough, alas! None ever mines.

And we have been on many thousand lines,
And we have shown, on each, spirit and power;
But hardly have we, for one little hour,
Been on our own line, have we been ourselves—
Hardly had skill to utter one of all
The nameless feelings that course through our breast,
But they course on forever unexpressed.
And long we try in vain to speak and act
Our hidden self, and what 'we say and do
Is eloquent, is well—but 'tis not true!
And then we will no more be racked
With inward striving, and demand
Of all the thousand nothings of the hour
Their stupefying power;
Ah yes, and they benumb us at our call!
Yet still, from time to time, vague and forlorn,
From the soul's subterranean depth upborne
As from an infinitely distant land,
Come airs, and floating echoes, and convey
A melancholy into all our day.

Only—but this is rare—
When a belovéd hand is laid in ours,
When, jaded with the rush and glare
Of the interminable hours,
Our eyes can in another's eyes read clear,
When our world-deafened ear
Is by the tones of a loved voice caressed—
A bolt is shot back somewhere in our breast,
And a lost pulse of feeling stirs again.
The eye sinks inward, and the heart lies plain,
And what we mean, we say, and what we would, we know.
A man becomes aware of his life's flow,
And hears its winding murmur; and he sees
The meadows where it glides, the sun, the breeze.

And there arrives a lull in the hot race
Wherein he doth for ever chase
That flying and elusive shadow, rest.
An air of coolness plays upon his face,
And an unwonted calm pervades his breast.
And then he thinks he knows
The hills where his life rose,
And the sea where it goes.

EMILY DICKINSON 1830–1886

DARE YOU SEE A SOUL AT THE WHITE HEAT?

Dare you see a soul at the white heat?
Then crouch within the door.
Red is the fire's common tint;
But when the vivid ore
Has vanquished flame's conditions,
It quivers from the Forge
Without a color but the light
Of unanointed blaze.
Least village has its blacksmith
Whose anvil's even ring
Stands symbol for the finer forge
That soundless tugs within,
Refining these impatient ores
With hammer and with blaze,
Until the designated light
Repudiate the Forge.

THE BRAIN IS WIDER THAN THE SKY

The brain is wider than the sky,
For, put them side by side,
The one the other will include
With ease, and you beside.
The brain is deeper than the sea,
For, hold them, Blue to Blue,
The one the other will absorb,
As sponges, buckets do.
The brain is just the weight of God,
For, heft1 them, pound for pound,
And they will differ, if they do,
As syllable from sound.

RABINDRANATH TAGORE 1861–1941

20

On the day when the lotus bloomed, alas, my mind was stray-
ing, and I knew it not. My basket was empty and the flower
remained unheeded.

Only now and again a sadness fell upon me, and I started

up from my dream and felt a sweet trace of a strange fragrance in the south wind.

That vague sweetness made my heart ache with longing and it seemed to me that it was the eager breath of the summer seeking for its completion.

I knew not then that it was so near, that it was mine, and that this perfect sweetness had blossomed in the depth of my own heart.

—from *Gitanjali*

31

"Prisoner, tell me, who was it that bound you?"

"It was my master," said the prisoner. "I thought I could outdo everybody in the world in wealth and power, and I amassed in my own treasure-house the money due to my king. When sleep overcame me I lay upon the bed that was for my lord, and on waking up I found I was a prisoner in my own treasure-house."

"Prisoner, tell me who was it that wrought this unbreakable chain?"

"It was I," said the prisoner, "who forged this chain very carefully. I thought my invincible power would hold the world captive leaving me in a freedom undisturbed. Thus night and day I worked at the chain with huge fires and cruel hard strokes. When at last the work was done and the links were complete and unbreakable, I found that it held me in its grip."

—from *Gitanjali*

C.D. BALMONT 1867–1942

WITH MY ASPIRATION I CAUGHT
THE DISAPPEARING SHADOWS

With my aspiration I caught the disappearing shadows,
The disappearing shadows of the fading day,
I climbed the tower, and the stairs trembled,
And the stairs trembled under my feet.

And the higher I climbed, the clearer appeared,
The clearer appeared the figures in the distance,
And from that distance some noises came,
The noises came to me from Heaven and Earth.

The higher I rose, the brighter dazzled,
The brighter dazzled the peaks of the drowsing mountains,
As if caressing with this farewell glow,
As if caressing tenderly my misty eyes.

And beneath me the night came.
The night came for the sleeping Earth,
But for me the god of the daylight was shining,
The god of daylight was melting in the distance.

I found out how to catch the disappearing shadows,
The disappearing shadows of the fading day,
And I climbed higher, and the stairs trembled,
And the stairs trembled under my feet.

—Trans. Tatsiana DeRosa

V.Y. BRYUSOV 1873–1924

MY SPIRIT DID NOT BREAK IN THE DARKNESS OF CONTRADICTIONS

My spirit did not break in the darkness of contradictions,
My mind did not grow weaker in fateful opposition.
I love all dreams; all words are dear to me.
I dedicate my poem to all of the gods.

I prayed high prayers to Hecate[2] and Astarte,[3]
Like a priest, I shed the blood of a hundred calves,
And afterwards approached the crucifixes
And praised a love strong as death.

I visited the gardens of lyceums and academies,
On the wax I inscribed the wise men's speeches,
Like a diligent student I was adored by all of them,
But I only loved the conjunction of words.

On the Isle of Dream where there are statues and songs,
I walked all of the trails with torch and without torch.
Sometimes I worshiped those that are brighter,
Sometimes I eagerly looked forward to the shadows.

And I felt strange love for the darkness of contradictions,
With greed I began to search for fateful opposition.
All dreams are sweet to me; all words are precious,
And I dedicate my poem to all of the Gods.

—Trans. Tatsiana DeRosa

EDWARD FIELD 1924–

A JOURNEY

When he got up that morning everything was different:
He enjoyed the bright spring day
But he did not realize it exactly, he just enjoyed it.

And walking down the street to the railroad station
Past magnolia trees with dying flowers like old socks
It was a long time since he had breathed so simply.

Tears filled his eyes and it felt good
But he held them back
Because men didn't walk around crying in that town.

Waiting on the platform at the station
The fear came over him of something terrible about to happen:
The train was late and he recited the alphabet to keep hold.

And in its time it came screeching in
And as it went on making its usual stops,
People coming and going, telephone poles passing,

He hid his head behind a newspaper
No longer able to hold back the sobs, and willed his eyes
To follow the rational weavings of the seat fabric.

He didn't do anything violent as he had imagined.
He cried for a long time, but when he finally quieted down
A place in him that had been closed like a fist was open,

And at the end of the ride he stood up and got off that train:
And through the streets and in all the places he lived in later on
He walked, himself at last, a man among men,
With such radiance that everyone looked up and wondered.

WENDELL BERRY 1934–

I GO AMONG TREES AND SIT STILL

I go among trees and sit still.
All my stirring becomes quiet
around me like circles on water.
My tasks lie in their places
where I left them, asleep like cattle.

Then what is afraid of me comes
and lives a while in my sight.
What it fears in me leaves me,
and the fear of me leaves it.
It sings, and I hear its song.

Then what I am afraid of comes.
I live for a while in its sight.
What I fear in it leaves it,
and the fear of it leaves me.
It sings, and I hear its song.

After days of labor,
mute in my consternations,
I hear my song at last,
and I sing it. As we sing,
the day turns, the trees move.

JOYCE SNYDER 1945–

BALANCE

There is a part of me that is always weeping.
It is caused by the woes of the world.
If I look in a certain way, I can see her in this act.
I puzzle at this as I observe with sympathy
this expression of great pain.

There is a part of me that is always laughing.
Howling, almost, in foolish delight
at the joke life continually plays.
The mirth forever fed,
I am amused by the ways of the world.

There is a part of me that wants to scream.
Joyously. Hideously. Out of control.
I marvel at the restraint that keeps it in.
This calm becomes my virtue
and I acquiesce to pain.

The smile you see on my face
is the delicate balance of these idiot forces.

Joy Harjo 1951–

I Give You Back

I release you, my beautiful and terrible
fear. I release you. you were my beloved
and hated twin, but now, I don't know you
as myself. I release you with all the
pain I would know at the death of
my children.

You are not my blood anymore.

I give you back to the soldiers
who burned down my home, beheaded my children,
raped and sodomized my brothers and sisters.
I give you back to those who stole the
food from our plates when we were starving.

I release you, fear, because you hold
these scenes in front of me and I was born
with eyes that can never close.

I release you
I release you
I release you
I release you

I am not afraid to be angry.
I am not afraid to rejoice.
I am not afraid to be black.
I am not afraid to be white.
I am not afraid to be hungry.
I am not afraid to be full.
I am not afraid to be hated.
I am not afraid to be loved.

to be loved, to be loved, fear

Oh, you have chocked me, but I gave you the leash.
You have gutted me, but I gave you the knife.
You have devoured me, but I laid myself across the fire.

I take myself back, fear.
You are not my shadow any longer.
I won't hold you in my hands.
You can't live in my eyes, my ears, my voice

my belly, or in my heart my heart
my heart my heart

But come here, fear
I am alive and you are so afraid
of dying.

BHIKSHUNI WEISBROT 1953–

I JUST WANT TO BE HAPPY...

Whereas my mother said,
"Life is not about being happy,"
and there it was –
an impasse as big
as a Montana sky.

THE PLAY

You will forgive me
if I did not reveal myself to you
all at once,
but rather in fragments.

The freedom was exhilarating,
like the startling freshness of spring
plus there were no secrets.

I threw the flat stone of fear
far from me,
skipping, skipping
across a river of wide acceptance,
until
I held onto what I knew
was Your Love.

Strange how the mystery
of myself unveiled
humored me.

DANIEL WEEKS 1958–

A TENDERNESS HAS COME

It was as if he
were listening alone,

even with Clarissa
in his arms and
moving him with the sway
of her hips, listening
alone to the soft strain—
as if the music
were listening
to a deep something within,
a tenderness to be heard,
felt only when the music
had washed away the
world, and Clarissa
too radiating a
warmth to him,
making his mind
swim among the stars
with her fragrance,
like spring honeysuckle
and lilac wild in the hills,
where no man can touch it.
And the rhythm of her,
swaying with him in
that old moonlight
and starlight, the
rhythm, like mama's
rockin' near the fire
in a childhood
he remembered
only in his old
limestone bones,
brought him
now, at last,
to tenderness,
such that all the old mule stubbornness
he'd set against the world,
like the Presbyterian starch
that held him straight,
he set now
against the new-found
tenderness to keep
a tear from breaking free.

Cycle 5: Romantic Love and Lust

Hebrew Bible c. 900–200 BCE

You Are Beautiful

You are beautiful, my love, as
    Tirzah,[1]
  lovely as Jerusalem,
awesome as an army with
    banners.
Turn away your eyes from me,
    for they have overcome me.
Your hair is like a flock of goats,
    that lie along the side of
      Gilead.
Your teeth are like a flock of
      ewes,
    which have come up from
      the washing;
    of which every one has
      twins;
    none is bereaved among
      them.
Your temples are like a piece of a
    pomegranate behind
      your veil.
There are sixty queens, eighty
    concubines,
    and virgins without number.
My dove, my perfect one, is
    unique.
She is her mother's only
    daughter.
She is the favorite one of she
    who bore her.

84

The daughters saw her, and called
    her blessed;
    the queens and the
    concubines, and they
    praised her.
Who is she who looks forth as
    the morning,
    beautiful as the moon,
    clear as the sun,
    and awesome as an army
    with banners?

—from "Song of Solomon" 6:4–10

DANTE ALIGHIERI 1265–1321

SO KIND AND SO HONEST SHE SEEMS

So kind and so honest she seems
My lady, when she greets others
That every tongue must tremblingly go silent,
And eyes do not dare behold her.
She goes on, sensing that she is praised,
Graciously dressed in humility;
And she seems to be something that has come
From the sky to the earth, a miracle shown.

She shows herself, pleasing to those who admire her,
That she gives for the eyes a sweetness to the heart,
That no one can understand who has not tried;
And it seems that from her lips moves
A sweet spirit full of love,
Which tells the soul: "Sigh."

—Trans. Gabriella Basile

ROBERT HERRICK 1591–1674

UPON JULIA'S BREASTS

Display thy breasts, my Julia, there let me
Behold that circummortal[2] purity;
Between whose glories, there my lips I'll lay,
Ravished in that fair *Via Lactea*.[3]

UPON THE NIPPLES OF JULIA'S BREAST

Have ye beheld (with much delight)
A red rose peeping through a white?
Or else a cherry (double graced)
Within a lily center-placed?
Or ever marked the pretty beam
A strawberry shows half drowned in cream?
Or seen rich rubies blushing through
A pure smooth pearl, and orient too?
So like to this, nay all the rest,
Is each neat niplet of her breast.

TO THE VIRGINS, TO MAKE MUCH OF TIME

1

Gather ye rosebuds while ye may,
    Old Time is still a-flying,
And this same flower that smiles today
    Tomorrow will be dying.

2

The glorious lamp of heaven, the sun,
    The higher he's a-getting,
The sooner will his race be run,
    And nearer he's to setting.

3

That age is best which is the first,
    When youth and blood are warmer;
But, being spent, the worse and worst
    Times still succeed the former.

4

Then be not coy, but use your time,
    And, while ye may, go marry;
For, having lost but once your prime,
    You may for ever tarry.

THOMAS CAREW 1595–1640

BOLDNESS IN LOVE

Mark how the bashful morn, in vain
Courts the amorous Marigold,
With sighing blasts, and weeping rain;

Yet she refuses to unfold.
But when the Planet of the day,
Approacheth with his powerful ray,
Then she spreads, then she receives
His warmer beams into her virgin leaves.
So shalt thou thrive in love, fond Boy;
If thy tears, and sighs discover
Thy grief, thou never shalt enjoy
The just reward of a bold lover:
But when with moving accents, thou
Shalt constant faith, and service vow,
Thy Celia shall receive those charms
With open ears, and with unfolded arms.

ANDREW MARVELL 1621–1678

TO HIS COY MISTRESS

Had we but World enough, and Time,
This coyness Lady were no crime.
We would sit down, and think which way
To walk, and pass our long Love's Day.
Thou by the Indian Ganges'[4] side
Should'st Rubies find: I by the Tide
Of Humber[5] would complain. I would
Love you ten years before the Flood:
And you should if you please refuse
Till the Conversion of the Jews.
My vegetable Love should grow
Vaster than Empires, and more slow.
An hundred years should go to praise
Thine Eyes, and on thy Forehead Gaze.
Two hundred to adore each Breast:
But thirty thousand to the rest.
An Age at least to every part,
And the last Age should show your Heart.
For Lady you deserve this State;
Nor would I love at a lower rate.
    But at my back I always hear
Times wingèd Chariot hurrying near:
And yonder all before us lie
Deserts of vast Eternity.

Thy Beauty shall no more be found;
Nor, in thy marble Vault, shall sound
My ecchoing Song: then Worms shall try
That long preserv'd Virginity:
And your quaint Honour turn to dust;
And into ashes all my Lust.
The Grave's a fine and private place,
But none I think do there embrace.
    Now, therefore, while the youthful hue
Sits on thy skin like morning dew,
And while thy willing Soul transpires
At every pore with instant Fires,
Now let us sport us while we may;
And now, like am'rous birds of prey,
Rather at once our Time devour,
Than languish in his slow-chapt pow'r.[6]
Let us roll all our Strength, and all
Our sweetness, up into one Ball:
And tear our Pleasures with rough strife,
Thorough the Iron gates of Life.
Thus, though we cannot make our Sun
Stand still, yet we will make him run.

JOHANN WOLFGANG VON GOETHE 1749–1832

THE BRIDEGROOM

At midnight, as I slept, my heart full of love
Lay awake in my chest, as if it were daylight;
When morning came it felt like night,
But I did not care what the day might bring.

I missed her, and for her alone I endured my
Toil and struggle through the burning
Heat of day; but what refreshing life awaited me
In the cool evening! It was worth it and good!

The sun went down, and, hand in hand,
We greeted the last blessed view,
And her eyes spoke straight into mine:
Just hope that from the East it will rise again.

At midnight, bright starlight guides me, as
In a sweet dream, to the doorstep where she rests.

How I wish to find a resting place there, too;
However it turns out, life is good.

—Trans. Gert Niers

Secret Understanding

All the people stand amazed
At the look in my darling's eyes;
I, however, know better,
I know rather well what it means.

This is what it says: I love this man,
And not that one or the other.
Good people, give up
Your surprise and curiosity!

Yes, with enormous strength
She throws her glance around;
But she tries to reveal only
To him the next sweet hour.

—Trans. Gert Niers

Robert Burns 1759–1796

A Red, Red Rose

Oh my luve is like a red, red rose,
  That's newly sprung in June:
Oh my luve is like the melodie,
  That's sweetly play'd in tune.

As fair art thou, my bonie lass,
  So deep in luve am I;
And I will luve thee still, my dear,
  Till a' the seas gang dry.

Till a' the seas gang dry, my dear,
  And the rocks melt wi' the sun;
And I will luve thee still, my dear,
  While the sands o' life shall run.

And fare thee weel, my only luve!
  And fare thee weel a while!
And I will come again, my luve,
  Tho' it were ten thousand mile!

Thomas Moore 1779–1852

Believe Me, If All Those Endearing Young Charms

Believe me, if all those endearing young charms,
    Which I gaze on so fondly to-day,
Were to change by to-morrow, and fleet in my arms,
    Like fairy-gifts fading away,
Thou wouldst still be ador'd, as this moment thou art
    Let thy loveliness fade as it will,
And around the dear ruin each wish of my heart
    Would entwine itself verdantly still.

It is not while beauty and youth are thine own,
    And thy cheeks unprofan'd by a tear,
That the fervor and faith of a soul can be known,
    To which time will but make thee more dear;
No, the heart that truly lov'd never forgets,
    But as truly loves on to the close,
As the sun-flower turns on her god, when he sets,
    The same look which she turn'd when he rose.

Alexander S. Pushkin 1799–1837

Oh My Maiden-Rose, I Am in Shackles

Oh my maiden-rose, I am in shackles;
But I am not ashamed of your restraints:
So the nightingale in the bay tree,
Feathered tzar of sylvan singers,
Near the honored and lovely rose,
Lives in blissful captivity
And tenderly sings songs to her
In the darkness of the passionate night.

    —Trans. Tatsiana DeRosa

Elizabeth Barrett Browning 1806–1861

XXII

When our two souls stand up erect and strong,
Face to face, silent, drawing nigh and nigher,

Until the lengthening wings break into fire
At either curvèd point,—what bitter wrong
Can the earth do to us, that we should not long
Be here contented? Think. In mounting higher,
The angels would press on us and aspire
To drop some golden orb of perfect song
Into our deep, dear silence. Let us stay
Rather on earth, Belovèd,—where the unfit
Contrarious moods of men recoil away
And isolate pure spirits, and permit
A place to stand and love in for a day,
With darkness and the death-hour rounding it.

ROBERT BROWNING 1812–1889

MEETING AT NIGHT

1

The gray sea and the long black land;
And the yellow half-moon large and low;
And the startled little waves that leap
In fiery ringlets from their sleep,
As I gain the cove with pushing prow,
And quench its speed i' the slushy sand.

2

Then a mile of warm sea-scented beach;
Three fields to cross till a farm appears;
A tap at the pane, the quick sharp scratch
And blue spurt of a lighted match,
And a voice less loud, through its joys and fears,
Than the two hearts beating each to each!

WALT WHITMAN 1819–1892

I AM HE THAT ACHES WITH LOVE

I am he that aches with amorous love;
Does the earth gravitate? does not all matter, aching, attract all
    matter?
So the body of me to all I meet or know.

WE TWO BOYS TOGETHER CLINGING

We two boys together clinging,
One the other never leaving,
Up and down the roads going, North and South excursions
    making,
Power enjoying, elbows stretching, finger clutching,
Arm'd and fearless, eating, drinking, sleeping, loving,
No law less than ourselves owning, sailing, soldiering, thieving,
    threatening,
Misers, menials, priests alarming, air breathing, water, drinking,
    on the turf or the sea-beach dancing,
Cities wrenching, ease scorning, statutes mocking, feebleness chasing,
Fulfilling our foray.

DANTE GABRIEL ROSSETTI 1828–1882

HEART'S COMPASS

Sometimes thou seem'st not as thyself alone,
    But as the meaning of all things that are;
    A breathless wonder, shadowing forth afar
Some heavenly solstice hushed and halcyon;
Whose unstirred lips are music's visible tone;
    Whose eyes the sun-gate of the soul unbar,
    Being of its furthest fires oracular;—
The evident heart of all life sown and mown.

Even such Love is; and is not thy name Love?
    Yea, by thy hand the Love-god rends apart
    All gathering clouds of Night's ambiguous art;
Flings them far down, and sets thine eyes above;
And simply, as some gage of flower or glove,
    Stakes with a smile the world against thy heart.

JAMES THOMSON 1834–1882

THE BRIDGE

"O, what are you waiting for here, young man?
    What are you looking for over the bridge?"
A little straw hat with the streaming blue ribbons
    Is soon to come dancing over the bridge.

Her heart beats the measure that keeps her feet dancing,
    Dancing along like a wave o' the sea;
Her heart pours the sunshine with which her eyes glancing
    Light up strange faces in looking for me.

The strange faces brighten in meeting her glances;
    The strangers all bless her, pure, lovely, and free:
She fancies she walks, but her walk skips and dances,
    Her heart makes such music in coming to me.

O, thousands and thousands of happy young maidens
    Are tripping this morning their sweethearts to see;
But none whose heart beats to a sweeter love-cadence
    Than hers who will brighten the sunshine for me.

"O, what are you waiting for here, young man?
    What are you looking for over the bridge?"
A little straw hat with the streaming blue ribbons;
    —And here it comes dancing over the bridge!

OSCAR WILDE 1854–1900

IN THE GOLD ROOM
A HARMONY

Her ivory hands on the ivory keys
    Strayed in a fitful fantasy,
Like the silver gleam when the poplar trees
    Rustle their pale leaves listlessly,
    Or the drifting foam of a restless sea
When the waves show their teeth in the flying breeze.

Her gold hair fell on the wall of gold
    Like the delicate gossamer tangles spun
On the burnished disk of the marigold,
    Or the sunflower turning to meet the sun
    When the gloom of the dark blue night is done,
And the spear of the lily is aureoled.

And her sweet red lips on these lips of mine
    Burned like the ruby fire set
In the swinging lamp of a crimson shrine,
    Or the bleeding wounds of the pomegranate,
    Or the heart of the lotus drenched and wet
With the spilt-out blood of the rose-red wine.

V.Y. Bryusov 1873–1924

Pompeian Woman

"My first husband was a wealthy merchant,
The second was a poet, the third—a piteous mime,
The forth—a consul, the fifth, the current one, is a eunuch,
But Caesar himself was the matchmaker this time.

"The owner of the empire greatly loved me
But I fancied one Nubian slave.
For many my belt was too weak, and I don't
Expect 'Casta et Pudica'[7] above my grave.

"But you, my friend, the shy one from Mysia!
Forever forever I am loyal only to you.
Darling, don't believe that all women are liars:
There is a faithful one among them!"

And so she spoke, pale and breathless,
Lydia, a matron, as in a dream of haze,
Forgetting that all Pompei was in terror
And the sky above Vesuvius was in flame.

And when exhausted lovers became quiet
And were conquered by a heady sleep,
Upon the city a mass of gray dust fell,
And the city was under ashes buried.

Centuries passed, and as from hungry jawbones,
We tore the past from the earth,
And found as a sign of immortal passion
Two well preserved bodies in a lovers' embrace.

Raise the sacred monument higher,
Living sculpture of eternal bodies,
So memory will not fade in the Universe
Of a passion which outlived its boundaries.

—Trans. Tatsiana De Rosa

D.H. Lawrence 1885–1930

Gloire de Dijon

When she rises in the morning
I linger to watch her;

She spreads the bath-cloth underneath the window
And the sunbeams catch her
Glistening white on the shoulders,
While down her sides the mellow
Golden shadow glows as
She stoops to the sponge, and her swung breasts
Sway like full-blown yellow
Gloire de Dijon roses.
She drips herself with water, and her shoulders
Glisten as silver, they crumple up
Like wet and falling roses, and I listen
For the sluicing of their rain-dishevelled petals.
In the window full of sunlight
Concentrates her golden shadow
Fold on fold, until it glows as
Mellow as the glory roses.

MYSTERY

Now I am all
One bowl of kisses,
Such as the tall
Slim votaresses[8]
Of Egypt filled
For a God's excesses.

I lift to you
My bowl of kisses,
And through the temple's
Blue recesses
Cry out to you
In wild caresses.

And to my lips'
Bright crimson rim
The passion slips,
And down my slim
White body drips
The shining hymn.

And still before
The altar I
Exult the bowl
Brimful, and cry

To you to stoop
And drink, Most High.

Oh drink me up
That I may be
Within your cup
Like a mystery,
Like wine that is still
In ecstasy.

Glimmering still
In ecstasy,
Commingled wines
Of you and me
In one fulfill
The mystery.

E.E. Cummings 1894–1962

45: I Love You Much(Most Beautiful Darling)

i love you much(most beautiful darling)

more than anyone on the earth and i
like you better than everything in the sky
—sunlight and singing welcome your coming

although winter may be everywhere
with such a silence and such a darkness
noone can quite begin to guess

(except my life)the true time of year—

and if what calls itself a world should have
the luck to hear such singing(or glimpse such
sunlight as will leap higher than high
through gayer than gayest someone's heart at your each

nearerness)everyone certainly would(my
most beautiful darling)believe in nothing but love

Conrad Aiken 1889–1973

Music I Heard with You

Music I heard with you was more than music,
And bread I broke with you was more than bread;

Now that I am without you, all is desolate;
All that was once so beautiful is dead.

Your hands once touched this table and this silver,
And I have seen your fingers hold this glass.
These things do not remember you, belovèd, –
And yet your touch upon them will not pass.

For it was in my heart you moved among them,
And blessed them with your hands and with your eyes;
And in my heart they will remember always,—
They knew you once, O beautiful and wise.

PABLO NERUDA 1904–1973

FULL WOMAN, FLESH APPLE, HOT MOON

Full woman, flesh apple, hot moon,
thick seaweed scent, crushed mud and light,
what dark clarity opens between your columns?
What ancient night does man touch with his senses?

Oh, loving is a journey with water and with stars,
with smothered air and rough flour tempests:
loving is a lightning battle
and two bodies defeated by one honey.

Kiss by kiss I travel your small infinity,
your margins, your rivers, your tiny villages,
and the genital fire transformed into deliciousness

Courses through blood's thin paths
until it precipitates like a nocturnal carnation,
until being and not being only a flash in the shadows.

—Trans. Sandra Kunanele

KEVIN CLARK 1950–

"LE SECRET"
—after Rodin

I'd just stepped out of The Classical Tradition
When I saw her looking at the two marble-
White hands poised the instant before touching.

I hadn't noticed the column between them yet.
Her beauty was a given, but the discretion
In her gaze drew me like the dark avenues
Of her pleated print skirt. She'd tipped her head
To see something. The palm-high column at once
Joining and separating the right hands? Each one
Glowed near what it couldn't know.
                                    How easy
To imagine those nights we'd lock together,
Sitting up, riding the pre-tremors
As candles flared shadows between us,
Our posture bolt straight as if emanating
From both of us at once, how we'd lift and drop,
Dive for the plummet promised in each iris,
How every finger anticipates the swoon
Beyond first touch.
                             She hadn't seen me.
She slid her weight from left hip to right,
Slowly circled the stand, her skirt circling
Before winding back. Could I be sure her gaze
Was a deep form into which I'd been invited?
When I stole up close to try the scent of her hair,
She didn't once turn her eyes from the hands, but
Slipped her fingers into the spaces between mine.
It was our twentieth anniversary. We'd come for art.

DORIANNE LAUX 1952–

THE THIEF

What is it when your man sits on the floor
in sweatpants, his latest project
set out in front of him like a small world, maps
and photographs, diagrams and plans, everything
he hopes to build, invent or create,
and you believe in him as you always have,
even after the failures, even more now
as you set your coffee down
and move toward him, to where he sits
oblivious of you, concentrating
in a square of sun—
you step over the rulers and blue graph-paper
to squat behind him, and he barely notices,

though you're still in your robe
which falls open a little as you reach
around his chest, feel for the pink
wheel of each nipple, the slow beat
of his heart, your ear pressed to his back
to listen—and you are torn,
not wanting to interrupt his work
but unable to keep your fingers
from dipping into the ditch in his pants,
torn again with tenderness
for the way his flesh grows unwillingly
toward your curved palm, toward the light,
as if you had planted it, this sweet root,
your mouth already an echo of its shape—
you slip your tongue into his ear
and he hears you, calling him away
from his work, the angled lines of his thoughts,
into the shapeless place you are bound
to take him, over bridges of bone, beyond
borders of skin, climbing over him
into the world of the body, its labyrinth
of ladders and stairs—and you love him
like the first time you loved him,
with equal measures of expectancy
and fear and awe, taking him with you
into the soft geometry of the flesh, the earth
before its sidewalks and cities,
its glistening spires,
stealing him back from the world he loves
into this other world he cannot build without you.

ALLISON JOSEPH 1967–

LEARNING TO LAUGH

At first I laughed to hide my nervousness,
my hand closed over my mouth
to silence that titter,
an uncertain sound
I didn't, couldn't control.

Breasts exposed, thighs
uncovered, I'd been found out,
caught, held up under daylight

for inspection, my chest
rising and falling with each

sharp intake of breath.
Then I learned to melt
into your hands, sliding
into pleasure when your lips
met mine, labia parted

for your tongue, mouth
open as I gasped, nerves
signaling bliss. I pulled
you closer in, reveled
in joy so profound

that I couldn't help laughing
a full-bodied laugh that rang
through the dormant building,
waking the sleeping, the drunk.
I laughed so low, so deep,

that I couldn't believe such a sound
could come from my naked body,
the same flesh that once
could only titter in shame.
What finally did it? Your hands,

those fingers, that didn't stop
touching every sexual place:
nape of the neck, bare lower
back, undersides of breasts.
Determined, those hands

set loose a woman not sated
with quick meeting, mating,
worked corners, crevices—
until that laugh came bubbling
out of me, sudden rapture

I didn't deny, a sound that would never
be furtive again, proud and loud instead,
so loud that neighbors must wonder
what it is you're giving me,
their ears burning when they hear

the laughs that just keep
coming, rising out of me

to stop traffic on the boulevard,
drivers slowing to listen
to the most joy they've ever heard.

RACHEL JAMISON WEBSTER 1974–

NEBULA

My life assigns me its life
and I am like an orb
rounding its curves until

light comes in and splits my eyes,
sparks a living star and
I don't know who you are,

your name or mine or
how long we've been
contracted into time, or why.

It helps if you circle your hand
on the back of my head,
and I can imagine coming in again,

a kind of spiraling but slowly—
in that whirring spin
that makes a kind of keening.

We can't see the universe's edges,
but we can see it breathe.
It is not that we pour down into body

from the stars, not that our spines are
laddered stars, but when
we first kissed, I tasted it—

dust of the space that makes us.

BRIAN THORNTON 1975–

PARADOX OF PERIPHERAL VISION

*"The peripheral retina is very sensitive to dim objects
and relative motion. When the central retina is dam-
aged, the patient may not be able to see faces straight*

ahead but may see stars in the sky or a speck of paper
on the floor."
—excerpt from awareness brochure distributed by
the Macular Degeneration Foundation

I'm not really sure about your eyes,
but your ears look lovely in this light.
Your smile, I'm told, could make a blind man see.
Sorry. But the bit of tikka in your teeth
shows you have sophisticated taste.
Please forgive my staring at your waist,
but the periphery mountains are amazing—
little lint sheep in meadows grazing
on steep cliffs; some resting in the shade
of a Mirabelle tree in late
September across your shoulder, now asleep.
How I want so bad to be a sheep
instead of me pretending to see the ewe—
the you those ewes are holding tightly to.

Cycle 6: Language, Inspiration and the Imagination

Jane Colman Turell 1708–1735

To My Muse, December 29, 1725

Come, gentle muse, and once more lend thine aid,
O bring thy succor to a humble maid!
How often dost thou liberally dispense
To our dull breast thy quick'ning influence!
By thee inspir'd, I'll cheerful tune my voice,
And love and sacred friendship make my choice.
In my pleas'd bosom you can freely pour,
A greater treasure than Jove's golden shower.
Come now, fair muse, and fill my empty mind
With rich ideas, great and unconfin'd.
Instruct me in those secret arts that lie
Unseen to all but to a poet's eye.
O let me burn with Sappho's noble fire,
But not like her for faithless man expire.
And let me rival great Orinda's[1] fame,
Or like sweet Philomela's[2] be my name.
Go lead the way, my muse, nor must you stop,
'Till we have gain'd Parnassus'[3] shady top:
'Till I have view'd those fragrant soft retreats,
Those fields of bliss, the muses' sacred seats.
I'll then devote thee to fair virtue's fame,
And so be worthy of a poet's name.

Johann Wolfgang von Goethe 1749–1832

Beloved, just look

Beloved, just look
At the branches full of clusters!
Let me show you the fruits
Housed in prickly, green shells.

Round and silent, they hang for a
Long time unaware of each other,
A swinging bough
Rocks them patiently.

But always from within the
Brown kernel ripens and swells,
It wants to breathe the air
And longs to see the sun.

The shell bursts and
Joyfully breaks loose;
That's how my songs, one after
Another, fall into your lap.

—Trans. Gert Niers

William Wordsworth 1770–1850

Lines Composed a Few Miles above Tintern Abbey, on Revisiting the Banks of the Wye during a Tour. July 13, 1798

Five years have past; five summers, with the length
Of five long winters! And again I hear
These waters, rolling from their mountain-springs
With a soft inland murmur. – Once again
Do I behold these steep and lofty cliffs,
That on a wild secluded scene impress
Thoughts of more deep seclusion; and connect
The landscape with the quiet of the sky.
The day is come when I again repose
Here, under this dark sycamore, and view
These plots of cottage-ground, these orchard-tufts,
Which at this season, with their unripe fruits,
Are clad in one green hue, and lose themselves

'Mid groves and copses. Once again I see
These hedgerows, hardly hedgerows, little lines
Of sportive wood run wild: these pastoral farms,
Green to the very door; and wreaths of smoke
Sent up, in silence, from among the trees!
With some uncertain notice, as might seem
Of vagrant dwellers in the houseless woods,
Or some of Hermit's cave, where by his fire
The Hermit sits alone.
                These beauteous forms,
Through a long absence, have not been to me
As is a landscape to a blind man's eye:
But oft, in lonely rooms, and 'mid the din
Of towns and cities, I have owed to them
In hours of weariness, sensations sweet,
Felt in the blood, and felt along the heart;
And passing even into my purer mind,
With tranquil restoration: – feelings too
Of unremembered pleasure: such, perhaps,
As have no slight or trivial influence
On that best portion of a good man's life,
His little, nameless, unremembered, acts
Of kindness and of love. Nor less, I trust,
To them I may have owed another gift,
Of aspect more sublime; that blessed mood,
In which the burden of the mystery,
In which the heavy and the weary weight
Of all this unintelligible world,
Is lightened: – that serene and blessed mood,
In which the affections gently lead us on, –
Until, the breath of this corporeal frame
And even the motion of our human blood
Almost suspended, we are laid asleep
In body, and become a living soul:
While with an eye made quiet by the power
Of harmony, and the deep power of joy,
We see into the life of things.
                        If this

Be but a vain belief, yet, oh! How oft –
In darkness and amid the many shapes
Of joyless daylight; when the fretful stir
Unprofitable, and the fever of the world,
Have hung upon the beatings of my heart –

How oft, in spirit, have I turned to thee,
O sylvan Wye! Thou wanderer through the woods,
How often has my spirit turned to thee!
And now, with gleams of half-extinguished thought,
With many recognitions dim and faint,
And somewhat of a sad perplexity,
The picture of the mind revives again:
While here I stand, not only with the sense
Of present pleasure, but with pleasing thoughts
That in this moment there is life and food
For future years. And so I dare to hope,
Though changed, no doubt, from what I was when first
I came among these hills; when like a roe
I bounded o'er the mountains, by the sides
Of the deep rivers, and the lonely streams,
Wherever nature led: more like a man
Flying from something that he dreads, than one
Who sought the thing he loved. For nature then
(The coarser pleasures of my boyish days,
And their glad animal movements all gone by)
To me was all in all.—I cannot paint
What then I was. The sounding cataract
Haunted me like a passion: the tall rock,
The mountain, and the deep and gloomy wood,
Their colours and their forms, were then to me
An appetite; a feeling and a love,
That had no need of a remoter charm,
By thought supplied, nor any interest
Unborrowed from the eye. – That time is past,
And all its aching joys are now no more,
And all its dizzy raptures. Not for this
Faint I, nor mourn nor murmur; other gifts
Have followed; for such loss, I would believe,
Abundant recompense. For I have learned
To look on nature, not as in the hour
Of thoughtless youth; but hearing oftentimes
The still, sad music of humanity,
Nor harsh nor grating, though of ample power
To chasten and subdue. And I have felt
A presence that disturbs me with the joy
Of elevated thoughts; a sense sublime
Of something far more deeply interfused,
Whose dwelling is the light of setting suns,

And the round ocean and the living air,
And the blue sky, and in the mind of man:
A motion and a spirit, that impels
All thinking things, all objects of all thought,
And rolls through all things. Therefore am I still
A lover of the meadows and the woods,
And mountains; and of all that we behold
From this green earth: of all the mighty world
Of eye, and ear, – both what they half create,
And what perceive; well pleased to recognize
In nature and the language of the sense,
The anchor of my purest thoughts, the nurse,
The guide, the guardian of my heart, and soul
Of all my moral being.

                                        Nor perchance,
If I were not thus taught, should I the more
Suffer my genial spirits to decay:
For thou art with me here upon the banks
Of this fair river; thou my dearest Friend,
My dear, dear Friend; and in thy voice I catch
The language of my former heart, and read
My former pleasures in the shooting lights
Of thy wild eyes. Oh! Yet a little while
May I behold in thee what I was once,
My dear, dear Sister! And this prayer I make,
Knowing that Nature never did betray
The heart that loved her; 'tis her privilege,
Through all the years of this our life, to lead
From joy to joy: for she can so inform
The mind that is within us, so impress
With quietness and beauty, and so feed
With lofty thoughts, that neither evil tongues,
Rash judgments, nor the sneers of selfish men,
Nor greetings where no kindness is, nor all
The dreary intercourse of daily life,
Shall e'er prevail against us, or disturb
Our cheerful faith, that all which we behold
Is full of blessings. Therefore let the moon
Shine on thee in thy solitary walk;
And let the misty mountain-winds be free
To blow against thee: and, in after years,
When these wild ecstasies shall be matured
Into a sober pleasure; when thy mind

Shall be a mansion for all lovely forms,
Thy memory be as a dwelling-place
For all sweet sounds and harmonies; oh! Then,
If solitude, or fear, or pain, or grief,
Should be thy portion, with what healing thoughts
Of tender joy wilt thou remember me,
And these my exhortations! Nor, perchance –
If I should be where I no more can hear
Thy voice, nor catch from thy wild eyes these gleams
Of past existence—wilt thou then forget
That on the banks of this delightful stream
We stood together; and that I, so long
A worshipper of Nature, hither came
Unwearied in that service; rather say
With warmer love—oh! With far deeper zeal
Of holier love. Nor wilt thou then forget,
That after many wanderings, many years
Of absence, these steep woods and lofty cliffs,
And this green pastoral landscape, were to me
More dear, both for themselves and for thy sake!

I WANDERED LONELY AS A CLOUD

I wandered lonely as a cloud
That floats on high o'er vales and hills,
When all at once I saw a crowd,
A host, of golden daffodils;
Beside the lake, beneath the trees,
Fluttering and dancing in the breeze.

Continuous as the stars that shine
And twinkle on the milky way,
They stretched in never-ending line
Along the margin of a bay:
Ten thousand saw I at a glance,
Tossing their heads in sprightly dance.

The waves beside them danced; but they
Out-did the sparkling waves in glee:
A poet could not but be gay,
In such a jocund company:
I gazed—and gazed—but little thought
What wealth the show to me had brought:

For oft, when on my couch I lie
In vacant or in pensive mood,
They flash upon that inward eye
Which is the bliss of solitude;
And then my heart with pleasure fills,
And dances with the daffodils.

PERCY BYSSHE SHELLEY 1792–1822

TO A SKY-LARK

Hail to thee, blithe Spirit!
Bird thou never wert—
That from Heaven, or near it,
Pourest thy full heart
In profuse strains of unpremeditated art.

Higher still and higher
From the earth thou springest
Like a cloud of fire;
The blue deep thou wingest,
And singing still dost soar, and soaring ever singest.

In the golden lightning
Of the sunken Sun—
O'er which clouds are bright'ning,
Thou dost float and run,
Like an unbodied joy whose race is just begun.

The pale purple even
Melts around thy flight;
Like a star of Heaven
In the broad day-light
Thou art unseen,—but yet I hear thy shrill delight:

Keen as are the arrows
Of that silver sphere,
Whose intense lamp narrows
In the white dawn clear
Until we hardly see—we feel that it is there.

All the earth and air
With thy voice is loud.
As, when night is bare,
From one lonely cloud
The moon rains out her beams—and heaven is overflowed.

What thou art we know not;
What is most like thee?
From rainbow clouds there flow not
Drops so bright to see
As from thy presence showers a rain of melody.

Like a poet hidden
In the light of thought,
Singing hymns unbidden,
Till the world is wrought
To sympathy with hopes and fears it heeded not:

Like a high-born maiden
In a palace tower,
Soothing her love-laden
Soul in secret hour
With music sweet as love—which overflows her bower:

Like a glow-worm golden
In a dell of dew,
Scattering unbeholden
Its aerial hue
Among the flowers and grass, which screen it from the view:

Like a rose embowered
In its own green leaves—
By warm winds deflowered—
Till the scent it gives
Makes faint with too much sweet these heavy-winged thieves.

Sound of vernal showers
On the twinkling grass,
Rain-awakened flowers,
All that ever was
Joyous, and clear, and fresh, thy music doth surpass.

Teach us, Sprite or Bird,
What sweet thoughts are thine:
I have never heard
Praise of love or wine
That panted forth a flood of rapture so divine.

Chorus hymeneal
Or triumphal chaunt
Matched with thine, would be all
But an empty vaunt,
A thing wherein we feel there is some hidden want.

What objects are the fountains
Of thy happy strain?
What fields, or waves, or mountains?
What shapes of sky or plain?
What love of thine own kind? What ignorance of pain?

With thy clear keen joyance
Languor cannot be—
Shadow of annoyance
Never came near thee:
Thou lovest—but ne'er knew love's sad satiety.

Waking or asleep,
Thou of death must deem
Things more true and deep
Than we mortals dream,
Or how could thy notes flow in such a crystal stream?

We look before and after,
And pine for what is not—
Our sincerest laughter
With some pain is fraught—
Our sweetest songs are those that tell of saddest thought.

Yet if we could scorn
Hate, and pride, and fear;
If we were things born
Not to shed a tear,
I know not how thy joy we ever should come near.

Better than all measures
Of delightful sound—
Better than all treasures
That in books are found—
Thy skill to poet were, thou Scorner of the ground!

Teach me half the gladness
That thy brain must know,
Such harmonious madness
From my lips would flow
The world should listen then—as I am listening now!

ODE TO THE WEST WIND

I

O wild West Wind, thou breath of Autumn's being,
Thou, from whose unseen presence the leaves dead

Are driven, like ghosts from an enchanter fleeing,
Yellow, and black, and pale, and hectic red,
Pestilence-stricken multitudes: O thou,
Who chariotest to their dark wintry bed
The wingèd seeds, where they lie cold and low,
Each like a corpse within its grave, until
Thine azure sister of the Spring shall blow
Her clarion o'er the dreaming earth, and fill
(Driving sweet buds like flocks to feed in air)
With living hues and odours plain and hill:
Wild Spirit, which art moving everywhere;
Destroyer and preserver; hear, oh, hear!

					II

Thou on whose stream, mid the steep sky's commotion,
Loose clouds like earth's decaying leaves are shed,
Shook from the tangled boughs of Heaven and Ocean,
Angels of rain and lightning: there are spread
On the blue surface of thine aëry surge,
Like the bright hair uplifted from the head
Of some fierce Maenad,[4] even from the dim verge
Of the horizon to the zenith's height,
The locks of the approaching storm. Thou dirge
Of the dying year, to which this closing night
Will be the dome of a vast sepulchre,
Vaulted with all thy congregated might
Of vapours, from whose solid atmosphere
Black rain, and fire, and hail will burst: oh, hear!

					III

Thou who didst waken from his summer dreams
The blue Mediterranean, where he lay,
Lulled by the coil of his crystàlline streams,
Beside a pumice isle in Baiae's bay,[5]
And saw in sleep old palaces and towers
Quivering within the wave's intenser day,
All overgrown with azure moss and flowers
So sweet, the sense faints picturing them! Thou
For whose path the Atlantic's level powers
Cleave themselves into chasms, while far below
The sea-blooms and the oozy woods which wear
The sapless foliage of the ocean, know
Thy voice, and suddenly grow gray with fear,
And tremble and despoil themselves: oh, hear!

IV

If I were a dead leaf thou mightest bear;
If I were a swift cloud to fly with thee;
A wave to pant beneath thy power, and share
The impulse of thy strength, only less free
Than thou, O uncontrollable! If even
I were as in my boyhood, and could be
The comrade of thy wanderings over Heaven,
As then, when to outstrip thy skiey speed
Scarce seemed a vision; I would ne'er have striven
As thus with thee in prayer in my sore need.
Oh, lift me as a wave, a leaf, a cloud!
I fall upon the thorns of life! I bleed!
A heavy weight of hours has chained and bowed
One too like thee: tameless, and swift, and proud.

V

Make me thy lyre, even as the forest is:
What if my leaves are falling like its own!
The tumult of thy mighty harmonies
Will take from both a deep, autumnal tone,
Sweet though in sadness. Be thou, Spirit fierce,
My spirit! Be thou me, impetuous one!
Drive my dead thoughts over the universe
Like withered leaves to quicken a new birth!
And, by the incantation of this verse,
Scatter, as from an unextinguished hearth
Ashes and sparks, my words among mankind!
Be through my lips to unawakened earth
The trumpet of a prophecy! O, Wind,
If Winter comes, can Spring be far behind?

ELIZABETH BARRETT BROWNING 1806–1861

TO GEORGE SAND
A DESIRE

Thou large-brained woman and large-hearted man,
Self-called George Sand![6] whose soul, amid the lions
   Of thy tumultuous senses, moans defiance
   And answers roar for roar, as spirits can:
   I would some mild miraculous thunder ran
   Above the applauded circus, in appliance

Of thine own nobler nature's strength and science,
Drawing two pinions, white as wings of swan,
From thy strong shoulders, to amaze the place
With holier light! that thou to woman's claim
And man's, mightst join bedside the angel's grace
Of a pure genius sanctified from blame,
Till child and maiden pressed to thine embrace
To kiss upon thy lips a stainless fame.

ALFRED, LORD TENNYSON 1809–1892

THE POET'S MIND

I

Vex not thou the poet's mind
    With thy shallow wit:
Vex not thou the poet's mind;
    For thou canst not fathom it.
Clear and bright it should be ever,
Flowing like a crystal river;
Bright as light, and clear as wind.

II

Dark-brow'd sophist, come not anear;
    All the place is holy ground;
    Hollow smile and frozen sneer
        Come not here.
    Holy water will I pour
    Into every spicy flower
Of the laurel-shrubs that hedge it around.
The flowers would faint at your cruel cheer.
    In your eye there is death,
    There is frost in your breath
    Which would blight the plants.
        Where you stand you cannot hear
           From the groves within
           The wild-bird's din.
In the heart of the garden the merry bird chants.
It would fall to the ground if you came in.
    In the middle leaps a fountain
        Like sheet lightning,
        Ever brightening
    With a low melodious thunder;

All day and all night it is ever drawn
    From the brain of the purple mountain
    Which stands in the distance yonder:
It springs on a level of bowery lawn,
And the mountain draws it from Heaven above,
And it sings a song of undying love;
And yet, tho' its voice be so clear and full,
You never would hear it; your ears are so dull;
So keep where you are: you are foul with sin;
It would shrink to the earth if you came in.

WALT WHITMAN 1819–1892

ROOTS AND LEAVES THEMSELVES ALONE

Roots and leaves themselves alone are these,
Scents brought to men and women from wild woods and
    pond-side,
Breast-sorrel and pinks of love, fingers that wind around
    tighter than vines,
Gushes from the throats of birds hid in the foliage of trees as
    the sun is risen,
Breezes of land and love set from living shores to you on the
    living sea, to you O sailors!
Frost-mellow'd berries and Third-month twigs offer'd fresh to
    young persons wandering out in the fields when the
    winter breaks up,
Love-buds put before you and within you whoever you are,
Buds to be unfolded on the old terms,
If you bring the warmth of the sun to them they will open and
    bring form, color, perfume, to you,
If you become the aliment and the wet they will become
    flowers, fruits, tall branches and trees.

FRANCES ELLEN WATKINS HARPER 1824–1911

LEARNING TO READ

Very soon the Yankee teachers
    Came down and set up school;
But, oh! how the Rebs did hate it,–
    It was agin' their rule.

Our masters always tried to hide
    Book learning from our eyes;
Knowledge did'nt agree with slavery–
    'Twould make us all too wise.

But some of us would try to steal
    A little from the book,
And put the words together,
    And learn by hook or crook.

I remember Uncle Caldwell,
    Who took pot liquor fat
And greased the pages of his book,
    And hid it in his hat.

And had his master ever seen
    The leaves upon his head,
He'd have thought them greasy papers,
    But nothing to be read.

And there was Mr. Turner's Ben,
    Who heard the children spell,
And picked the words right up by heart,
    And learned to read 'em well.

Well, the Northern folks kept sending
    The Yankee teachers down;
And they stood right up and helped us,
    Though Rebs did sneer and frown.

And I longed to read my Bible,
    For precious words it said;
But when I begun to learn it,
    Folks just shook their heads,

And said there is no use trying,
    Oh! Chloe, you're too late;
But as I was rising sixty,
    I had no time to wait.

So I got a pair of glasses,
    And straight to work I went,
And never stopped till I could read
    The hymns and Testament.

Then I got a little cabin
    A place to call my own–

And I felt as independent
As the queen upon her throne.

Dante Gabriel Rossetti 1828–1882

A Sonnet

A Sonnet is a moment's monument,—
Memorial from the Soul's eternity
To one dead deathless hour. Look that it be,
Whether for lustral rite or dire portent,
Of its own arduous fulness reverent:
Carve it in ivory or in ebony,
As Day or Night may rule; and let Time see
Its flowering crest impearled and orient.

A Sonnet is a coin: its face reveals
The soul,—its converse, to what Power 'tis due:—
Whether for tribute to the august appeals
Of Life, or dower in Love's high retinue,
It serve; or, 'mid the dark wharf's cavernous breath,
In Charon's[7] palm it pay the toll to Death.

Authur Rimbaud 1854–1891

My Bohemia

I wandered, my hands in my torn coat pockets;
And my overcoat became ideal;
I wandered under the sky, Muse! and I was your troubadour;
Oh! lá lá! what splendid loves I dreamed!

My only pants had a large hole.
—Petit-Poucet[8] dreamer, I sowed along my way
My tumbling rhymes. My shelter was Ursa Major.[9]
—My stars in heaven rustled softly

And I listened, sitting at the edge of the road,
Those fair September evenings where I felt on my forehead
Dewdrops, like a wine of vigor;

Where while rhyming amidst the shadowy fantasy,
I plucked, like the strings of a lyre, the laces
Of my worn-out shoes, one foot near to my heart!
—Trans. Kelly Johnson

Vyacheslav Ivanovich Ivanov 1866–1949

Alpine Horn

Among deaf mountains I met a shepherd,
Who blew a long alpine horn.
His song pleasantly poured forth; though sonorous,
The horn was just a tool to wake
A captivating echo in the mountains.
And each time after making a few sounds,
The shepherd waited for the echo.
It travelled through ravines with such
An unspeakably sweet chime
It seemed like an invisible choir of spirits
That with unearthly instruments translated
The tongue of earth into the words of heaven.
And I thought: 'Oh, genius, like this horn
You must sing the song of earth
To wake another song in human hearts.
Blessed is he who hears.'
And from the mountains the voice replied:
'Nature is a symbol like this horn.
It sounds just for the reply. And the reply is God.
Blessed is he who hears both the song and the reply.'

—Trans. Tatsiana De Rosa

James Weldon Johnson 1871–1938

O Black and Unknown Bards

O Black and unknown bards of long ago,
How came your lips to touch the sacred fire?
How, in your darkness, did you come to know
The power and beauty of the minstrel's lyre?
Who first from midst his bonds lifted his eyes?
Who first from out the still watch, lone and long,
Feeling the ancient faith of prophets rise
Within his dark-kept soul, burst into song?
Heart of what slave poured out such melody
As "Steal away to Jesus"?[10] On its strains
His spirit must have nightly floated free,
Though still about his hands he felt his chains.

Who heard great "Jordan roll"? And who was he
That breathed that comforting, melodic sigh,
"Nobody knows de trouble I see"?

What merely living clod, what captive thing,
Could up toward God through all its darkness grope,
And find within its deadened heart to sing
These songs of sorrow, love, and faith, and hope?
How did it catch that subtle undertone,
That note in music heard not with the ears?
How sound the elusive reed, so seldom blown,
Which stirs the soul or melts the heart to tears?

Not that great German master in his dream
Of harmonies that thundered 'mongst the stars
At the creation, ever heard a theme
Nobler than "Go down, Moses." Mark its bars,
How like a mighty trumpet-call they stir
The blood. Such are the notes that men have sung,
Going to valorous deeds; such tones there were
That helped make history when Time was young.

There is a wide, wide wonder in it all,
That from degraded rest and service toil
The fiery spirit of the seer should call
These simple children of the sun and soil.
O black slave singers, gone, forgot, unfamed,
You—you alone, of all the long, long line
Of those who've sung untaught, unknown, unnamed,
Have stretched out upward, seeking the divine.

You sang not deeds of heroes or of kings;
No chant of bloody war, no exulting paean
Of arms-won triumphs; but your humble strings
You touched in chord with music empyrean.[11]
You sang far better than you knew; the songs
that for your listeners' hungry hearts sufficed
Still live,—but more than this to you belongs:
You sang a race from wood and stone to Christ.

PAUL LAWRENCE DUNBAR 1872–1906

A CHOICE

They please me not—these solemn songs
That hint of sermon covered up.
'Tis true the world should heed its wrongs,
    But in a poem let me sup,
Not simples brewed to cure or ease
Humanity's confessed disease,
But the spirit-wine of a singing line,
    Or a dew-drop in a honey cup!

HILDA DOOLITTLE 1886–1961

HOLY SATYR

Most holy Satyr,[12]
like a goat,
with horns and hooves
to match thy coat
of russet brown,
I make leaf-circlets
and a crown of honey-flowers
for thy throat;
where the amber petals
drip to ivory,
I cut and slip
each stiffened petal
in the rift
of carven petal:
honey horn
has wed the bright
virgin petal of the white
flower cluster: lip to lip
let them whisper,
let them lilt, quivering:
Most holy Satyr,
like a goat,
hear this our song,
accept our leaves,
love-offering,
return our hymn;

like echo fling
a sweet song,
answering note for note.

MOONRISE

Will you glimmer on the sea?
will you fling your spear-head
on the shore?
what note shall we pitch?
we have a song,
on the bank we share our arrows;
the loosed string tells our note:

O flight,
bring her swiftly to our song.
She is great,
we measure her by the pine trees.

PABLO NERUDA 1904–1973

THE WORD

It was born
the word in the blood,
it grew in the dark body, pulsing,
and it flew with the lips and the mouth.

Further and closer
still more, still more came
from dead parents and from wandering races,
from territories that became stone,
that tired from their poor tribes,
because when pain came out to the path
the people traveled and arrived
and reunited new soil and water
to plant anew their word.
And such is the inheritance:
this is the air that connects us
with the buried person and with the dawn
of new beings yet unrisen.

Still the atmosphere trembles
with the first word
produced

with panic and groan.
It came out
of the fogs
and until now there is no thunder
that thunders still its iron sound
like that word,
the first
pronounced word:
maybe it was just a whisper, a drop,
and it falls and falls, still it cascades.

Then meaning filled the word.
It became pregnant and filled with lives,
all became birth and sounds:
affirmation, clarity, strength,
negation, destruction, death:
the verb assumed all the powers
and fused existence with essence
in the electricity of its beauty.

Human word, syllable, hip
of long light and hard silver,
hereditary cup that receives
the blood's communications:
here the silence was integrated
by the whole of the human word
and not to speak is to die from others:
we make ourselves full of language,
the mouth speaks without moving its lips:
suddenly the eyes are words.

I take the word and explore it
as if it were only human form,
its lines delight me and I sail
in each resonance of language:
I pronounce and am, and,
without speech, I am moved closer
to the end of words to silence.

I drink to the word raising
a word or clear glass,
in it I drink
the language-wine
or the endless water,
maternal fountain of words,

and glass and water and wine
bring forth my song
because verb is origin
and pours life. It is blood,
the blood that expresses its substance
and its development is thus disposed:
give glass to glass, blood to blood,
and the words give life to life.

—Trans. Sandra Kunanele

STEPHEN SPENDER 1909–1995

I THINK CONTINUALLY OF THOSE WHO WERE TRULY GREAT

I think continually of those who were truly great.
Who, from the womb, remembered the soul's history
Through corridors of light where the hours are suns,
Endless and singing. Whose lovely ambition
Was that their lips, still touched with fire,
Should tell of the Spirit clothed from head to foot in song.
And who hoarded from the Spring branches
The desires falling across their bodies like blossoms.

What is precious is never to forget
The essential delight of the blood drawn from ageless springs
Breaking through rocks in worlds before our earth.
Never to deny its pleasure in the morning simple light
Nor its grave evening demand for love.
Never to allow gradually the traffic to smother
With noise and fog, the flowering of the spirit.

Near the snow, near the sun, in the highest fields
See how these names are fêted by the waving grass
And by the streamers of white cloud
And whispers of wind in the listening sky.
The names of those who in their lives fought for life,
Who wore at their hearts the fire's centre.
Born of the sun, they traveled a short while towards the sun,
And left the vivid air singed with their honour.

ALLEN GINSBERG 1926–1997

VISION 1948

Dread spirit in me that I ever try
    With written words to move,
Hear thou my plea, at last reply
    To my impotent pen:
Should I endure, and never prove
    Yourself and me in love,
Tell me, spirit, tell me, O what then?

And if not love, why, then, another passion
    For me to pass in image:
Shadow, shadow, and blind vision.
    Dumb roar of the white trance,
Ecstatic shadow out of rage,
    Power out of passage.
Dance, dance, spirit, spirit, dance!

Is it my fancy that the world is still,
    So gentle in her dream?
Outside, great Harlems of the will
    Move under black sleep:
Yet in spiritual scream,
    The saxophones the same
As me in madness call thee from the deep.

I shudder with intelligence and I
    Wake in the deep light
And hear a vast machinery
    Descending without sound,
Intolerable to me, too bright,
    And shaken in the sight
The eye goes blind before the world goes round.

DANIEL WEEKS 1958–

HE LAY DOWN IN GREEN TIMOTHY

John Coleman lay down
hidden in green timothy,
awake to the dull throb
of the day's dull work

in arm and thigh,
lay listening to the
silence come out of
the late afternoon air,
like a hawk gliding
noiseless and slow
above the tree crowns,
a silence soft and calming
in the thick and heated
air. He lay listening,
old John Coleman, till
the tired sun hid
its fire, too, and the
soft churring of
the insects rose and
rose in the darkening
air where silence
was, till old John
Coleman's ear, cocked
like an old Delaware
scout's, began to compose
a wild music from that
humming, a mountain tune
borne off the summer air—
a strange old music
borne off on this
summer air.

Cycle 7: Relatedness to the Environment, Flora and Fauna

THOMAS GRAY 1716–1771

ODE ON THE DEATH OF A FAVOURITE CAT DROWNED IN A TUB OF GOLDFISHES

'Twas on a lofty vase's side,
Where China's gayest art had dyed
   The azure flowers that blow;
Demurest of the tabby kind,
The pensive Selima, reclined,
   Gazed on the lake below.

Her conscious tail her joy declared;
The fair round face, the snowy beard,
   The velvet of her paws,
Her coat, that with the tortoise vies,
Her ears of jet, and emerald eyes,
   She saw; and purred applause.

Still had she gazed; but 'midst the tide
Two angel forms were seen to glide,
   The genii of the stream;
Their scaly armour's Tyrian hue[1]
Through richest purple to the view
   Betrayed a golden gleam.

The hapless nymph with wonder saw;
A whisker first and then a claw,
   With many an ardent wish,
She stretched in vain to reach the prize.
What female heart can gold despise?
   What cat's averse to fish?

Presumptuous maid! with looks intent
Again she stretch'd, again she bent,
   Nor knew the gulf between.
(Malignant Fate sat by, and smiled)
The slippery verge her feet beguiled,
   She tumbled headlong in.
Eight times emerging from the flood
She mewed to every watery god,
   Some speedy aid to send.
No dolphin came, no Nereid[2] stirred;
Nor cruel Tom, nor Susan heard;
   A Favourite has no friend!
From hence, ye beauties, undeceived,
Know, one false step is ne'er retrieved,
   And be with caution bold.
Not all that tempts your wandering eyes
And heedless hearts, is lawful prize;
   Nor all that glisters, gold.

JOHANN WOLFGANG VON GOETHE 1749–1832

TO THE RISING FULL MOON

Do you want to leave me so soon?
For a moment, were so close.
Heavy clouds surround you with darkness,
And now you are gone altogether.

But you feel how sad I am,
As your rim beams like a rising star!
You prove to me that I am loved,
No matter how far my darling is.

Shine on then! Bright and brighter,
On a clear course, in all your splendor!
Though my heart races in pain,
The night is overcome with bliss.

—Trans. Gert Niers

MAY SONG

How radiant Nature
Appears to me!

How bright the sunlight!
How joyful the field!

Buds emerge
From every twig,
And a thousand voices
From the thicket,

And joy and gladness
From every breast.
O earth, o sun,
O joy, o delight,

O love, my love,
In golden beauty
Like the morning clouds
Upon those hills

In glory you bless
The fresh field –
The fragrance of flowers
Fills the world!

O girl, dearest girl,
How I love you!
How your eyes gleam,
How you love me!

As the lark loves
Song and air,
And morning flowers love
The scent of the sky,

That's how I love you,
With the warmth of my blood
I love you who gives me
Youth and joy and courage

To create new
Songs and dances.
Be happy always in
The way you love me.

—Trans. Gert Niers

AT MIDNIGHT

At midnight, as a little boy, I passed,
Not really willingly, that church yard
To my father's house, the parish; star next to
Star—they all were shining in full splendor;
    At midnight.

Much later in my life when,
Under her spell, I had to see my dearest,
Stars and Northern Lights competed with each other,
And I, coming and going, inhaled eternal bliss;
    At midnight.

Until at last the light of the full moon
With all its power broke into my darkness,
And my thoughts, both reasonable and quick,
Embraced past and future;
    At midnight.

—Trans. Gert Niers

ON THE LAKE

And so I draw in from the wide world
New blood and fresh nourishment;
So kind and good is Nature
Who holds me to her breast!
The waves rock our boat
To the beat of the rowing oars,
And mountains in sky-high clouds
Meet our onward course.

My eyes, why are you looking down?
Golden dreams—are you coming back?
Go away, dream, as golden as you are:
Love and life are also right here.

On the lake twinkle
Thousands of dancing stars,
Soft fog surrounds
The staggering distance;
Morning wind sends its wings
Over the bay still dipped in shadow;
And the surface of the lake
Reflects the ripening fruit.

—Trans. Gert Niers

PHILIP FRENEAU 1752–1832

ON THE RELIGION OF NATURE

The power, that gives with liberal hand
    The blessings man enjoys, while here,
And scatters through a smiling land
    Abundant products of the year;
            That power of nature, ever blessed,
            Bestowed religion with the rest.

Born with ourselves, her early sway
    Inclines the tender mind to take
The path of right, fair virtue's way
    Its own felicity to make.
            This universally extends
            And leads to no mysterious ends.

Religion, such as nature taught,
    With all divine perfection suits;
Had all mankind this system sought
    Sophists[3] would cease their vain disputes,
            And from this source would nations know
            All that can make their heaven below.

This deals not curses on mankind,
    Or dooms them to perpetual grief,
If from its aid no joys they find,
    It damns them not for unbelief;
            Upon a more exalted plan
            Creatress nature dealt with man—

Joy to the day, when all agree
    On such grand systems to proceed,
From fraud, design, and error free,
    And which to truth and goodness lead:
            Then persecution will retreat
            And man's religion be complete.

WILLIAM WORDSWORTH 1770–1850

MY HEART LEAPS UP

My heart leaps up when I behold
    A rainbow in the sky:
So was it when my life began;

So is it now I am a man;
So be it when I shall grow old,
  Or let me die!
The Child is father of the Man;
And I could wish my days to be
Bound each to each by natural piety.

Samuel Taylor Coleridge 1772–1834

To Nature

It may indeed be phantasy, when I
  Essay to draw from all created things
  Deep, heartfelt, inward joy that closely clings;
And trace in leaves and flowers that round me lie
Lessons of love and earnest piety.
  So let it be; and if the wide world rings
  In mock of this belief, it brings
Nor fear, nor grief, nor vain perplexity.
So will I build my altar in the fields,
  And the blue sky my fretted dome shall be,
And the sweet fragrance that the wild flower yields
  Shall be the incense I will yield to Thee,
Thee only God! and thou shalt not despise
Even me, the priest of this poor sacrifice.

This Lime-Tree Bower My Prison
Addressed to Charles Lamb,
of the India House, London

*In the June of 1797 some long-expected friends paid a visit
to the author's cottage; and on the morning of their arrival,
he met with an accident, which disabled him from walking
during the whole time of their stay. One evening, when they
had left him for a few hours, he composed the following lines
in the garden-bower.*

Well, they are gone, and here must I remain,
This lime-tree bower my prison! I have lost
Beauties and feelings, such as would have been
Most sweet to my remembrance even when age
Had dimmed mine eyes to blindness! They, meanwhile,
Friends, whom I never more may meet again,
On springy heath, along the hill-top edge,

Wander in gladness, and wind down, perchance,
To that still roaring dell,[4] of which I told;
The roaring dell, o'erwooded, narrow, deep,
And only speckled by the mid-day sun;
Where its slim trunk the ash from rock to rock
Flings arching like a bridge;—that branchless ash,
Unsunned and damp, whose few poor yellow leaves
Ne'er tremble in the gale, yet tremble still,
Fanned by the water-fall! and there my friends
Behold the dark green file of long lank weeds,
That all at once (a most fantastic sight!)
Still nod and drip beneath the dripping edge
Of the blue clay-stone.
                            Now, my friends emerge
Beneath the wide wide Heaven—and view again
The many-steepled tract magnificent
Of hilly fields and meadows, and the sea,
With some fair bark, perhaps, whose sails light up
The slip of smooth clear blue betwixt two Isles
Of purple shadow! Yes! they wander on
In gladness all; but thou, methinks, most glad,
My gentle-hearted Charles! for thou hast pined
And hungered after Nature, many a year,
In the great City pent, winning thy way
With sad yet patient soul, through evil and pain
And strange calamity! Ah! slowly sink
Behind the western ridge, thou glorious Sun!
Shine in the slant beams of the sinking orb,
Ye purple heath-flowers! richlier burn, ye clouds!
Live in the yellow light, ye distant groves!
And kindle, thou blue Ocean! So my friend
Struck with deep joy, may stand, as I have stood,
Silent with swimming sense; yea, gazing round
On the wide landscape, gaze till all doth seem
Less gross than bodily, and of such hues
As veil the Almighty Spirit, when yet he makes
Spirits perceive his presence.
                            A delight
Comes sudden on my heart, and I am glad
As I myself were there! Nor in this bower,
This little lime-tree bower, have I not marked
Much that has soothed me. Pale beneath the blaze
Hung the transparent foliage; and I watched

Some broad and sunny leaf, and loved to see
The shadow of the leaf and stem above
Dappling its sunshine! And that walnut-tree
Was richly tinged, and a deep radiance lay
Full on the ancient ivy, which usurps
Those fronting elms, and now, with blackest mass
Makes their dark branches gleam a lighter hue
Through the late twilight: and though now the bat
Wheels silent by, and not a swallow twitters,
Yet still the solitary humble-bee
Sings in the bean-flower! Henceforth I shall know
That Nature ne'er deserts the wise and pure;
No plot so narrow, be but Nature there,
No waste so vacant, but may well employ
Each faculty of sense, and keep the heart
Awake to Love and Beauty! and sometimes
'Tis well to be bereft of promised good,
That we may lift the soul, and contemplate
With lively joy the joys we cannot share.
My gentle-hearted Charles! when the last rook
Beat its straight path along the dusky air
Homewards, I blest it! deeming its black wing
(Now a dim speck, now vanishing in light)
Had crossed the mighty Orb's dilated glory,
While thou stood'st gazing; or, when all was still,
Flew creeking o'er thy head, and had a charm
For thee, my gentle-hearted Charles, to whom
No sound is dissonant which tells of Life.

GEORGE GORDON, LORD BYRON 1788–1824

XIII

Where rose the mountains, there to him were friends;
    Where rolled the ocean, thereon was his home;
    Where a blue sky, and glowing clime, extends,
    He had the passion and the power to roam;
    The desert, forest, cavern, breaker's foam,
    Were unto him companionship; they spake
    A mutual language, clearer than the tome
    Of his land's tongue, which he would oft forsake
For nature's pages glassed by sunbeams on the lake.

—from *Childe Harold's Pilgrimage*—Canto III

LXXV

Are not the mountains, waves, and skies a part
　　Of me and of my soul, as I of them?
　　Is not the love of these deep in my heart
　　With a pure passion? Should I not contemn
　　All objects, if compared with these? And stem
　　A tide of suffering, rather than forego
　　Such feelings for the hard and worldly phlegm[5]
　　Of those whose eyes are only turned below,
Gazing upon the ground, with thoughts which dare not glow?

　　　　　　　　—from Childe Harold's Pilgrimage—Canto III

LXXXVIII

Ye stars! Which are the poetry of heaven,
　　If in your bright leaves we would read the fate
　　Of men and empires,—'tis to be forgiven,
　　That in our aspirations to be great,
　　Our destinies o'erleap their mortal state,
　　And claim a kindred with you; for ye are
　　A beauty and a mystery, and create
　　In us such love and reverence from afar,
That fortune, fame, power, life, have named themselves a star.

　　　　　　　　—from Childe Harold's Pilgrimage—Canto III

XCIII

And this is in the night:—Most glorious night!
　　Thou wert not sent for slumber! Let me be
　　A sharer in thy fierce and far delight—
　　A portion of the tempest and of thee!
　　How the lit lake shines, a phosphoric sea,
　　And the big rain comes dancing to the earth!
　　And now again 'tis black, and now, the glee
　　Of the loud hills shakes with its mountain-mirth,
As if they did rejoice o'er a young earthquake's birth.

　　　　　　　　—from Childe Harold's Pilgrimage—Canto III

RALPH WALDO EMERSON 1803–1882

THE RHODORA[6]
ON BEING ASKED, WHENCE IS THE FLOWER?

In May, when sea-winds pierced our solitudes,
I found the fresh Rhodora in the woods,

Spreading its leafless blooms in a damp nook,
To please the desert and the sluggish brook.
The purple petals, fallen in the pool,
Made the black water with their beauty gay;
Here might the red-bird come his plumes to cool,
And court the flower that cheapens his array.
Rhodora! if the sages ask thee why
This charm is wasted on the earth and sky,
Tell them, dear, that if eyes were made for seeing,
Then Beauty is its own excuse for being:
Why thou were there, O rival of the rose!
I never thought to ask, I never knew:
But, in my simple ignorance, suppose
The self-same Power that brought me there brought you.

ELIZABETH BARRETT BROWNING 1806–1881

TO FLUSH, MY DOG

Yet, my pretty sportive friend,
Little is't to such an end
That I praise thy rareness!
Other dogs may be thy peers
Haply in these drooping ears,
And this glossy fairness.

But of thee it shall be said,
This dog watched beside a bed
Day and night unweary—
Watched within a curtained room,
Where no sunbeam brake the gloom
Round the sick and dreary.

Roses, gathered for a vase,
In that chamber died apace,
Beam and breeze resigning.
This dog only, waited on,
Knowing that when light is gone
Love remains for shining.

Other dogs in thymy dew
Tracked the hares, and followed through
Sunny moor or meadow.
This dog only, crept and crept

Next a languid cheek that slept,
Sharing in the shadow.

Other dogs of loyal cheer
Bounded at the whistle clear,
Up the woodside hieing.[7]
This dog only, watched in reach
Of a faintly uttered speech,
Or a louder sighing.

And if one or two quick tears
Dropped upon his glossy ears,
Or a sigh came double—
Up he sprang in eager haste,
Fawning, fondling, breathing fast,
In a tender trouble.

And this dog was satisfied
If a pale thin hand would glide
Down his dewlaps sloping—
Which he pushed his nose within,
After—platforming his chin
On the palm left open.

JOHN GREENLEAF WHITTIER 1807–1892

THE WORSHIP OF NATURE

The harp at Nature's advent strung
Has never ceased to play;
The song the stars of morning sung
Has never died away.

And prayer is made, and praise is given,
By all things near and far;
The ocean looketh up to heaven,
And mirrors every star.

Its waves are kneeling on the strand,
As kneels the human knee,
Their white locks bowing to the sand,
The priesthood of the sea!

They pour their glittering treasures forth,
Their gifts of pearl they bring,

And all the listening hills of earth
Take up the song they sing.

The green earth sends its incense up
From many a mountain shrine;
From folded leaf and dewy cup
She pours her sacred wine.

The mists above the morning rills[8]
Rise white as wings of prayer;
The altar-curtains of the hills
Are sunset's purple air.

The winds with hymns of praise are loud,
Or low with sobs of pain,—
The thunder-organ of the cloud,
The dropping tears of rain.

With drooping head and branches crossed
The twilight forest grieves,
Or speaks with tongues of Pentecost
From all its sunlit leaves.

The blue sky is the temple's arch,
Its transept[9] earth and air,
The music of its starry march
The chorus of a prayer.

So Nature keeps the reverent frame
With which her years began,
And all her signs and voices shame
The prayerless heart of man.

ALFRED, LORD TENNYSON 1809–1892

COME DOWN, O MAID, FROM YONDER MOUNTAIN HEIGHT

Come down, O maid, from yonder mountain height:
What pleasure lives in height (the shepherd sang)
In height and cold, the splendour of the hills?
But cease to move so near the Heavens, and cease
To glide a sunbeam by the blasted Pine,
To sit a star upon the sparkling spire;
And come, for Love is of the valley, come,
For Love is of the valley, come thou down

And find him; by the happy threshold, he,
Or hand in hand with Plenty in the maize,
Or red with spirted purple of the vats,
Or foxlike in the vine; nor cares to walk
With Death and Morning on the silver horns,
Nor wilt thou snare him in the white ravine,
Nor find him dropt upon the firths of ice,
That huddling slant in furrow-cloven falls
To roll the torrent out of dusky doors:
But follow; let the torrent dance thee down
To find him in the valley; let the wild
Lean-headed Eagles yelp alone, and leave
The monstrous ledges there to slope, and spill
Their thousand wreaths of dangling water-smoke,
That like a broken purpose waste in air:
So waste not thou; but come; for all the vales
Await thee; azure pillars of the hearth
Arise to thee; the children call, and I
Thy shepherd pipe, and sweet is every sound,
Sweeter thy voice, but every sound is sweet;
Myriads of rivulets hurrying thro' the lawn,
The moan of doves in immemorial elms,
And murmuring of innumerable bees.

HENRY DAVID THOREAU 1817–1862

NATURE

O nature I do not aspire
To be the highest in thy quire,[10]
To be a meteor in the sky
Or comet that may range on high,
Only a zephyr that may blow
Among the reeds by the river low.
Give me thy most privy place
Where to run my airy race.
In some withdrawn unpublic mead
Let me sigh upon a reed,
Or in the woods with leafy din
Whisper the still evening in,
For I had rather be thy child
And pupil in the forest wild

Than be the king of men elsewhere
And most sovereign slave of care
To have one moment of thy dawn
Than share the city's year forlorn.
Some still work give me to do
Only be it near to you.

WALT WHITMAN 1819–1892

WE TWO, HOW LONG WE WERE FOOL'D

We two, how long we were fool'd,
Now transmuted, we swiftly escape as Nature escapes,
We are Nature, long have we been absent, but now we return,
We become plants, trunks, foliage, roots, bark,
We are bedded in the ground, we are rocks,
We are oaks, we grow in the openings side by side,
We browse, we are two among the wild herds spontaneous as any,
We are two fishes swimming in the sea together,
We are what locust blossoms are, we drop scent around lanes
     mornings and evenings,
We are also the coarse smut of beasts, vegetables, minerals,
We are two predatory hawks, we soar above and look down,
We are two resplendent suns, we it is who balance ourselves
     orbic and stellar, we are as two comets,
We prowl fang'd and four-footed in the woods, we spring on prey,
We are two clouds forenoons and afternoons driving overhead,
We are seas mingling, we are two of those cheerful waves
     rolling over each other and interwetting each other,
We are what the atmosphere is, transparent, receptive,
     pervious, impervious,
We are snow, rain, cold, darkness, we are each product and
     influence of the globe,
We have circled and circled till we have arrived home again,
     we two,
We have voided all but freedom and all but our own joy.

A SONG OF THE ROLLING EARTH

1

A song of the rolling earth, and of words according,
Were you thinking that those were the words, those upright
     lines? those curves, angles, dots?

No, those are not the words, the substantial words are in the
    ground and sea,
They are in the air, they are in you.

Were you thinking that those were the words, those delicious
    sounds out of your friends' mouths?
No, the real words are more delicious than they.

Human bodies are words, myriads of words,
(In the best poems re-appears the body, man's or woman's,
    well-shaped, natural, gay,
Every part able, active, receptive, without shame or the need of
    shame.)

Air, soil, water, fire—those are words,
I myself am a word with them—my qualities interpenetrate
    with theirs—my name is nothing to them,
Though it were told in the three thousand languages, what
    would air, soil, water, fire, know of my name?

A healthy presence, a friendly or commanding gesture, are
    words, sayings, meanings,
The charms that go with the mere looks of some men and
    women, are sayings and meanings also.

The workmanship of souls is by those inaudible words of the
    earth,
The masters know the earth's words and use them more than
    audible words.

Amelioration is one of the earth's words,
The earth neither lags nor hastens,
It has all attributes, growths, effects, latent in itself from the jump,
It is not half beautiful only, defects and excrescences show just
    as much as perfections show.

The earth does not withhold; it is generous enough,
The truths of the earth continually wait, they are not so
    conceal'd either,
they are calm, subtle, untransmissible by print,
They are imbued through all things conveying themselves
    willingly,
Conveying a sentiment and invitation, I utter and utter,
I speak not, yet if you hear me not of what avail am I to you?
To bear, to better, lacking these of what avail am I?

(Accouche! Accouchez![11]

Will you rot your own fruit in yourself there?
Will you squat and stifle there?)

The earth does not argue,
Is not pathetic, has no arrangements,
Does not scream, haste, persuade, threaten, promise,
Make no discriminations, has no conceivable failures,
Closes nothing, refuses nothing, shuts none out,
Of all the powers, objects, states, it notifies, shuts none out.

The earth does not exhibit itself nor refuse to exhibit itself,
    possesses still underneath,
Underneath the ostensible sounds, the august chorus of
    heroes, the wail of slaves,
Persuasions of lovers, curses, gasps of the dying, laughter of
    young people, accents of bargainers,
Underneath these possessing words that never fail.

To her children the words of the eloquent dumb great mother
    never fail,
The true words do not fail, for motion does not fail and
    reflection does not fail,
Also the day and night do not fail, and the voyage we pursue
    does not fail.

Of the interminable sisters,
Of the ceaseless cotillions of sisters,
Of the centripetal and centrifugal sisters, the elder and
    younger sisters,
The beautiful sister we know dances on with the rest.

With her ample back towards every beholder,
With the fascinations of youth and the equal fascinations of age,
Sits she whom I too love like the rest, sits undisturb'd,
Holding up in her hand what has the character of a mirror,
    while her eyes glance back from it,
Glance as she sits, inviting none, denying none,
Holding a mirror day and night tirelessly before her own face.

Seen at hand or seen at distance,
Duly the twenty-four appear in public every day,
Duly approach and pass with their companions or a
    companion,
Looking from no countenances of their own, but from the
    countenances of those who are with them,
From the countenances of children or women or the manly

countenance,
From the open countenances of animals or from inanimate
    things,
From the landscape or waters or from the exquisite apparition
    of the sky,
From our countenances, mine and yours, faithfully returning
    them,
Every day in public appearing without fail, but never twice
    with the same companions.

Embracing man, embracing all, proceed the three hundred and
    sixty-five resistlessly round the sun;
Embracing all, soothing, supporting, follow close three
    hundred and sixty-five offsets of the first, sure and
    necessary as they.

Tumbling on steadily, nothing, dreading,
Sunshine, storm, cold, heat, forever withstanding, passing,
    carrying,
The soul's realization and determination still inheriting,
The fluid vacuum around and ahead still entering and dividing,
No balk retarding, no anchor anchoring, on no rock striking,
Swift, glad, content, unbrereav'd, nothing losing,
Of all able and ready at any time to give strict account,
The divine ship sails the divine sea.

2

Whoever you are! motion and reflection are especially for you,
The divine ship sails the divine sea for you.

Whoever you are! you are he or she for whom the earth is
    solid and liquid,
You are he or she for whom the sun and moon hang in the sky,
For no one more than you are the present and the past,
For none more than you is immortality.
Each man to himself and each woman to herself, is the word
    of the past and present, and the true word of immortality;
No one can acquire for another—not one,
Not one can grow for another—not one.

The song is to the singer, and comes back most to him,
The teaching is to the teacher, and comes back most to him,
The murder is to the murderer, and comes back most to him,
The theft is to the thief, and comes back most to him,
The love is to the lover, and comes back most to him,
The gift is to the giver, and comes back most to him—it

cannot fail,
The oration is to the orator, the acting is to the actor and
   actress not to the audience,
And no man understand any greatness or goodness but his
   own, or the indication of his own.

3

I swear the earth shall surely be complete to him or her who
   shall be complete,
The earth remains jagged and broken only to him or here who
   remains jagged and broken.

I swear there is no greatness or power that does not emulate
   those of the earth,
There can be no theory of any account unless it corroborate
   the theory of the earth,
No politics, song, religion, behavior, or what not, is of account,
   unless it compare with the amplitude of the earth,
Unless it face the exactness, vitality, impartiality, rectitude of
   the earth.

I swear I begin to see love with sweeter spasms than that
   which responds love,
It is that which contains itself, which never invites and never
   refuses.
I swear I begin to see little or nothing in audible words,
All merges toward the presentation of the unspoken meanings
   of the earth,
Toward him who sings the songs of the body and of the truths
   of the earth,
Toward him who makes the dictionaries of words that print
   cannot touch.

I swear I see what is better than to tell the best,
It is always to leave the best untold.

When I undertake to tell the best I find I cannot,
My tongue is ineffectual on its pivots,
My breath will not be obedient to its organs,
I become a dumb man.

The best of the earth cannot be told anyhow, all or any is best,
It is not what you anticipated, it is cheaper, easier, nearer,
things are not dismiss'd from the places they held before,
Facts, religions, improvements, politics, trades, are as real as
   before,

But the soul is also real, it too is positive and direct,
No reasoning, no proof has establish'd it,
Undeniable growth has establish'd it.

4

These to echo the tones of souls and the phrases of souls,
(If they did not echo the phrases of souls what were they then?
If they had not reference to you in especial what were they
    then?)

I swear I will never henceforth have to do with the faith that
    tells the best,
I will have to do only with that faith that leaves the best
    untold.

Say on, sayers! sing on, singers!
Delve! mould! pile the words of the earth!
Work on, age after age, nothing is to be lost,
It may have to wait long, but it will certainly come in use,
When the materials are all prepared and ready, the architects
    shall appear.

I swear to you the architects shall appear without fail,
I swear to you they will understand you and justify you,
The greatest among them shall be he who best knows you, and
    encloses all and is faithful to all,
He and the rest shall not forget you, they shall perceive that
    you are not an iota less then they,
You shall be fully glorified in them.

Gerard Manley Hopkins 1844–1889

Binsey Poplars
felled 1879

My aspens dear, whose airy cages quelled,
    Quelled or quenched in leaves the leaping sun,
    All felled, felled, are all felled;
        Of a fresh and following folded rank
            Not spared, not one
            That dandled a sandalled
        Shadow that swam or sank
On meadow & river & wind-wandering weed-winding bank.

O if we but knew what we do
        When we delve or hew—

Hack and rack the growing green!
　　Since country is so tender
　　To touch, her being só slender,
　　That, like this sleek and seeing ball
　　But a prick will make no eye at all,
　　Where we, even where we mean
　　　　To mend her we end her,
　　　When we hew or delve:
After-comers cannot guess the beauty been.
　　Ten or twelve, only ten or twelve
　　　Strokes of havoc unselve
　　　　The sweet especial scene,
　　　Rural scene, a rural scene,
　　Sweet especial rural scene.

W.B. Yeats 1865–1939

The Lake Isle of Innisfree

I will arise and go now, and go to Innisfree,
And a small cabin build there, of clay and wattles made:
Nine bean-rows will I have there, a hive for the honey-bee,
And live alone in the bee-loud glade.

And I shall have some peace there, for peace comes dropping slow,
Dropping from the veils of the morning to where the cricket sings;
There midnight's all a glimmer, and noon a purple glow,
And evening full of the linnet's wings.

I will arise and go now, for always night and day
I hear lake water lapping with low sounds by the shore;
While I stand on the roadway, or on the pavements grey,
I hear it in the deep heart's core.

Robert Frost 1874–1963

The Tuft of Flowers

I went to turn the grass once after one
Who mowed it in the dew before the sun.

The dew was gone that made his blade so keen
Before I came to view the leveled scene.

I looked for him behind an isle of trees;
I listened for his whetstone on the breeze.

But he had gone his way, the grass all mown,
And I must be, as he had been,—alone,

"As all must be," I said within my heart,
"Whether they work together or apart."

But as I said it, swift there passed me by
On noiseless wing a 'wildered butterfly,

Seeking with memories grown dim o'er night
Some resting flower of yesterday's delight.

And once I marked his flight go round and round,
As where some flower lay withering on the ground.

And then he flew as far as eye could see,
And then on tremulous wing came back to me.

I thought of questions that have no reply,
And would have turned to toss the grass to dry;

But he turned first, and led my eye to look
At a tall tuft of flowers beside a brook,

A leaping tongue of bloom the scythe had spared
Beside a reedy brook the scythe had bared.

I left my place to know them by their name,
Finding them butterfly weed when I came.

The mower in the dew had loved them thus,
By leaving them to flourish, not for us,

Nor yet to draw one thought of ours to him.
But from sheer morning gladness at the brim.

The butterfly and I had lit upon,
Nevertheless, a message from the dawn,

That made me hear the wakening birds around,
And hear his long scythe whispering to the ground,

And feel a spirit kindred to my own;
So that henceforth I worked no more alone;

But glad with him, I worked as with his aid,
And weary, sought at noon with him the shade;

And dreaming, as it were, held brotherly speech
With one whose thought I had not hoped to reach.

"Men work together," I told him from the heart,
"Whether they work together or apart."

E.E. CUMMINGS 1894–1962

O SWEET SPONTANEOUS

O sweet spontaneous
earth how often have
the doting

       fingers of
prurient philosophies pinched
and
poked

thee
has the naughty thumb
of science prodded
thy

    beauty   how
often have religions taken
thee upon their scraggy
knees squeezing and

buffeting thee that thou mightest conceive
gods
    but
true

to the incomparable
couch of death thy
rhythmic
lover

    thou answerest

them only with

        spring

SPRING OMNIPOTENT GODDESS THOU

spring omnipotent goddess Thou
dost stuff parks

with overgrown pimply
chevaliers and gumchewing giggly

damosels Thou dost
persuade to serenade
his lady the musical tom-cat
Thou dost inveigle

into crossing sidewalks the
unwary june-bug and the frivolous
angleworm
Thou dost hang canary birds in parlour windows

Spring slattern of seasons
you have soggy legs
and a muddy petticoat
drowsy

is your hair your
eyes are sticky with
dream and you have a
sloppy body from

being brought to bed of crocuses
when you sing in your whisky voice
the grass rises on the head of the earth
and all the trees are put on edge

spring
of the excellent jostle of
thy hips
and the superior

slobber of your breasts i
am so very fond that my
soul inside of me hollers

                                        for thou comest

and your hands are the snow and thy
fingers are the rain
and your
feet O your feet

freakish
feet feet incorrigible

ragging the world

Pablo Neruda   1904–1973

Horses

From the window I saw the horses.

It was in Berlin, in winter. The light
was without light, without sky the sky.

The air white like wet bread.

And from my window a solitary arena
bitten by winter's teeth.

Suddenly, led by a man,
ten horses went out into the fog.

Barely they undulated when they went, like fire,
but to my eyes they occupied the world,
empty till that hour. Perfect, ablaze,
They were like ten gods with long pure hooves,
with manes resembling the dream of the salt.

Their rumps were worlds and oranges.

Their color was honey, amber, a-blaze.

Their necks were towers
cut on the stone of pride,
and through their furious eyes peeked
like a prisoner, power.

And there in silence, in the middle
of the day, of the dirty and disorderly winter,
the intense horses were the blood,
the rhythm, the instigating treasure of life.

I looked, I looked and then was revived: without knowing
there was the fountain, the gold dance, the sky,
the fire that lived in beauty.

I have forgotten the winter in that dark Berlin.

I will not forget the light of the horses.

—Trans. Sandra Kunanele

DYLAN THOMAS 1914–1953

THE FORCE THAT THROUGH THE GREEN FUSE DRIVES THE FLOWER

The force that through the green fuse drives the flower
Drives my green age; that blasts the roots of trees
Is my destroyer.
And I am dumb to tell the crooked rose
My youth is bent by the same wintry fever.

The force that drives the water through the rocks
Drives my red blood; that dries the mouthing streams
Turns mine to wax.
And I am dumb to mouth unto my veins
How at the mountain spring the same mouth sucks.

The hand that whirls the water in the pool
Stirs the quicksand; that ropes the blowing wind
Hauls my shroud sail.
And I am dumb to tell the hanging man
How of my clay is made the hangman's lime.

The lips of time leech to the fountain head;
Love drips and gathers, but the fallen blood
Shall calm her sores.
And I am dumb to tell a weather's wind
How time has ticked a heaven round the stars.

And I am dumb to tell the lover's tomb
How at my sheet goes the same crooked worm.

NIKKI GIOVANNI 1943–

WINTER POEM

once a snowflake fell
on my brow and i loved
it so much and i kissed
it and it was happy and called its cousins
and brothers and a web
of snow engulfed me then
i reached to love them all
and i squeezed them and they became

a spring rain and i stood perfectly
still and was a flower

ADELE KENNY 1948–

OF OTHER

It isn't now or this patch of blue autumn,
light skimmed like milk without substance
(its ghost on my lips). Or the way trees darken

before the sky, the way light slants through
pines (my neighbor's lamp or the moon).
It's not the way night feels when I walk in

March, when snow melts into mud, and I
smell grass again; when I know, without seeing,
that tight buds open high in the branches. It's

not the expected order of things but moments of
other (when something startles you into knowing
something other), and the heaviness lifts inside you.

Tonight, wind pulled leaves from the sky
to my feet and, suddenly (without warning) a
deer leapt from the thicket behind me—leapt

and disappeared—past me as I passed myself,
my body filled with absence, with air,
a perfect mold of the light gone through it.

SUSANNA RICH 1951–

WINTER TREES

Not for their boasting blossoms
or closed ranks of summer green,
nor for their autumn flames—neon

yellow, raging orange, chartreuse—
did I learn to love the trees, but for their
empty twigs, the scar where pulsed

a bud, the nests in crooks of branches,
the thorns, the single linden leaf
dangling its berry. Here trunk runes

speak tulip poplar, white oak, shag
bark hickory. The chestnut declares itself
in silhouetted scoops, the dogwood

in the curl and wave of onion caps and
praying hands. When trees turn into
themselves, when I can wonder at the single

catkin, pod, or key—the names stretch-marked
onto the weeping beech—I can be as they are—
abundant with the sky gathered in my arms.

LAURELS ON THE APPALACHIAN TRAIL

As if life were perpetual morning, wild
mountain laurels lure me with their impossibly
many heads—tight pin-cushions, tiny
clappered bells, thronging pink-white clusters
bursting into full unfurling umbrellas tempting sun.
I brought two cameras and take and take
and take as if only the flutter of my lens
could kiss these laurels to ache forth
their blossoms. Bush upon bush rises into
choirs—like alpine hillocks growing into hills,
into ridges, peaks and peaks—as if eons
of spring, tiers of ancestors were waking
at once... They bloom—bloom—regardless
that only I (or no one) walks this trail—
these crowds of miniature speakers, these
half-shells drenching me helpless in their rain,
these laurels and I—petals and petals, limbs and
and and and—gathering each other in.

WALKING HOLLY DOWN A WOODED LANE

I've tried sneaking by the house
next door, not to wake
Holly from her sphinx-pawed sleep.

I don't know how to be
with the joy in her clinking tags
soon after I round

the corner of her drive—
the tongue-lolling beast
galloping behind me,

ears back, tail whipping.
Decades, now, since I rescued
a retriever, like her, beaten

in the street. I lived
in an apartment, so I placed her
on a farm. I still think of her,

and all the lovers, family, friends
who were not to be, for lack of
time, or courage, or means.

What have I abandoned
that Holly should so surprise me?
I turn and call to this golden creature.

I won't walk as many hills:
she might bolt into the road
when we've passed these woods,

or her people might come home
and catch us in this mutual
kidnapping. Yesterday, I

stole past.
Halfway down the lane
I heard her clink-clinking:

Love knows when we're
trying to slip away, and follows—
regardless—then takes the lead.

DORIANNE LAUX 1952–

THE ORGASMS OF ORGANISMS

Above the lawn the wild beetles mate
and mate, skew their tough wings
and join. They light in our hair,
on our arms, fall twirling and twinning
into our laps. And below us, in the grass,
the bugs are seeking each other out,
antennae lifted and trembling, tiny legs
scuttling, then the infinitesimal
ah's of their meeting, the awkward joy
of their turnings around. O end to end

they meet again and swoon as only bugs can.
This is why, sometimes, the grass feels electric
under our feet, each blade quivering, and why
the air comes undone over our heads
and washes down around our ears like rain.
But it has to be spring, and you have to be
in love—acutely, painfully, achingly in love—
to hear the black-robed choir of their sighs.

BHIKSHUNI WEISBROT 1953–

SPRING AGAIN

Earth moves in
a metronome of rotation,
she cannot stop herself
nor her splendors—
the warmth of maternal embrace,
bare shoulders open to light.

Cycle 8: Hope, Optimism and Idealism

HEBREW BIBLE C. 900–200 BCE

PSALM 23

A Psalm by David.

The LORD is my shepherd:
    I shall lack nothing.
He makes me lie down in green
    pastures.
He leads me beside still
    waters.
He restores my soul.
    He guides me in the paths of
    righteousness for his
    name's sake.
Even though I walk through the
    valley of the shadow
    of death,
    I will fear no evil, for you
    are with me.
    Your rod and your staff, they
    comfort me.
You prepare a table before me in
    the presence of my
    enemies.
You anoint my head with oil.
    My cup runs over.
Surely goodness and loving
    kindness shall follow
    me all the days of my
    life,

and I will dwell in the
LORD's house forever.

JOHN DONNE 1572–1631

DEATH, BE NOT PROUD

Death, be not proud, though some have callèd thee
Mighty and dreadful, for thou art not so;
For those whom thou think'st thou dost overthrow
Die not, poor Death, nor yet canst thou kill me.
From rest and sleep, which but thy pictures be,
Much pleasure; then from thee much more must flow,
And soonest our best men with thee do go,
Rest of their bones, and soul's delivery.
Thou'rt slave to fate, chance, kings, and desperate men,
And dost with poison, war, and sickness dwell;
And poppy or charms can make us sleep as well
And better than thy stroke; why swell'st thou then?
One short sleep past, we wake eternally,
And death shall be no more: Death, thou shalt die.

JOHANN WOLFGANG VON GOETHE 1749–1832

PHENOMENON

When the sun god Phoebus
Embraces a wall of rain
An arch drenched in radiant colors
Rises into the sky.

I see another arch
Drawn into fog,
Although in white,
It is still heavenly.

Therefore, my good old man,
You should not worry:
Though your hair is white,
You will love again.

—Trans. Gert Niers

SAMUEL TAYLOR COLERIDGE 1772–1834

PANTISOCRACY[1]

No more my visionary soul shall dwell
On joys that were; no more endure to weigh
The shame and anguish of the evil day,
Wisely forgetful! O'er the ocean swell
Sublime of Hope, I seek the cottag'd dell
Where Virtue calm with careless step may stray,
And dancing to the moonlight roundelay,
The wizard Passions weave an holy spell.
Eyes that have ach'd with Sorrow! Ye shall weep
Tears of doubt-mingled joy, like theirs who start
From Precipices of distemper'd sleep,
On which the fierce-eyed Fiends their revels keep,
And see the rising Sun, and feel it dart
New rays of pleasance trembling to the heart.

JOHN CLARE 1793–1864

SONG: LOVE LIVES BEYOND THE TOMB

Love lives beyond
The tomb, the earth, which fades like dew –
I love the fond,
The faithful, and the true.

Love lives in sleep,
'Tis happiness of healthy dreams,
Eve's dews may weep,
But love delightful seems.

'Tis seen in flowers,
And in the even's pearly dew
On earth's green hours,
And in the heaven's eternal blue.

'Tis heard in spring
When light and sunbeams, warm and kind,
On angel's wing
Brings love and music to the wind.

And where's the voice
So young, so beautiful, and sweet

As nature's choice,
Where spring and lovers meet?

Love lives beyond
The tomb, the earth, the flowers, and dew.
I love the fond,
The faithful, young, and true.

George Moses Horton 1797–1884

Imploring to Be Resigned at Death

Let me die and not tremble at death,
  But smile at the close of my day,
And then at the flight of my breath,
  Like a bird of the morning in May,
    Go chanting away.

Let me die without fear of the dead,
  No horrors my soul shall dismay,
And with faith's pillow under my head,
  With defiance to mortal decay,
    Go chanting away.

Let me die like a son of the brave,
  And martial distinction display,
Nor shrink from a thought of the grave,
  No, but with a smile from the clay,
    Go chanting away.

Let me die glad, regardless of pain,
  No pang to this world betray,
And the spirit cut loose from its chains,
  So loath in the flesh to delay,
    Go chanting away.

Let me die, and my worst foe forgive,
  When death veils the last vital ray;
Since I have but a moment to live,
  Let me, when the last debt I pay,
    Go chanting away.

ALFRED, LORD TENNYSON 1809–1892

NOTHING WILL DIE

When will the stream be aweary of flowing
      Under my eye?
When will the wind be aweary of blowing
      Over the sky?
When will the clouds be aweary of fleeting?
When will the heart be aweary of beating?
      And nature die?
Never, oh! never, nothing will die;
        The stream flows,
        The wind blows,
        The cloud fleets,
        The heart beats,
        Nothing will die.

Nothing will die;
All things will change
Thro' eternity.
'Tis the world's winter;
Autumn and summer
Are gone long ago;
Earth is dry to the centre,
But spring, a new comer,
A spring rich and strange,
Shall make the winds blow
Round and round,
Thro' and thro',
      Here and there,
      Till the air
And the ground
Shall be fill'd with life anew.

The world was never made;
It will change, but it will not fade.
So let the wind range;
For even and morn
      Ever will be
      Thro' eternity.
Nothing was born;
Nothing will die;
All things will change.

CHARLOTTE BRONTË 1816–1855

LIFE

Life, believe, is not a dream
So dark as sages say;
Oft a little morning rain
Foretells a pleasant day.
Sometimes there are clouds of gloom,
But these are transient all;
If the shower will make the roses bloom,
O why lament its fall?
Rapidly, merrily,
Life's sunny hours flit by,
Gratefully, cheerily
Enjoy them as they fly!
What though Death at times steps in,
And calls our Best away?
What though sorrow seems to win,
O'er hope, a heavy sway?
Yet Hope again elastic springs,
Unconquered, though she fell;
Still buoyant are her golden wings,
Still strong to bear us well.
Manfully, fearlessly,
The day of trial bear,
For gloriously, victoriously,
Can courage quell despair!

WALT WHITMAN 1819–1892

A CLEAR MIDNIGHT

This is thy hour O Soul, thy free flight into the wordless,
Away from books, away from art, the day erased, the lesson
    done,
Thee fully forth emerging, silent, gazing, pondering the themes
    thou lovest best,
Night, sleep, death and the stars.

OVER THE CARNAGE ROSE PROPHETIC A VOICE

Over the carnage rose prophetic a voice,
Be not dishearten'd, affection shall solve the problems of

freedom yet,
Those who love each other shall become invincible,
They shall yet make Columbia victorious.

Sons of the Mother of All, you shall be victorious,
You shall yet laugh to scorn the attacks of all the remainder of
    the earth.

No danger shall balk Columbia's lovers,
If need be a thousand shall sternly immolate themselves for one.

One from Massachusetts shall be a Missourian's comrade,
From Maine and from hot Carolina, and another an
    Oregonese, shall be friends triune,
More precious to each other than all the riches of the earth.

To Michigan, Florida perfumes shall tenderly come,
Not the perfumes of flowers, but sweeter, and wafted beyond death.

It shall be customary in the houses and streets to see manly
    affection,
The most dauntless and rude shall touch face to face lightly,
The dependence of Liberty shall be lovers,
The continuance of Equality shall be comrades.

These shall tie you and band you stronger than hoops of iron,
I, ecstatic, O partners! O lands! with the love of lovers tie you.

(Were you looking to be held together by lawyers?
Or by an agreement on a paper? or by arms?
Nay, nor the world, nor any living thing, will so cohere.)

EMILY DICKINSON 1830–1886

HOPE IS THE THING WITH FEATHERS

"Hope" is the thing with feathers –
That perches in the soul –
And sings the tune without the words –
And never stops—at all –

And sweetest—in the Gale—is heard –
And sore must be the storm –
That could abash the little Bird
That kept so many warm –

I've heard it in the chillest land –

And on the strangest Sea –
Yet, never, in Extremity,
It asked a crumb—of Me.

Thomas Hardy 1840–1928

The Darkling Thrush

I leant upon a coppice gate
    When Frost was spectre-grey,
And Winter's dregs made desolate
    The weakening eye of day.
The tangled bine-stems scored the sky
    Like strings of broken lyres,
And all mankind that haunted nigh
    Had sought their household fires.

The land's sharp features seemed to be
    The Century's corpse outleant,
His crypt the cloudy canopy,
    The wind his death-lament.
The ancient pulse of germ and birth
    Was shrunken hard and dry,
And every spirit upon earth
    Seemed fervourless as I.

At once a voice arose among
    The bleak twigs overhead
In a full-hearted evensong
    Of joy illimited;
An aged thrush, frail, gaunt, and small,
    In blast-beruffled plume,
Had chosen thus to fling his soul
    Upon the growing gloom.

So little cause for carolings
    Of such ecstatic sound
Was written on terrestrial things
    Afar or nigh around,
That I could think there trembled through
    His happy good-night air
Some blessed Hope, whereof he knew
    And I was unaware.

OSCAR WILDE 1854–1900

VITA NUOVA[2]

I stood by the unvintageable sea
    Till the wet waves drenched face and hair with spray;
    The long red fires of the dying day
Burned in the west; the wind piped drearily;
And to the land the clamorous gulls did flee:
    'Alas!' I cried, 'my life is full of pain,
    And who can garner fruit or golden grain
From these waste fields which travail ceaselessly!'
My nets gaped wide with many a break and flaw,
    Nathless I threw them as my final cast
    Into the sea, and waited for the end.
When lo! a sudden glory! and I saw
    From the black waters of my tortured past
    The argent splendour of white limbs ascend!

STEPHEN CRANE 1871–1900

I WALKED IN A DESERT

I walked in a desert.
And I cried:
"Ah, God, take me from this place!"
A voice said: "It is no desert."
I cried: "Well, but –
The sand, the heat, the vacant horizon."
A voice said: "It is no desert."

PAUL LAWRENCE DUNBAR 1872–1906

HE HAD HIS DREAM

He had his dream, and all through life,
Worked up to it through toil and strife.
Afloat fore'er before his eyes,
It colored for him all his skies:
    The storm-cloud dark
    Above his bark,
The calm and listless vault of blue

Took on its hopeful hue,
It tinctured every passing beam—
    He had his dream.

He labored hard and failed at last,
His sails too weak to bear the blast,
The raging tempests tore away
And sent his beating bark astray.
    But what cared he
    For wind or sea!
He said, "the tempest will be short,
My bark will come to port."
He saw through every cloud a gleam—
    He had his dream.

DANIEL WEBSTER DAVIS 1862–1913

I CAN TRUST

I can not see why trials come,
And sorrows follow thick and fast;
I can not fathom His designs,
Nor why my pleasures can not last,
Nor why my hopes so soon are dust,
But, I can trust.

When darkest clouds my sky o'er hang,
And sadness seems to fill the land,
I calmly trust His promise sweet,
And cling to his ne'er failing hand,
And, in life's darkest hour, I'll just
Look up and trust.

I know my life with Him is safe,
And all things still must work for good
To those who love and serve our God,
And lean on Him as children should,
Though hopes decay and turn to dust,
I still will trust.

CLAUDE MCKAY 1889–1948

AMERICA

Although she feeds me bread of bitterness,
And sinks into my throat her tiger's tooth,
Stealing my breath of life, I will confess
I love this cultured hell that tests my youth!
Her vigor flows like tides into my blood,
Giving me strength erect against her hate.
Her bigness sweeps my being like a flood.
Yet as a rebel fronts a king in state,
I stand within her walls with not a shred
Of terror, malice, not a word of jeer.
Darkly I gaze into the days ahead,
And see her might and granite wonders there,
Beneath the touch of Time's unerring hand,
Like priceless treasures sinking in the sand.

CHINMOY KUMAR GHOSE 1931–2007

START A NEW BEGINNING

When the answer does not seem to come,
Do not give up.
Try to wait a little more.
When the answer does not come at all,
Do not give up.
Start a new beginning.
This time
Smite your heart with your throbbing cries,
And
Break your face with your illumining smiles.

THERE WAS A TIME

There was a time when I stumbled and stumbled,
But now I only climb and climb beyond
And far beyond my Goal's endless Beyond,
And yet my Captain commands: "Go on, go on!"

EMILY LEWIS PENN 1953–

NACHTMUSIK SONNET

Even though I am old enough to forget
the name of my first grade teacher –
Have I blocked out the memory
of a school house, the antiseptic smell,
a concrete playground, metal swings and seesaws,
packets of two-cent seeds you bought in May,
five-cent containers of warm white milk?
Now I sit in this house with Mozart
and the sounds of traffic, a steady rain,
the feel of an impending storm
that tightens the stomach.
Still, there is something to be said for the music,
for the secret knowledge that the weather will change
and we will give a standing ovation to tomorrow.

Cycle 9: Childhood, Innocence, Wonder and Awe

ANDREW MARVELL 1621–1628

THE GARDEN

How vainly men themselves amaze[1]
To win the palm, the oak, or bays,[2]
And their uncessant labours see
Crown'd from some single herb or tree,
Whose short and narrow vergèd shade
Does prudently their toils upbraid;
While all flow'rs and all trees do close
To weave the garlands of repose.

Fair Quiet, have I found thee here,
And Innocence, thy sister dear!
Mistaken long, I sought you then
In busy companies of men;
Your sacred plants, if here below,[3]
Only among the plants will grow.
Society is all but rude,
To this delicious solitude.

No white nor red[4] was ever seen
So am'rous as this lovely green.
Fond lovers, cruel as their flame,
Cut in these trees their mistress' name;
Little, alas, they know or heed
How far these beauties hers exceed!
Fair trees! wheres'e'er your barks I wound,
No name shall but your own be found.

When we have run our passion's heat,
Love hither makes his best retreat.

167

The gods, that mortal beauty chase,
Still[5] in a tree did end their race:
Apollo hunted Daphne so,
Only that she might laurel grow;
And Pan did after Syrinx speed,
Not as a nymph, but for a reed.

What wond'rous life in this I lead!
Ripe apples drop about my head;
The luscious clusters of the vine
Upon my mouth do crush their wine;
The nectarine and curious[6] peach
Into my hands themselves do reach;
Stumbling on melons as I pass,
Ensnar'd with flow'rs, I fall on grass.

Meanwhile the mind, from pleasure less,
Withdraws into its happiness;
The mind, that ocean where each kind
Does straight its own resemblance find,[7]
Yet it creates, transcending these,
Far other worlds, and other seas;
Annihilating all that's made
To a green thought in a green shade.

Here at the fountain's sliding foot,
Or at some fruit tree's mossy root,
Casting the body's vest[8] aside,
My soul into the boughs does glide;
There like a bird it sits and sings,
Then whets[9] and combs its silver wings;
And, till prepar'd for longer flight,
Waves in its plumes the various light.

Such was that happy garden-state,
While man there walk'd without a mate;
After a place so pure and sweet,
What other help could yet be meet!
But 'twas beyond a mortal's share
To wander solitary there:
Two paradises 'twere in one
To live in paradise alone.

How well the skillful gard'ner drew
Of flow'rs and herbs this dial[10] new,
Where from above the milder sun

Does through a fragrant zodiac run;
And as it works, th' industrious bee
Computes its time as well as we.
How could such sweet and wholesome hours
Be reckon'd but with herbs and flow'rs!

THOMAS TRAHERNE 1637–1674

WONDER

How like an angel came I down!
How bright are all things here!
When first among His works I did appear
O how their glory me did crown!
The world resembled his Eternity,
In which my soul did walk;
And ev'ry thing that I did see
Did with me talk.

The skies in their magnificence,
The lively, lovely air;
Oh how divine, how soft, how sweet, how fair!
The stars did entertain my sense,
And all the works of God, so bright and pure,
So rich and great did seem,
As if they ever must endure
In my esteem.

A native health and innocence
Within my bones did grow,
And while my God did all His Glories show,
I felt a vigor in my sense
That was all Spirit. I within did flow
With seas of life, like wine;
I nothing in the world did know
But 'twas divine.

Harsh ragged objects were concealed,
Oppressions tears and cries,
Sins, griefs, complaints, dissensions, weeping eyes
Were hid, and only things revealed
Which heav'nly Spirits, and the Angels prize.
The state of innocence

And bliss, not trades and poverties,
Did fill my sense.

The streets were paved with golden stones,
The boys and girls were mine,
Oh how did all their lovely faces shine!
The sons of men were holy ones,
In joy and beauty they appeared to me,
And everything which here I found,
While like an angel I did see,
Adorned the ground.

Rich diamond and pearl and gold
In ev'ry place was seen;
Rare splendors, yellow, blue, red, white and green,
Mine eyes did everywhere behold.
Great wonders clothed with glory did appear,
Amazement was my bliss,
That and my wealth was ev'ry where:
No joy to this!

Cursed and devised proprieties,
With envy, avarice
And fraud, those fiends that spoil even Paradise,
Flew from the splendor of mine eyes,
And so did hedges, ditches, limits, bounds,
I dreamed not aught of those,
But wandered over all men's grounds,
And found repose.

Proprieties themselves were mine,
And hedges ornaments;
Walls, boxes, coffers, and their rich contents
Did not divide my joys, but all combine.
Clothes, ribbons, jewels, laces, I esteemed
My joys by others worn:
For me they all to wear them seemed
When I was born.

TO THE SAME PURPOSE

To the same purpose: he, not long before
    Brought home from nurse, going to the door
        To do some little thing
        He must not do within,
            With wonder cries,

As in the skies
He saw the moon, "O yonder is the moon,
Newly come after me to town,
That shined at Lugwardin but yesternight,
Where I enjoyed the self-same sight."
As if it had ev'n twenty thousand faces,
It shines at once in many places;
To all the earth so wide
God doth the stars divide,
With so much art
The moon impart,
They serve us all; serve wholly every one
As if they served him alone.
While every single person hath such store,
'Tis want of sense that makes us poor.

ANN ELIZA BLEECKER 1752–1783

ON THE IMMENSITY OF CREATION

Oh! Could I borrow some celestial plume,
This narrow globe should not confine me long
In its contracted sphere—the vast expanse,
Beyond where thought can reach, or eye can glance,
My curious spirit, charm'd should traverse o'er,
New worlds to find, new systems to explore:
When these appear'd, again I'd urge my flight
Till all creation open'd to my sight.
    Ah! Unavailing wish, absurd and vain,
Fancy return and drop thy wing again;
Could'st thou more swift than light move steady on,
Thy sight as broad, and piercing as the sun,
And Gabriel's years too added to thy own;
Nor Gabriel's sight, nor thought, nor rapid wing,
Can pass the immense domains of th'eternal King;
The greatest seraph in his bright abode
Can't comprehend the labours of a God.
Proud reason fails, and is confounded here;
—Man how contemptible thou dost appear!
What art thou in this scene?—Alas! No more
Than a small atom to the sandy shore,
A drop of water to a boundless sea,
A single moment to eternity.

WILLIAM BLAKE 1757–1827

INFANT JOY

'I have no name:
I am but two days old.'
What shall I call thee?
'I happy am,
Joy is my name.'
Sweet joy befall thee!

Pretty joy!
Sweet joy, but two days old.
Sweet joy I call thee:
Thou dost smile,
I sing the while,
Sweet joy befall thee!

THE ECHOING GREEN

The Sun does arise,
And make happy the skies;
The merry bells ring
To welcome the Spring;
The skylark and thrush,
The birds of the bush,
Sing louder around
To the bells' cheerful sound,
While our sports shall be seen
On the Echoing Green.

Old John with white hair,
Does laugh away care,
Sitting under the oak,
Among the old folk.
They laugh at our play,
And soon they all say:
'Such, such were the joys
When we all, girls & boys,
In our youth time were seen
On the Echoing Green.'

Till the little ones, weary,
No more can be merry;
The sun does descend,
And our sports have an end.

Round the laps of their mothers
Many sisters and brothers,
Like birds in their nest,
Are ready for rest,
And sport no more seen
On the darkening Green.

WILLIAM WORDSWORTH 1770–1850

COMPOSED UPON WESTMINSTER BRIDGE, SEPTEMBER 3, 1802

Earth has not anything to show more fair:
Dull would he be of soul who could pass by
A sight so touching in its majesty:
This City now doth, like a garment, wear
The beauty of the morning; silent, bare,
Ships, towers, domes, theatres and temples lie
Open unto the fields, and to the sky;
All bright and glittering in the smokeless air.
Never did sun more beautifully steep
In his first splendor, valley, rock, or hill;
Ne'er saw I, never felt, a calm so deep!
The river glideth at his own sweet will:
Dear God! The very houses seem asleep;
And all that mighty heart is lying still!

ODE: INTIMATIONS OF IMMORTALITY FROM RECOLLECTIONS OF EARLY CHILDHOOD

The Child is Father of the Man;
And I could wish my days to be
Bound each to each by natural piety.

I

There was a time when meadow, grove, and stream,
The earth, and every common sight,
        To me did seem
        Apparelled in celestial light,
The glory and the freshness of a dream.
It is not now as it hath been of yore;-
        Turn wheresoe'er I may,
            By night or day,
The things which I have seen I now can see no more.

II

The Rainbow comes and goes,
And lovely is the Rose;
The Moon doth with delight
Look round her when the heavens are bare;
Waters on a starry night
Are beautiful and fair;
The sunshine is a glorious birth;
But yet I know, where'er I go,
That there hath past away a glory from the earth.

III

Now, while the birds thus sing a joyous song,
And while the young lambs bound
As to the tabor's sound,
To me alone there came a thought of grief:
A timely utterance gave that thought relief,
And I again am strong:
The cataracts blow their trumpets from the steep;
No more shall grief of mine the season wrong;
I hear the Echoes through the mountains throng,
The Winds come to me from the fields of sleep,
And all the earth is gay;
Land and sea
Give themselves up to jollity,
And with the heart of May
Doth every Beast keep holiday;-
Thou Child of Joy,
Shout round me, let me hear thy shouts, thou happy
Shepherd-boy!

IV

Ye blessèd Creatures, I have heard the call
Ye to each other make; I see
The heavens laugh with you in your jubilee;
My heart is at your festival,
My head hath its coronal,
The fulness of your bliss, I feel—I feel it all.
Oh evil day! if I were sullen
While Earth herself is adorning,
This sweet May-morning,
And the Children are culling
On every side,
In a thousand valleys far and wide,
Fresh flowers; while the sun shines warm,

And the Babe leaps up on his Mother's arm: –
　　I hear, I hear, with joy I hear!
　　– But there's a Tree, of many, one,
A single Field which I have looked upon,
Both of them speak of something that is gone:
　　　The Pansy at my feet
　　　Doth the same tale repeat:
Whither is fled the visionary gleam?
Where is it now, the glory and the dream?

V

Our birth is but a sleep and a forgetting:
The Soul that rises with us, our life's Star,
　　　Hath had elsewhere its setting,
　　　　And cometh from afar:
　　　Not in entire forgetfulness,
　　　And not in utter nakedness,
But trailing clouds of glory do we come
　　　From God, who is our home:
Heaven lies about us in our infancy!
Shades of the prison-house begin to close
　　　Upon the growing Boy,
　　　　But He
Beholds the light, and whence it flows,
　　　He sees it in his joy;
The Youth, who daily farther from the east
　　　Must travel, still is Nature's Priest,
　　　And by the vision splendid
　　　Is on his way attended;
At length the Man perceives it die away,
And fade into the light of common day.

VI

Earth fills her lap with pleasures of her own;
Yearnings she hath in her own natural kind,
And, even with something of a Mother's mind,
　　　And no unworthy aim,
　　　The homely Nurse doth all she can
To make her Foster-child, her Inmate Man,
　　　Forget the glories he hath known,
And that imperial palace whence he came.

VII

Behold the Child among his new-born blisses,
A six years' Darling of a pigmy size!
See, where 'mid work of his own hand he lies,

Fretted by sallies of his mother's kisses,
With light upon him from his father's eyes!
See, at his feet, some little plan or chart,
Some fragment from his dream of human life,
Shaped by himself with newly-learned art;
    A wedding or a festival,
    A mourning or a funeral;
        And this hath now his heart,
    And unto this he frames his song:
        Then will he fit his tongue
To dialogues of business, love, or strife;
    But it will not be long
    Ere this be thrown aside,
    And with new joy and pride
The little Actor cons another part;
Filling from time to time his 'humorous stage'
With all the Persons, down to palsied Age,
That Life brings with her in her equipage;
    As if his whole vocation
    Were endless imitation.

VIII

Thou, whose exterior semblance doth belie
    Thy Soul's immensity;
Thou best Philosopher, who yet dost keep
Thy heritage, thou Eye among the blind,
That, deaf and silent, read'st the eternal deep,
Haunted for ever by the eternal mind, –
    Mighty Prophet! Seer blest!
    On whom those truths do rest,
Which we are toiling all our lives to find,
In darkness lost, the darkness of the grave;
Thou, over whom thy Immortality
Broods like the Day, a Master o'er a Slave,
A Presence which is not to be put by;
Thou little Child, yet glorious in the might
Of heaven-born freedom on thy being's height,
Why with such earnest pains dost thou provoke
The years to bring the inevitable yoke,
Thus blindly with thy blessedness at strife?
Full soon thy Soul shall have her earthly freight,
And custom lie upon thee with a weight,
Heavy as frost, and deep almost as life!

IX

O joy! that in our embers
Is something that doth live,
That nature yet remembers
What was so fugitive!
The thought of our past years in me doth breed
Perpetual benediction: not indeed
For that which is most worth to be blest;
Delight and liberty, the simple creed
Of Childhood, whether busy or at rest,
With new-fledged hope still fluttering in his breast: –
Not for these I raise
The song of thanks and praise;
But for those obstinate questionings
Of sense and outward things,
Fallings from us, vanishings;
Blank misgivings of a Creature
Moving about in worlds not realized,
High instincts before which our mortal Nature
Did tremble like a guilty Thing surprised:
But for those first affections,
Those shadowy recollections,
Which, be they what they may,
Are yet the fountain, light of all our day,
Are yet a master light of all our seeing;
Uphold us, cherish, and have power to make
Our noisy years seem moments in the being
Of the eternal Silence: truths that wake,
To perish never;
Which neither listlessness, nor mad endeavour,
Nor Man nor Boy,
Nor all that is at enmity with joy,
Can utterly abolish or destroy!
Hence in a season of calm weather
Though inland far we be,
Our Souls have sight of that immortal sea
Which brought us hither,
Can in a moment travel thither,
And see the Children sport upon the shore,
And hear the mighty waters rolling evermore.

X

Then sing, ye Birds, sing, sing a joyous song!
And let the young Lambs bound

As to the tabor's sound!
We in thought will join your throng,
        Ye that pipe and ye that play,
        Ye that through your hearts today
        Feel the gladness of the May!
What though the radiance which was once so bright
Be now for ever taken from my sight,
        Though nothing can bring back the hour
Of splendour in the grass, of glory in the flower;
        We will grieve not, rather find
        Strength in what remains behind;
        In the primal sympathy
        Which having been must ever be;
        In the soothing thoughts that spring
        Out of human suffering;
        In the faith that looks through death,
In years that bring the philosophic mind.

                    XI
And O, ye Fountains, Meadows, Hills, and Groves,
Forebode not any severing of our loves!
Yet in my heart of hearts I feel your might;
I only have relinquished one delight
To live beneath your more habitual sway.
I love the Brooks which down their channels fret,
Even more than when I tripped lightly as they;
The innocent brightness of a new-born Day
        Is lovely yet;
The Clouds that gather round the setting sun
Do take a sober colouring from an eye
That hath kept watch o'er man's mortality;
Another race hath been, and other palms are won.
Thanks to the human heart by which we live,
Thanks to its tenderness, its joys, and fears,
To me the meanest flower that blows can give
Thoughts that do often lie too deep for tears.

WALT WHITMAN 1819–1892

MIRACLES

Why, who makes much of a miracle?
As to me I know of nothing else but miracles,

Whether I walk the streets of Manhattan,
Or dart my sight over the roofs of houses toward the sky,
Or wade with naked feet along the beach just in the edge of the
    water,
Or stand under trees in the woods,
Or talk by day with any one I love, or sleep in the bed at night
    with any one I love,
Or sit at table at dinner with the rest,
Or look at strangers opposite me riding in the car,
Or watch honey-bees busy around the hive of a summer forenoon,
Or animals feeding in the fields,
Or birds, or the wonderfulness of insects in the air,
Or the wonderfulness of the sundown, or of stars shining so quiet
    and bright,
Or the exquisite delicate thin curve of the new moon in spring;
These with the rest, one and all, are to me miracles,
The whole referring, yet each distinct and in its place.

To me every hour of light and dark is a miracle,
Every cubic inch of space is a miracle,
Every square yard of the surface of the earth is spread with the same,
Every foot of the interior swarms with the same.

To me the sea is a continual miracle,
The fishes that swarm—the rocks—the motion of the waves –
    the ships with men in them,
What stranger miracles are there?

SPARKLES FROM THE WHEEL

Where the city's ceaseless crowd moves on the livelong day,
Withdrawn I join a group of children watching, I pause aside with
    them.
By the curb toward the edge of the flagging,
A knife-grinder works at his wheel sharpening a great knife,
Bending over he carefully holds it to the stone, by foot and knee,
With measure'd tread he turns rapidly, as he presses with light but
    firm hand,
Forth issue then in copious golden jets,
Sparkles from the wheel.

The scene and all its belongings, how they seize and affect me,
The sad sharp-chinn'd old man with worn clothes and broad
    shoulder-band of leather,
Myself effusing and fluid, a phantom curiously floating, now here

absorb'd and arrested,
The group, (an unminded point set in a vast surrounding,)
The attentive, quiet children, the loud, proud, restive base of the
    streets,
The low hoarse purr of the whirling stone, the light-press'd blade,
Diffusing, dropping, sideways-darting, in tiny showers of gold,
Sparkles from the wheel.

WHEN I HEARD THE LEARN'D ASTRONOMER

When I heard the learn'd astronomer,
When the proofs, the figures, were ranged in columns before me,
When I was shown the charts and diagrams, to add, divide,
    and measure them,
When I sitting heard the astronomer where he lectured with
    much applause in the lecture-room,
How soon unaccountable I became tired and sick,
Till rising and gliding out I wander'd off by myself,
In the mystical moist night-air, and from time to time,
Look'd up in perfect silence at the stars.

GERARD MANLEY HOPKINS 1844–1889

SPRING AND FALL
to a young child

Márgarét, áre you gríeving
Over Goldengrove unleaving?
Leáves like the things of man, you
With your fresh thoughts care for, can you?
Ah! ás the heart grows older
It will come to such sights colder
By and by, nor spare a sigh
Though worlds of wanwood leafmeal lie;
And yet you wíll weep and know why.
Now no matter, child, the name:
Sórrow's spríngs áre the same.
Nor mouth had, no nor mind, expressed
What heart heard of, ghost guessed:
It ís the blight man was born for,
It is Margaret you mourn for.

SPRING

Nothing is so beautiful as Spring—
   When weeds, in wheels, shoot long and lovely and lush;
   Thrush's eggs look little low heavens, and thrush
Through the echoing timber does so rinse and wring
The ear, it strikes like lightnings to hear him sing;
   The glassy peartree leaves and blooms, they brush
   The descending blue; that blue is all in a rush
With richness; the racing lambs too have fair their fling.

What is all this juice and all this joy?
   A strain of the earth's sweet being in the beginning
In Eden garden. – Have, get, before it cloy,
   Before it cloud, Christ, lord, and sour with sinning,
Innocent mind and Mayday in girl and boy,
   Most, O maid's child, thy choice and worthy the winning.

RABINDRANATH TAGORE 1861–1941

95

I was not aware of the moment when I first crossed the
threshold of this life.

   What was the power that made me open out into this vast
mystery like a bud in the forest at midnight!

   When in the morning I looked upon the light I felt in a
moment that I was no stranger in this world, that the
inscrutable without name and form had taken me in its arms
in the form of my own mother.

   Even so, in death the same unknown will appear as ever
known to me. And because I love this life, I know I shall love
death as well.

   The child cries out when from the right breast the mother
takes it away, in the very next moment to find in the left one
its consolation.

–from Gitanjali

D.H. LAWRENCE 1885–1930

PIANO

Softly, in the dusk, a woman is singing to me;
Taking me back down the vista of years, till I see

A child sitting under the piano, in the boom of the tingling strings
And pressing the small, poised feet of a mother who smiles as she sings.

In spite of myself, the insidious mastery of song
Betrays me back, till the heart of me weeps to belong
To the old Sunday evenings at home, with winter outside
And hymns in the cosy parlour, the tinkling piano our guide.

So now it is vain for the singer to burst into clamour
With the great black piano appassionato.[11] The glamour
Of childish days is upon me, my manhood is cast
Down in the flood of remembrance, I weep like a child for the past.

DYLAN THOMAS 1914–1953

FERN HILL

Now as I was young and easy under the apple boughs
About the lilting house and happy as the grass was green,
  The night above the dingle[12] starry,
    Time let me hail and climb
  Golden in the heydays of his eyes,
And honoured among wagons I was prince of the apple towns
And once below a time I lordly had the trees and leaves
    Trail with daisies and barley
  Down the rivers of the windfall light.

And as I was green and carefree, famous among the barns
About the happy yard and signing as the farm was home,
  In the sun that is young once only,
    Time let me play and be
  Golden in the mercy of his means,
And green and golden I was huntsman and herdsman, the calves
Sang to my horn, the foxes on the hills barked clear and cold,
    And the sabbath rang slowly
  In the pebbles of the holy streams.

All the sun long it was running, it was lovely, the hay
Fields high as the house, the tunes from the chimneys, it was air
    And playing, lovely and watery
      And fire green as grass.
    And nightly under the simple stars
As I rode to sleep the owls were bearing the farm away,
All the moon long I heard, blessed among stables, the nightjars
    Flying with the ricks, and the horses

Flashing into the dark.
And then to awake, and the farm, like a wanderer white
With the dew, come back, the cock on his shoulder: it was all
    Shining, it was Adam and maiden,
        The sky gathered again
    And the sun grew round that very day.
So it must have been after the birth of the simple light
In the first, spinning place, the spellbound horses walking warm
    Out of the whinnying green stable
        On to the fields of praise.

And honoured among foxes and pheasants by the gay house
Under the new made clouds and happy as the heart was long,
    In the sun born over and over,
        I ran my heedless ways,
    My wishes raced through the house high hay
And nothing I cared, at my sky blue trades, that time allows
In all his tuneful turning so few and such morning songs
    Before the children green and golden
        Follow him out of grace,

Nothing I cared, in the lamb white days, that time would take me
Up to the swallow thronged loft by the shadow of my hand,
    In the moon that is always rising,
        Nor that riding to sleep
    I should hear him fly with the high fields
And wake to the farm forever fled from the childless land.
Oh as I was young and easy in the mercy of his means,
        Time held me green and dying
    Though I sang in my chains like the sea.

RACHEL JAMISON WEBSTER 1974–

KAUAI

We've come back
to the site of her
conception.

She calls it *why*
and cries all night sleepless, wild.

It seems the way is always
floating and the goal:

to live so the ghosts we were
don't trail us and echo.
I think we are inside a flower,
under a pollen of stars vast as scattered sand.

The air pulses with perfume,
flowers calling to flowers and the ferrying air.

But my eyes are thin and elsewhere.

I am thinking
even coming into the soul is a difficult birth,
squeezed in the body's vise.

My bent legs like pincers
or the vegetable petals of some tropical flower.
Even my mind gripped by the folds of the flesh,

how the cell keeps doubling itself out into
complexity...

The tulip trees of the valley
spread their bone canopies into slick green
leaves and fire flowers deep as cups.

Their cups fill with rain, rain
drinks the leaves drinking rain.

I can't begin to explain.

How on this porous peak of stone in the sea
our daughter came into me.

Little flick of a fish I could not see.

I was just learning to be human
and upright among all that life.

And what was real was stranger
than this night with its dust of unnamed suns.

It was the beyond in him, in me, in us.
And she was.

Cycle 10: Sensory Delights, Vitality and Mindfulness

ROBERT HERRICK 1591–1674

UPON JACK AND JILL. EPIGRAM

When Jill complains to Jack for want of meat,
Jack kisses Jill, and bids her freely eat.
Jill says, Of what? Says Jack, On that sweet kiss,
Which full of nectar and ambrosia is,
The food of poets. So I thought, says Jill;
That makes them look so lank, so ghost-like still.
Let poets feed on air or what they will;
Let me feed full till that I fart, says Jill.

THOMAS CAREW 1595–1640

PERSUASIONS TO ENJOY

If the quick spirits in your eye
Now languish, and anon must die;
If every sweet, and every grace,
Must fly from that forsaken face:
    Then (*Celia*) let us reap our joys,
    E're time such goodly fruit destroys.

Or, if that golden fleece must grow
For ever, free from aged snow;
If those bright Suns must know no shade,
Nor your fresh beauties ever fade:
Then fear not (*Celia*) to bestow,
What still being gather'd, still must grow.

Thus, either *Time* his Sickle brings
In vain, or else in vain his wings.

ALEXANDER S. PUSHKIN 1799–1837

BACCHIC SONG[1]

Voice of mirth, why are you silent?
Resonate, bacchanalian refrains!
Here is a toast to the tender maidens
And young wives who loved us!
Fill up your glass!
    Throw the ritual rings
    Against the clinking bottom
    Into the thick wine!
Let us raise our glasses and bring them together!
Here is a toast to the Muses, and a toast to reason!
    Flame you, oh sacred sun![2]
    As this lamp gets pale
    Before the bright rise of the dawn,
Thus false wisdom twinkles and fades
    Before the immortal sun of the mind.
Hail to the sun, let darkness evanesce!
                —Trans. Tatsiana DeRosa

EMILY BRONTË 1818–1849

A LITTLE WHILE, A LITTLE WHILE

A little while, a little while,
The weary task is put away,
And I can sing and I can smile,
Alike, while I have holiday.

Where wilt thou go, my harassed heart—
What thought, what scene invites thee now
What spot, or near or far apart,
Has rest for thee, my weary brow?

There is a spot, 'mid barren hills,
Where winter howls, and driving rain;
But, if the dreary tempest chills,
There is a light that warms again.

The house is old, the trees are bare,
Moonless above bends twilight's dome;
But what on earth is half so dear—
So longed for—as the hearth of home?

The mute bird sitting on the stone,
The dank moss dripping from the wall,
The thorn-trees gaunt, the walks o'ergrown,
I love them—how I love them all!

Still, as I mused, the naked room,
The alien firelight died away;
And from the midst of cheerless gloom,
I passed to bright, unclouded day.

A little and a lone green lane
That opened on a common wide;
A distant, dreamy, dim blue chain
Of mountains circling every side.

A heaven so clear, an earth so calm,
So sweet, so soft, so hushed an air;
And, deepening still the dream-like charm,
Wild moor-sheep feeding everywhere.

That was the scene, I knew it well;
I knew the turfy pathway's sweep,
That, winding o'er each billowy swell,
Marked out the tracks of wandering sheep.

Could I have lingered but an hour,
It well had paid a week of toil;
But Truth has banished Fancy's power:
Restraint and heavy task recoil.

Even as I stood with raptured eye,
Absorbed in bliss so deep and dear,
My hour of rest had fleeted by,
And back came labor, bondage, care.

WALT WHITMAN 1819–1892

I SING THE BODY ELECTRIC

1

I sing the body electric,

The armies of those I love engirth me and I engirth them,
They will not let me off till I go with them, respond to them,
And discorrupt them, and charge them full with the charge of
    the soul.

Was it doubted that those who corrupt their own bodies
    conceal themselves?
And if those who defile the living are as bad as they who defile
    the dead?
And if the body does not do fully as much as the soul?
And if the body were not the soul, what is the soul?

2

The love of the body of man or woman balks account, the
    body itself balks account,
That of the male is perfect, and that of the female is perfect.

The expression of the face balks account,
But the expression of a well-made man appears not only in his
    face,
It is in his limbs and joints also, it is curiously in the joints of
    his hips and wrists,
It is in his walk, the carriage of his neck, the flex of his waist
    and knees, dress does not hide him,
The strong sweet quality he has strikes through the cotton and
    broadcloth,
To see him pass conveys as much as the best poem, perhaps more,
You linger to see his back, and the back of his neck and
    shoulder-side.

The sprawl and fullness of babes, the bosoms and heads of
    women, the folds of their dress, their style as we pass in
    the street, the contour of their shape downwards,
The swimmer naked in the swimming-bath, seen as he swims
    through the transparent green-shine, or lies with his face
    up and rolls silently to and fro in the heave of the water,
The bending forward and backward of rowers in row-boats, the
    horseman in his saddle,
Girls, mothers, house-keepers, in all their performances,
The group of laborers seated at noon-time with their open
    dinner-kettles, and their wives waiting,
The female soothing a child, the farmer's daughter in the
    garden or cow-yard,
The wrestle of wrestlers, two apprentice-boys, quite grown,
    lusty, good-natured, native-born, out on the vacant lot at

sun-down after work,
The coats and caps thrown down, the embrace of love and resistance,
The upper-hold and under-hold, the hair rumpled over and
  blinding the eyes;
The march of firemen in their own costumes, the play of
  masculine muscle through clean-setting trowsers and
  waist-straps,
The slow return from the fire, the pause when the bell strikes
  suddenly again, and the listening on the alert,
The natural, perfect, varied attitudes, the bent head, the curv'd
  neck and the counting;
Such-like I love—I loosen myself, pass freely, am at the
  mother's breast with the little child,
Swim with the swimmers, wrestle with wrestlers, march in line
  with the firemen, and pause, listen, count.

3

I knew a man, a common farmer, the father of five sons,
And in them the fathers of sons, and in them the fathers of sons.

This man was of wonderful vigor, calmness, beauty of person,
The shape of his head, the pale yellow and white of his hair
  and beard, the immeasurable meaning of his black eyes,
  the richness and breath of his manners,
These I used to go and visit him to see, he was wise also,
He was six feet tall, he was over eighty years old, his sons were
  massive, clean, bearded, tan-faced, handsome,
They and his daughters loved him, all who saw him loved him,
They did not love him by allowance, they loved him with
  personal love,
He drank water only, the blood show'd like scarlet through the
  clear-brown skin of his face,
He was a frequent gunner and fisher, he sail'd his boat
  himself, he had a fine one presented to him by a ship-
  joiner, he had fowling-pieces presented to him by men
  that loved him,
When he went with his five sons and many grand-sons to hunt
  or fish, you would pick him out as the most beautiful and
  vigorous of the gang,
You would wish long and long to be with him, you would wish
  to sit by him in the boat that you and he might touch
  each other.

4

I have perceiv'd that to be with those I like is enough,

To stop in company with the rest at evening is enough,
To be surrounded by beautiful, curious, breathing, laughing
    flesh is enough,
To pass among them or touch any one, or rest my arm ever so
    lightly round his or her neck for a moment, what is this
    then?
I do not ask any more delight, I swim in it as in a sea.

There is something in staying close to men and women and
looking on them, and in the contact and odor of them,
    that pleases the soul well,
All thing please the soul, but these please the soul well.

5

This is the female form,
A divine nimbus exhales from it from head to foot,
It attracts with fierce undeniable attraction,
I am drawn by its breath as if I were no more than a helpless
    vapor, all falls aside but myself and it,
Books, art, religion, time, the visible and solid earth, and what
    was expected of heaven or fear'd of hell, are now
    consumed,
Mad filaments, ungovernable shoots play out of it, the
    response likewise ungovernable,
Hair, bosom, hips, band of legs, negligent falling hands all
    diffused, mine too diffused,
Ebb stung by the flow and flow stung by the ebb, love-flesh
    swelling and deliciously aching
Limitless limpid jets of love hot and enormous, quivering jelly
    of love, white-blow and delirious juice,
Bridegroom night of love working surely and softly into the
    prostrate dawn,
Undulating into the willing and yielding day,
Lost in the cleave of the clasping and sweet-flesh'd day.

This the nucleus—after the child is born of woman, man is
    born of woman,
This the bath of birth, this the merge of small and large, and
    the outlet again.
Be not ashamed women, your privilege encloses the rest, and
    is the exit of the rest,
You are the gates of the body, and you are the gates of the soul.
The female contains all qualities and tempers them,
She is in her place and moves with perfect balance,
She is all things duly veil'd, she is both passive and active,

She is to conceive daughters as well as sons, and sons as well
as daughters.

As I see my soul reflected in Nature,
As I see through a mist, One with inexpressible completeness,
sanity, beauty,
See the bent head and arms folded over the breast, the Female
I see.

6

The male is not less the soul nor more, he too is in his place,
He too is all qualities, he is action and power,
The flush of the known universe is in him,
Scorn becomes him well, and appetite and defiance become
him well,
The wildest largest passions, bliss that is utmost, sorrow that is
utmost become him well, pride is for him,
The full-spread pride of man is calming and excellent to the
soul,
Knowledge becomes him, he likes it always, he brings every
thing to the test of himself,
Whatever the survey, whatever the sea and the sail he strikes
soundings at last only here,
(Where else does he strike soundings except here?)

The man's body is sacred and the woman's body is sacred,
No matter who it is, it is sacred—is the meanest one in the
laborers' gang?
Is it one of the dull-faced immigrants just landed on the wharf?
Each belongs here or anywhere just as much as the well-off,
just as much as you,
Each has his or her place in the procession.

(All is a procession,
The universe is a procession with measured and perfect
motion.)

Do you know so much yourself that you call the meanest
ignorant?
Do you suppose you have a right to a good sight, and he or
she has no right to a sight?
Do you think matter has cohered together from its diffuse
float, and the soil is on the surface, and water runs and
vegetation sprouts,
For you only, and not for him and her?

7

A man's body at auction,
(For before the war I often go to the slave-mart and watch the
    sale)
I help the auctioneer, the sloven does not half know his business.

Gentlemen look on this wonder,
Whatever the bids of the bidders they cannot be high enough for it,
For it the globe lay preparing quintillions of years without one
    animal or plant,
For it the revolving cycles truly and steadily roll'd.

In this head the all-baffling brain,
In it and below it the making of heroes.

Examine these limbs, red, black, or white, they are cunning in
    tendon and nerve,
They shall be stript that you may see them.

Exquisite senses, life-lit eyes, pluck, volition,
Flakes of breast-muscle, pliant backbone and neck, flesh not
    flabby, good-sized arms and legs,
And wonders within there yet.

Within there runs blood,
The same old blood! The same red-running blood!
There swells and jets a heart, there all passions, desires,
    reachings, aspirations,
(Do you think they are not there because they are not
    express'd in parlors and lecture-rooms?)

This is not only one man, this is the father of those who shall be
    fathers in their turns,
In him the start of populous states and rich republics,
Of him countless immortal lives with countless embodiments
    and enjoyments.

How do you know who shall come from the offspring of his
    offspring through the centuries?
(Who might you find you have come from yourself, if you
    could trace back through the centuries?)

8

A woman's body at auction,
She too is not only herself, she is the teeming mother of mothers,
She is the bearer of them that shall grow and be mates to the
    mothers.

Have you ever loved the body of a woman?
Have you ever loved the body of a man?
Do you not see that these are exactly the same to all in all
      nations and times all over the earth?

If any thing is sacred the human body is sacred,
And the glory and sweet of a man is the token of manhood
      untainted,
And in man or woman a clean, strong, firm-fibred body, is
      more beautiful than the most beautiful face.

Have you seen the fool that corrupted his own live body? Or
      the fool that corrupted her own live body?
For they do not conceal themselves, and cannot conceal
      themselves.

9

O my body! I dare not desert the likes of you in other men and
      women, nor the likes of the parts of you,
I believe the likes of you are to stand or fall with the likes of
      the soul, (and that they are the soul,)
I believe the likes of you shall stand or fall with my poems,
      and that they are my poems,
Man's, woman's, child's, youth's, wife's, husband's, mother's,
      father's, young man's, young woman's poems,
Head, neck, hair, ears, drop and tympan of the ears,
Eyes, eye-fringes, iris of the eye, eyebrows, and the waking or
      sleeping of the lids,
Mouth, tongue, lips, teeth, roof of the mouth, jaws, and the
      jaw-hinges,
Nose, nostrils of the nose, and the partition,
Cheeks, temples, forehead, chin, throat, back of the neck,
      neck-slue,
Strong shoulders, manly beard, scapula, hind-shoulders, and
      the ample side-round of the chest,
Upper-arm, armpit, elbow-socket, lower-arm, arm-sinews, arm-bones,
Wrist and wrist-joints, hand, palm, knuckles, thumb,
      forefinger, finger-joints, finger-nails,
Broad breast-front, curling hair of the breast, breast-bone,
      breast-side,
Ribs, belly, backbone, joints of the backbone,
Hips, hip-sockets, hip-strength, inward and outward round,
      man-balls, man-root,
Strong set of thighs, well carrying the trunk above,
Leg-fibres, knee, knee-pan, upper-leg, under-leg,

Ankles, instep, foot-ball, toes, toe-joints, the heel;
All attitudes, all the shapeliness, all the belongings of my or
    your body or of any one's body, male or female,
The lung-sponges, the stomach-sac, the bowels sweet and clean,
The brain in its folds inside the skull-frame,
Sympathies, heart-valves, palate-valves, sexuality, maternity,
Womanhood, and all that is a woman, and the man that comes
    from woman,
The womb, the teats, nipples, breast-milk, tears, laughter,
    weeping, love-looks, love-perturbations and risings,
The voice, articulation, language, whispering, shouting aloud;
Food, drink, pulse, digestion, sweat, sleep, walking, swimming,
Poise on the hips, leaping, reclining, embracing, arm-curving
    and tightening.
The continual changes of the flex of the mouth, and around
    the eyes,
The skin, the sunburnt shade, freckles, hair,
The curious sympathy one feels when feeling with the hand
    the naked meat of the body,
The circling rivers the breath, and breathing it in and out,
The beauty of the waist, and thence of the hips, and thence
    downward toward the knees,
The thin red jellies within you or within me, the bones and the
    marrow in the bones,
The exquisite realization of health;
O I say these are not the parts and poems of the body only,
    but of the soul,
O I say now these are the soul!

Rabindranath Tagore 1861–1941

57

Light, my light, the world-filling light, the eye-kissing light,
heart-sweetening light!
    Ah, the light dances, my darling, at the centre of my life;
the light strikes, my darling, the chords of my love; the sky
opens, the wind runs wild, laughter passes over the earth.
    The butterflies spread their sails on the sea of light. Lilies
and jasmines surge up on the crest of the waves of light.
    The light is shattered into gold on every cloud, my darling,
and it scatters gems in profusion.

Mirth spreads from leaf to leaf, my darling, and gladness without measure. The heaven's river has drowned its banks and the flood of joy is abroad.

—from *Gitanjali*

W.B. YEATS 1865–1939

THE FIDDLER OF DOONEY

When I play on my fiddle in Dooney,
Folk dance like a wave of the sea;
My cousin is priest in Kilvarnet,
My brother in Mocharabuiee.

I passed my brother and cousin:
They read in their books of prayer;
I read in my book of songs
I bought at the Sligo fair.

When we come at the end of time
To Peter sitting in state,
He will smile on the three old spirits,
But call me first through the gate;

For the good are always the merry,
Save by an evil chance,
And the merry love the fiddle,
And the merry love to dance:

And when the folk there spy me,
They will all come up to me,
With 'Here is the fiddler of Dooney!'
And dance like a wave of the sea.

C.D. BALMONT 1867–1942

THE SUNBEAM

I pierced my brain with a sunbeam.
I now look at the world. I remember nothing.
I see the light, and the colorful fog.
My spirit is in love, ecstatic, drunk.

How the sunbeam burns at my fingertips!
How sweet is this presence of fire for me!

Everything is fused. I have forgot all human affairs.
I am in the center of eternity's powers.
How joyful it is to be hot and bright!
How delightful it is to consume each moment!
With people of light I speak with light.
I reign. I burn. I thrive.

—Trans. Tatsiana DeRosa

THE LAW OF LIFE

I asked of the carefree wind:
What can I do to be young?
And the playful wind answered:
Be airy like wind, like smoke!

I asked of the mighty sea:
What is the great law of life?
And the sonorous sea answered:
Be always full of sound like me!

I asked of the empyreal[3] sun:
How can I shine brighter than dawn?
Nothing answered the sun,
But my soul heard: "Burn!"

—Trans. Tatsiana DeRosa

EDWIN ARLINGTON ROBINSON 1869–1935

MR. FLOOD'S PARTY

Old Eben Flood, climbing alone one night
Over the hill between the town below
And the forsaken upland hermitage
That held as much as he should ever know
On earth again of home, paused warily.
The road was his with not a native near;
And Eben, having leisure, said aloud,
For no man else in Tilbury Town to hear:

"Well, Mr. Flood, we have the harvest moon
Again, and we may not have many more;
The bird is on the wing, the poet says,
And you and I have said it here before.
Drink to the bird." He raised up to the light

the jug that he had gone so far to fill,
And answered huskily: "Well, Mr. Flood,
Since you propose it, I believe I will."

Alone, as if enduring to the end
A valiant armor of scarred hopes outworn,
He stood there in the middle of the road
Like Roland's ghost winding a silent horn.
Below him, in the town among the trees,
Where friends of other days had honored him,
A phantom salutation of the dead
Rang thinly till old Eben's eyes were dim.

Then, as a mother lays her sleeping child
Down tenderly, fearing it may awake,
He set the jug down slowly at his feet
With trembling care, knowing that most things break;
And only when assured that on firm earth
It stood, as the uncertain lives of men
Assuredly did not, he paced away,
And with his hand extended paused again:

"Well, Mr. Flood, we have not met like this
In a long time; and many a change has come
To both of us, I fear, since last it was
We had a drop together. Welcome home!"
Convivially returning with himself,
Again he raised the jug up to the light;
And with an acquiescent quaver said:
"Well, Mr. Flood, if you insist, I might.

"Only a very little, Mr. Flood –
For auld lang syne.[4] No more, sir; that will do."
So, for the time, apparently it did,
And Eben evidently thought so too;
For soon amid the silver loneliness
Of night he lifted up his voice and sang,
Secure, with only two moons listening,
Until the whole harmonious landscape rang –

"For auld lang syne." The weary throat gave out,
The last word wavered; and the song being done,
He raised again the jug regretfully
And shook his head, and was again alone.
There was not much that was ahead of him,

And there was nothing in the town below –
Where strangers would have shut the many doors
that many friends had opened long ago.

ROBERT FROST 1874–1963

PAN WITH US

Pan came out of the woods one day,—
His skin and his hair and his eyes were grey,
The gray of the moss of walls were they,—
    And stood in the sun and looked his fill
    At wooded valley and wooded hill.

He stood in the zephyr, pipes in hand,
On a height of naked pasture land;
In all the country he did command
    He saw no smoke and he saw no roof.
    That was well! and he stomped a hoof.

His heart knew peace, for none came here
To this lean feeding save once a year
Someone to salt the half-wild steer,
    Or homespun children with clicking pails
    Who see so little they tell no tales.

He tossed his pipes, too hard to teach
A new-world song, far out of reach,
For a sylvan sign that the blue jay's screech
    And the whimper of hawks beside the sun
    Were music enough for him, for one.

Times were changed from what they were:
Such pipes kept less of power to stir
The fruited bough of the juniper
    And the fragile bluets clustered there
    Than the merest aimless breath of air.

They were pipes of pagan mirth,
And the world had found new terms of worth.
He laid him down on the sun-burned earth
    And ravelled a flower and looked away—
    Play? Play?—What should he play?

TRUMBULL STICKNEY 1874–1904

LIVE BLINDLY

Live Blindly and upon the hour. The Lord,
Who was the Future, died full long ago.
Knowledge which is the Past is folly. Go,
Poor child, and be not to thyself abhorred.
Around thine earth sun-wingèd winds do blow
And planets roll; a meteor draws his sword;
The rainbow breaks his seven-coloured chord
And the long strips of river-silver flow:
Awake! Give thyself to the lovely hours.
Drinking their lips, catch thou the dream in flight
About their fragile hairs' aërial gold.
Thou art divine, thou livest, – as of old
Apollo springing naked to the light,
And all his island shivered into flowers.

JAMES JOYCE 1882–1941

X

Bright cap and streamers,
　　He sings in the hollow:
Come follow, come follow,
　　All you that love.
Leave dreams to the dreamers
　　That will not after,
　　That song and laughter
Do nothing move.

With ribbons streaming
　　He sings the bolder;
　　In troop at his shoulder
　　The wild bees hum.
And the time of dreaming
　　Dream is over—
　　As lover to lover,
　　Sweetheart, I come.

XX

In the dark pine-wood
　　I would we lay,

In deep cool shadow
    At noon of day.

How sweet to lie there,
    Sweet to kiss,
Where the great pine-forest
    Enaisled is!

Thy kiss descending
    Sweeter were
With a soft tumult
    Of thy hair.

O, unto the pine-wood
    At noon of day
Come with me now,
    Sweet love, away.

MINA LOY 1882–1966

THERE IS NO LIFE OR DEATH

There is no Life or Death,
Only activity
And in the absolute
Is no declivity.
There is no Love or Lust
Only propensity
Who would possess
Is a nonentity.
There is no First or Last
Only equality
And who would rule
Joins the majority.
There is no Space or Time
Only intensity,
And tame things
Have no immensity.

WILLIAM CARLOS WILLIAMS 1883–1963

DANSE RUSSE[5]

If when my wife is sleeping
and the baby and Kathleen
are sleeping
and the sun is a flame-white disc
in silken mists
above shinning trees,—
if I in my north room
dance naked, grotesquely
before my mirror
waving my shirt round my head
and singing softly to myself:
"I am lonely, lonely.
I was born to be lonely,
I am best so!"
If I admire my arms, my face,
my shoulders, flanks, buttocks
against the yellow drawn shades,—

Who shall say I am not
the happy genius of my household?

LOVE SONG

Sweep the house clean,
hang fresh curtains
in the windows
put on a new dress
and come with me!
The elm is scattering
its little loaves
of sweet smells
from a white sky!
Who shall hear of us
in the time to come?
Let him say there was
a burst of fragrance
from black branches.

EDNA ST. VINCENT MILLAY 1892–1950

MARIPOSA[6]

Butterflies are white and blue
In this field we wander through.
Suffer me to take your hand.
Death comes in a day or two.

All the things we ever knew
Will be ashes in that hour,
Mark the transient butterfly,
How he hangs upon the flower.

Suffer me to take your hand.
Suffer me to cherish you
Till the dawn is in the sky.
Whether I be false or true,
Death comes in a day or two.

E.E. CUMMINGS 1894–1962

22

you shall above all things be glad and young.
For if you're young, whatever life you wear
it will become you;and if you are glad
whatever's living will yourself become.
Girlboys may nothing more than boygirls need:
i can entirely her only love
whose any mystery makes every man's
flesh put space on;and his mind take off time
that you should ever think, may god forbid
and(in his mercy)your true lover spare:
for that way knowledge lies,the foetal grave
called progress,and negation's dead undoom.
I'd rather learn from one bird how to sing
than teach ten thousand stars how not to dance

WHEN GOD LETS MY BODY BE

when god lets my body be

From each brave eye shall sprout a tree
fruit that dangles there from

the purpled world will dance upon
Between my lips which did sing

a rose shall beget the spring
that maidens whom passion wastes

will lay between their little breasts
My strong fingers beneath the snow

Into strenuous birds shall go
my love walking in the grass

their wings will touch with her face
and all the while shall my heart be

With the bulge and nuzzle of the sea

65: I THANK YOU GOD FOR MOST THIS AMAZING

i thank You God for most this amazing
day:for the leaping greenly spirits of trees
and a blue true dream of sky;and for everything
which is natural which is infinite which is yes

(i who have died am alive again today,
and this is the sun's birthday;this is the birth
day of life and of love and wings:and of the gay
great happening illimitably earth)

how should tasting touching hearing seeing
breathing any—lifted from the no
of all nothing—human merely being
doubt unimaginable You?

(now the ears of my ears awake and
now the eyes of my eyes are opened)

ALDOUS HUXLEY 1894–1963

SCENES OF THE MIND

I have run where festival was loud
With drum and brass among the crowd
Of panic revellers, whose cries
Affront the quiet of the skies;
Whose dancing lights contract the deep
Infinity of night and sleep

To a narrow turmoil of troubled fire.
And I have found my heart's desire
In beechen caverns that autumn fills
With the blue shadowiness of distant hills;
Whose luminous grey pillars bear
The stooping sky: calm is the air,
Nor any sound is heard to mar
That crystal silence—as from far,
Far off a man may see
The busy world all utterly
Hushed as an old memorial scene.
Long evenings I have sat and been
Strangely content, while in my hands
I held a wealth of coloured strands,
Shimmering plaits of silk and skeins
Of soft bright wool. Each colour drains
New life at the lamp's round pool of gold;
Each sinks again when I withhold
The quickening radiance, to a wan
And shadowy oblivion
Of what it was. And in my mind
Beauty or sudden love has shined
And wakened colour in what was dead
And turned to gold the sullen lead
Of mean desires and everyday's
Poor thoughts and customary ways.
Sometimes in lands where mountains throw
Their silent spell on all below,
Drawing a magic circle wide
About their feet on every side,
Robbed of all speech and thought and act,
I have seen God in the cataract.
In falling water and in flame,
Never at rest, yet still the same,
God shows himself. And I have known
The swift fire frozen into stone,
And water frozen changelessly
Into the death of gems. And I
Long sitting by the thunderous mill
Have seen the headlong wheel made still,
And in the silence that ensued
Have known the endless solitude
Of being dead and utterly nought.

Inhabitant of mine own thought,
I look abroad, and all I see
Is my creation, made for me:
Along my thread of life are pearled
The moments that make up the world.

PABLO NERUDA 1904–1973

ODE TO LAZINESS

Yesterday I felt the ode
not rising from the ground.
It was time, it
should at least show
one green leaf.
I scratched the earth: "Rise,
sister ode
-I told her-
I have you promised,
do not fear me,
I am not going to shred you,
four-leaved ode,
four-handed ode,
you will drink tea with me.
Rise,
I am going to crown you
amongst the odes,
we will go out together
along the seashore,
on bicycle."
It was useless.

Then,
high up in the pines,
laziness
appeared nude,
she led me astonished
and drowsy,
she found me in the sand
small torn pieces
of oceanic substances,
woods, sea plants, rocks,
seabird feathers,
I searched without finding

yellow agates.
The sea
filled the spaces,
crumbling towers,
invading
my country's coasts,
gaining forward
successive foam catastrophes.
Alone on the sand
a group of flower petals
opened a ray.
I watched the silvered petrels[7]
cross
and like black crosses
the cormorants
diving among the rocks.
I liberated a bee
that nearly perished on
a spider thread.
I inserted a tiny stone
in a pocket,
it was smooth, tender
like a bird's chest,
meanwhile on the coast,
all afternoon,
sun and fog wrestled.
At times
fog became saturated
of light
like a topaz,
other times
a moist sun ray would drop
allowing yellow drops to fall.

In the night,
thinking about the duties of my
fugitive ode,
I took my shoes off
by the fire,
sand slipped out of them
and soon I began to fall
asleep.

—Trans. Sandra Kunanele

STANLEY KUNITZ 1905–2006

TOUCH ME

Summer is late, my heart.
Words plucked out of the air
some forty years ago
when I was wild with love
and torn almost in two
scatter like leaves this night
of whistling wind and rain.
It is my heart that's late,
it is my song that's flown.
Outdoors all afternoon
under a gunmetal sky
staking my garden down,
I kneeled to the crickets trilling
underfoot as if about
to burst from their crusty shells;
and like a child again
marveled to hear so clear
and brave a music pour
from such a small machine.
What makes the engine go?
Desire, desire, desire.
The longing for the dance
stirs in the buried life.
One season only,
           and it's done.
So let the battered old willow
thrash against the windowpanes
and the house timbers creak.
Darling, do you remember
the man you married? Touch me,
remind me who I am.

CHARLES BUKOWSKI 1920–1994

THE SHOWER

we like to shower afterwards
(I like the water hotter than she)
and her face is always soft and peaceful

and she'll wash me first
spread the soap over my balls
lift the balls
squeeze them,
then wash the cock:
"hey this thing is still hard!"
then get all the hair down there,—
the belly, the back, the neck, the legs,
I grin grin grin,
and then I wash her...
first the cunt, I
stand behind her, my cock in the cheeks of her ass
I gently soap up the cunt hairs,
wash there with a soothing motion,
I linger perhaps longer than necessary,
then I get the backs of the legs, the ass,
the back, the neck, I turn her, kiss her,
soap up the breasts, get them and the belly, the neck,
the fronts of the legs, the ankles, the feet,
and then the cunt, once more, for luck...
another kiss, and she gets out first,
toweling, sometimes singing while I stay in
turn the water on hotter
feeling the good times of love's miracle
I then get out...
it is usually mid-afternoon and quiet,
and getting dressed we talk about what else
there might be to do,
but being together solves most of it,
in fact, solves all of it
for as long as those things stay solved
in the history of woman and
man, it's different for each
better and worse for each—
for me, it's splendid enough to remember
past the marching of armies
and the horses that walk the streets outside
past the memories of pain and defeat and unhappiness:
Linda, you brought it to me,
when you take it away
do it slowly and easily
make it as if I were dying in my sleep instead of in
my life, amen.

KEVIN CLARK 1950–

SIXTIES NOIR

Smoke means cash, said the stoned collector.
Codie laughed, then paid
The toll with hash. We'd loaned
Ourselves each other, rode
Windowpane down the Jersey summer,
Her face gone jumpin jack flash,
Her crossroads aura
Sheer as her peasant blouse.

As she twirled the spliff in flame,
I blinked away
The bearded infant narcs
Winking from the starboard wing of the Impala.

By Wildwood, both of us loved
The life we'd worn.
On the starry beach, new friends
Riffed in whispers,
Knew never to Bogart.[8]

Heading home, her same smile
And the turnpike smog
Layered lacquer on my heart. Then,
Visions redux: Altar boys on bennies
Sang the Sanctus in double time.
Cops roved the rearview.
Straight as a line, I couldn't stop
Hallucinating. We drove
The surface roads, said we'd never pay a cent.

Codie held to the wheel, dropped me in Hackensack.
I cracked for good, then headed west.

SUSANNA RICH 1951–

FINDING RASPBERRIES BY THE ROAD

is all the proof of forgiveness I need—
tiny garnet drupelets clustered into berries;
clustered to other berries; crowded

onto shoots, canes, brambles, thickets—
these happy, red, multiple eyes peeking
from under teardrop leaves.

They hide. They dangle. They wait.
They test me with their woody spines,
their prickle and cling—to mark me

for themselves. Small touch—they release
into my curled palm—these gemmed-encrusted
cups hardly able to bear not having more

to give, tendering the gold nipples
they nestle in sepals[9]—like
stars—on the stem. They glow

in the offering of my hand—
perfect, shiny, whiskered mouths
meant for the chalice of my mouth.

Jane Hirshfield 1953–

The Dead Do Not Want Us Dead

The dead do not want us dead;
such petty errors are left for the living.
Nor do they want our mourning.
No gift to them—not rage, not weeping.
Return one of them, any one of them, to the earth,
and look: such foolish skipping,
such telling of bad jokes, such feasting!
Even a cucumber, even a single anise seed: feasting.
September 15, 2001

Daniel Weeks 1958–

Long Branch

I am here,
connected to the air,
not a lovely nor an unloved thing,
but akin to
a cardinal in the winged euonymous,[10]
the slender shoots of spring,

and the mint come up almost ready to razor greenly
the silver julep cup. This sunshine spread along the leaves
of maples across the road is made for me, as are the subtle
shadings the light's lack floods beneath the trees. Dianthus
flowers re-reddened with the May recall Balder's doom[11] and recreate
the hopping cardinal's ruddy feathers. I stand out unlovely in the lovely
weather, connected imperceptibly to the imperceptive air. There is
a sensation of starburnalong the skin of these uncovered arms and in
my face. There is
a wreath of sunlight in my hair. Terrible, inconsequent, laughing, mute,
or teared,
I am here.

SUSANNAH SPANTON 1959–

MOMENTS

Moments each a treasure
Like panes of glass we see through
As the day unfolds how do we measure
Nudging the meaning to emerge

A glance by chance
Fills the space within causing a stir
We are joined together in a dance
Slow sultry movements in stillness and light

Gifted with the sweetness of desire
The warmth burrows deep and wide
Giving birth to the blazing fire

Emitting streams of color to rapture

Cycle 11: Love, Gratitude, Compassion and Relatedness to Others

YUNUS EMRE C. 1228–1321

THE FLEETING LIFE

My lifetime has come and gone
As if it were a wind that blew and left.
Its passing now appears to me
All too brief, like the blinking of an eye.

To this word God is a witness,
The soul is a guest for this body.
One day it will go off and away
Like a bird escaped from a cage.

Life, my good man, can be likened
To the land that the farmer sows:
Lying scattered all over the soil,
Some of the seeds sprout, but some die.

My inside burns as a coal for a noble soul in this world.
The brave ones who die plant their crops on earth but harvest them in
    heaven.

If you have approached a sick person
And given a drop of water,
It will seem tomorrow as if
You have drunk a divine wine.

If you have seen a helpless one
Even if you have given a used item
Tomorrow it comes to you
As a heavenly sewn shroud.

Dear Yunus Emre in this world they say there are only two remains:
Al-Khidr and Elijah[1] it seems are the only ones who have drunk the
elixir of life.

—Trans. Melda Yildiz

ANONYMOUS NAHUATL C. 1500

POEM TO EASE BIRTH

in the house with the tortoise chair
   she will give birth to the pearl
               to the beautiful feather

in the house of the goddess who sits on a tortoise
   she will give birth to the necklace of pearls
               to the beautiful feathers we are

there she sits on the tortoise
swelling to give us birth

on your way on your way
   child be on your way to me here
               you whom I made new

come here child come be pearl
               be beautiful feather

—Trans. Daniel G. Brinton

THOMAS CAREW 1595–1640

A SONG

Ask me no more where Jove[2] bestows,
When June is past, the fading rose:
For in your beauty's orient deep,
These flowers, as in their causes, sleep.

Ask me no more whither doth stray
The golden atoms of the day;
For in pure love heaven did prepare
Those powders to enrich your hair.

Ask me no more whither doth haste
The nightingale when May is past;

For in your sweet dividing throat
She winters, and keeps warm her note.

Ask me no more where those stars light,
That downwards fall in dead of night;
For in your eyes they sit, and there
Fixed become, as in their sphere.

Ask me no more if east or west
the phoenix builds her spicy nest;
For unto you at last she flies,
And in your fragrant bosom dies.

Anne Bradstreet 1612–1672

To My Dear and Loving Husband

If ever two were one, then surely we.
If ever man were loved by wife, then thee;
If ever wife was happy in a man,
Compare with me ye women if you can.

I prize thy love more than whole Mines of Gold,
Or all the riches that the East doth hold.
My love is such that Rivers cannot quench,
Nor ought but love from thee, give recompense.

Thy love is such I can no way repay,
The heavens reward thee manifold I pray.
Then while we live, in love lets so persevere,
That when we live no more, we may live ever.

Before the Birth of One of Her Children

All things within this fading world hath end,
Adversity doth still our joys attend;
No ties so strong, no friends so dear and sweet,
But with death's parting blow is sure to meet.
The sentence past is most irrevocable,
A common thing, yet oh, inevitable.
How soon, my Dear, death may my steps attend.
How soon't may be thy lot to lose thy friend,
We both are ignorant, yet love bids me
These farewell lines to recommend to thee,
That when that knot's untied that made us one,

I may seem thine, who in effect am none.
And if I see not half my days that's due,
What nature would, God grant to yours and you;
The many faults that well you know
I have let be interred in my oblivious grave;
If any worth or virtue were in me,
Let that live freshly in thy memory
And when thou feel'st no grief, as I no harms,
Yet love thy dead, who long lay in thine arms.
And when thy loss shall be repaid with gains
Look to my little babes, my dear remains.
And if thou love thyself, or loved'st me,
These O protect from step-dame's injury.
And if chance to thine eyes shall bring this verse,
With some sad sighs honor my absent hearse;
And kiss this paper for thy love's dear sake,
Who with salt tears this last farewell did take.

WILLIAM BLAKE 1757–1827

THE DIVINE IMAGE

To Mercy Pity Peace and Love,
All pray in their distress:
And to these virtues of delight
Return their thankfulness.

For Mercy Pity Peace and Love
Is God our father dear:
And Mercy Pity Peace and Love
Is Man his child and care.

For Mercy has a human heart
Pity, a human face:
And Love, the human form divine,
And Peace, the human dress.

Then every man of every clime,
That prays in his distress,
Prays to the human form divine
Love Mercy Pity Peace.

And all must love the human form,
In heathen, turk or jew.

Where Mercy, Love & Pity dwell
There God is dwelling too.

A Cradle Song

Sweet dreams, form a shade
O'er my lovely infant's head;
Sweet dreams of pleasant streams
By happy, silent, moony beams.

Sweet Sleep, with soft down
Weave thy brows an infant crown.
Sweet Sleep, Angel mild,
Hover o'er my happy child.

Sweet smiles, in the night
Hover over my delight;
Sweet smiles, mother's smiles,
All the livelong night beguiles.

Sweet moans, dovelike sighs,
Chase not slumber from thy eyes.
Sweet moans, sweeter smiles,
All the dovelike moans beguiles.

Sleep, sleep, happy child,
All creation slept and smiled;
Sleep, sleep, happy sleep,
While o'er thee thy mother weep.

Sweet babe, in thy face
Holy image I can trace.
Sweet babe, once like thee,
Thy Maker lay and wept for me,

Wept for me, for thee, for all,
When He was an infant small.
Thou His image ever see,
Heavenly face that smiles on thee

Smiles on thee, on me, on all;
Who became an infant small.
Infant smiles are His own smiles;
Heaven and earth to peace beguiles.

WILLIAM WORDSWORTH 1770–1850

SIMON LEE, THE OLD HUNTSMAN

With an incident in which he was concerned.
In the sweet shire of Cardigan,
Not far from pleasant Ivor-hall,
An old Man dwells, a little man,—
'Tis said he once was tall.
Full five-and-thirty years he lived
A running huntsman merry;
And still the centre of his cheek
Is red as a ripe cherry.

No man like him the horn could sound,
And hill and valley rang with glee
When Echo bandied, round and round,
The halloo of Simon Lee.
In those proud days, he little cared
For husbandry or tillage;
To blither tasks did Simon rouse
The sleepers of the village.

He all the country could outrun,
Could leave both man and horse behind;
And often, ere the chase was done,
He reeled, and was stone-blind.
And still there's something in the world
At which his heart rejoices;
For when the chiming hounds are out,
He dearly loves their voices!

But, oh the heavy change!—bereft
Of health, strength, friends, and kindred, see!
Old Simon to the world is left
In liveried poverty.
His Master's dead,—and no one now
Dwells in the Hall of Ivor;
Men, dogs, and horses, all are dead;
He is the sole survivor.

And he is lean and he is sick;
His body, dwindled and awry,
Rests upon ankles swoln and thick;
His legs are thin and dry.

One prop he has, and only one,
His wife, an aged woman,
Lives with him, near the waterfall,
Upon the village Common.

Beside their moss-grown hut of clay,
Not twenty paces from the door,
A scrap of land they have, but they
Are poorest of the poor.
This scrap of land he from the heath
Enclosed when he was stronger;
But what to them avails the land
Which he can till no longer?

Oft, working by her Husband's side,
Ruth does what Simon cannot do;
For she, with scanty cause for pride,
Is stouter of the two.
And, though you with your utmost skill
From labour could not wean them,
'Tis little, very little—all
That they can do between them.

Few months of life has he in store
As he to you will tell,
For still, the more he works, the more
Do his weak ankles swell.
My gentle Reader, I perceive
How patiently you've waited,
And now I fear that you expect
Some tale will be related.

O Reader! had you in your mind
Such stores as silent thought can bring,
O gentle Reader! you would find
A tale in everything.
What more I have to say is short,
And you must kindly take it:
It is no tale; but, should you think,
Perhaps a tale you'll make it.

One summer-day I chanced to see
This old Man doing all he could
To unearth the root of an old tree,
A stump of rotten wood.

The mattock tottered in his hand;
So vain was his endeavour,
That at the root of the old tree
He might have worked for ever.
'You're overtasked, good Simon Lee,
Give me your tool,' to him I said;
And at the word right gladly he
Received my proffered aid.
I struck, and with a single blow
The tangled root I severed,
At which the poor old Man so long
And vainly had endeavoured.

The tears into his eyes were brought,
And thanks and praises seemed to run
So fast out of his heart, I thought
They never would have done.
—I've heard of hearts unkind, kind deeds
With coldness still returning;
Alas! the gratitude of men
Hath oftener left me mourning.

SAMUEL TAYLOR COLERIDGE 1772–1834

FROST AT MIDNIGHT

The Frost performs its secret ministry,
Unhelped by any wind. The owlet's cry
Came loud—and hark, again! loud as before.
The inmates[3] of my cottage, all at rest,
Have left me to that solitude, which suits
Abstruser musings: save that at my side
My cradled infant slumbers peacefully.
'Tis calm indeed! so calm, that it disturbs
And vexes meditation with its strange
And extreme silentness. Sea, hill, and wood,
This populous village! Sea, and hill, and wood,
With all the numberless goings-on of life,
Inaudible as dreams! the thin blue flame
Lies on my low-burnt fire, and quivers not;
Only that film, which fluttered on the grate,
Still flutters there, the sole unquiet thing.
Methinks, its motion in this hush of nature

Gives it dim sympathies with me who live,
Making it a companionable form,
Whose puny flaps and freaks the idling Spirit
By its own moods interprets, everywhere
Echo or mirror seeking of itself,
And makes a toy of Thought.

                    But O! how oft,
How oft, at school, with most believing mind,
Presageful, have I gazed upon the bars,
To watch that fluttering stranger!⁴ and as oft
With unclosed lids, already had I dreamt
Of my sweet birth-place, and the old church-tower,
Whose bells, the poor man's only music, rang
From morn to evening, all the hot Fair-day,
So sweetly, that they stirred and haunted me
With a wild pleasure, falling on mine ear
Most like articulate sounds of things to come!
So gazed I, till the soothing things, I dreamt,
Lulled me to sleep, and sleep prolonged my dreams!
And so I brooded all the following morn,
Awed by the stern preceptor's face, mine eye
Fixed with mock study on my swimming book:
Save if the door half opened, and I snatched
A hasty glance, and still my heart leaped up,
For still I hoped to see the stranger's face,
Townsman, or aunt, or sister more beloved,
My play-mate when we both were clothed alike!

     Dear Babe, that sleepest cradled by my side,
Whose gentle breathings, heard in this deep calm,
Fill up the interspersed vacancies
And momentary pauses of the thought!
My babe so beautiful! it thrills my heart
With tender gladness, thus to look at thee,
And think that thou shalt learn far other lore,
And in far other scenes! For I was reared
In the great city, pent 'mid cloisters dim,
And saw nought lovely but the sky and stars.
But thou, my babe! shalt wander like a breeze
By lakes and sandy shores, beneath the crags
Of ancient mountain, and beneath the clouds,
Which image in their bulk both lakes and shores
And mountain crags: so shalt thou see and hear

The lovely shapes and sounds intelligible
Of that eternal language, which thy God
Utters, who from eternity doth teach
Himself in all, and all things in himself.
Great universal Teacher! he shall mould
Thy spirit, and by giving make it ask.

    Therefore all seasons shall be sweet to thee,
Whether the summer clothe the general earth
With greenness, or the redbreast sit and sing
Betwixt the tufts of snow on the bare branch
Of mossy apple-tree, while the nigh thatch
Smokes in the sun-thaw; whether the eave-drops fall
Heard only in the trances of the blast,
Or if the secret ministry of frost
Shall hang them up in silent icicles,
Quietly shining to the quiet Moon.

ON RECEIVING A LETTER INFORMING ME OF THE BIRTH OF A SON

When they did greet me father, sudden awe
    Weigh'd down my spirit: I retired and knelt
    Seeking the throne of grace, but inly felt
No heavenly visitation upwards draw
My feeble mind, nor cheering ray impart.
    Ah me! before the Eternal Sire I brought
    Th' unquiet silence of confuséd thought
And shapeless feelings: my o'erwhelméd heart
Trembled, and vacant tears stream'd down my face.
And now once more, O Lord! to thee I bend,
    Lover of souls! and groan for future grace,
That ere my babe youth's perilous maze have trod,
    Thy overshadowing Spirit may descend,
    And he be born again, a child of God.

TO A FRIEND WHO ASKED, HOW I FELT WHEN THE NURSE FIRST PRESENTED MY INFANT TO ME

Charles! my slow heart was only sad, when first
    I scann'd that face of feeble infancy:
For dimly on my thoughtful spirit burst
    All I had been, and all my child might be!
But when I saw it on its mother's arm,
    And hanging at her bosom (she the while

Bent o'er its features with a tearful smile)
Then I was thrill'd and melted, and most warm
Impress'd a father's kiss: and all beguil'd
   Of dark remembrance and presageful fear,
   I seem'd to see an angel-form appear –
'Twas even thine, belovéd woman mild!
   So for the mother's sake the child was dear,
And dearer was the mother for the child.

HENRY WADSWORTH LONGFELLOW 1807–1882

THE BRIDGE

I stood on the bridge at midnight,
   As the clocks were striking the hour,
And the moon rose o'er the city,
   Behind the dark church-tower.

I saw her bright reflection
   In the waters under me,
Like a golden goblet falling
   And sinking into the sea.

And far in the hazy distance
   Of that lovely night in June,
The blaze of the flaming furnace
   Gleamed redder than the moon.

Among the long, black rafters
   The wavering shadows lay,
And the current that came from the ocean
   Seemed to lift and bear them away;

As, sweeping and eddying through them,
   Rose the belated tide,
And, streaming into the moonlight,
   The seaweed floated wide.

And like those waters rushing
   Among the wooden piers,
A flood of thoughts came o'er to me
   That filled my eyes with tears.

How often, O, how often,
   In the days that had gone by,

I had stood on that bridge at midnight
And gazed on that wave and sky!

How often, O, how often,
I had wished that the ebbing tide
Would bear me away on its bosom
O'er the ocean wild and wide!

For my heart was hot and restless,
And my life was full of care,
And the burden laid upon me
Seemed greater than I could bear.

But now it has fallen from me,
It is buried in the sea;
And only the sorrow of others
Throws its shadow over me.

Yet whenever I cross the river
On its bridge with wooden piers,
Like the odor of brine from the ocean
Comes the thought of other years.

And I think how many thousands
Of care-encumbered men,
Each bearing his burden of sorrow,
Have crossed the bridge since then.

I see the long procession
Still passing to and fro,
The young heart hot and restless,
And the old subdued and slow!

And forever and forever,
As long as the river flows,
As long as the heart has passions,
As long as life has woes;

The moon and its broken reflection
And its shadows shall appear,
As the symbol of love in heaven,
And its wavering image here.

WALT WHITMAN 1819–1892

TO YOU

Stranger, if you passing meet me and desire to speak to me,
     why should you not speak to me?
And why should I not speak to you?

MOTHER AND BABE

I see the sleeping babe nestling the breast of its mother,
The sleeping mother and babe—hush'd, I study them long and
     long.

TO A COMMON PROSTITUTE

Be composed—be at ease with me—I am Walt Whitman,
     liberal and lusty as Nature,
Not till the sun excludes you do I exclude you,
Not till the waters refuse to glisten for you and the leaves to rustle
     for you, do my words refuse to glisten and rustle for you.

My girl I appoint with you an appointment, and I charge you
     that you make preparation to be worthy to meet me,
And I charge you that you be patient and perfect till I come.
Till then I salute you with a significant look that you do not
     forget me.

BEAUTIFUL WOMEN

Women sit or move to and fro, some old, some young,
The young are beautiful—but the old are more beautiful than
     the young.

TO ONE SHORTLY TO DIE

From all the rest I single out you, having a message for you,
You are to die—let others tell you what they please, I cannot
     prevaricate,
I am exact and merciless, but I love you—there is no escape
     for you.

Softly I lay my right hand upon you, you just feel it,
I do not argue, I bend my head close and half envelop it,
I sit quietly by, I remain faithful,
I am more than nurse, more than parent or neighbor,
I absolve you from all except yourself spiritual bodily, that is
     eternal, you yourself will surely escape,

The corpse you will leave will be but excrementitious,
The sun bursts through in unlooked-for directions,
Strong thoughts fill you and confidence, you smile,
You forget you are sick, as I forget you are sick,
You do not see the medicines, you do not mind the weeping
    friends, I am with you,
I exclude others from you, there is nothing to be commiserated,
I do not commiserate, I congratulate you.

There Was a Child Went Forth

There was a child went forth every day,
And the first object he look'd upon, that object he became,
And that object became part of him for the day or a certain
    part of the day,
Or for many years or stretching cycles of years.

The early lilacs became part of this child,
And grass and white and red morning-glories, and white and
    red clover, and the song of the phœbe-bird,
And the Third-month lambs and the sow's pink-faint litter, and
    the mare's foal and the cow's calf,
And the noisy brood of the barnyard or by the mire of the pond-side,
    and the fish suspending themselves so curiously below there,
    and the beautiful curious liquid,
And the water-plants with their graceful flat heads, all became
    part of him.

The field-sprouts of Fourth-month and Fifth-month became
    part of him,
Winter-grain sprouts and those of the light-yellow corn, and
    the esculent roots of the garden,
And the apple-trees cover'd with blossoms and the fruit
    afterward, and wood-berries, and the commonest weeds by
    the road,
And the old drunkard staggering home from the outhouse of
    the tavern whence he had lately risen,
And the schoolmistress that pass'd, and the quarrelsome boys,
And the tidy and fresh-cheek'd girls, and the barefoot negro
    boy and girl,
And all the changes of city and country wherever he went.
His own parents, he that had father'd him and she that had
    conceiv'd him in her womb and birth'd him,
They gave this child more of themselves than that,
They gave him afterward every day, they became part of him.

The mother at home quietly placing the dishes on the suppertable,
The mother with mild words, clean her cap and gown, a
    wholesome odor falling off her person and clothes as she
    walks by,
The father strong, self-sufficient, manly, mean, anger'd, unjust,
The blow, the quick loud word, the tight bargain, the crafty
    lure,
The family usages, the language, the company, the furniture,
    the yearning and swelling heart,
Affection that will not be gainsay'd, the sense of what is real,
    the thought if after all it should prove unreal,
The doubts of day-time and the doubts of night-time, the
    curious whether and how,
Whether that which appears so is so, or is it all flashes and specks?
Men and women crowding fast in the streets, if they are not
    flashes and specks what are they?
The streets themselves and the façades of houses, and goods in
    the windows,
Vehicles, teams, the heavy-plank'd wharves, the huge crossing
    at the ferres,
The village on the highland seen from afar at sunset, the river
    between,
Shadows, aureola and mist, the light falling on roofs and
    gables of white or brown two miles off,
The schooner near by sleepily dropping down the tide, the
    little boat slack-tow'd astern,
The hurrying tumbling waves, quick-broken crests, slapping,
The strata of color'd clouds, the long bar of maroon-tint away
    solitary by itself, the spread of purity it lies motionless in,
The horizon's edge, the flying sea-crow, the fragrance of salt
    marsh and shore mud,
These became part of that child who went forth every day, and
    who now goes, and will always go forth every day.

A.E. HOUSMAN 1859–1936

XXXII

When I would muse in boyhood
    The wild green woods among,
And nurse resolves and fancies
    Because the world was young,

It was not foes to conquer,
　　Nor sweethearts to be kind,
But it was friends to die for
　　That I would seek and find.
I sought them far and found them,
　　The sure, the straight, the brave,
The hearts I lost my own to,
　　The souls I could not save.
They braced their belts about them,
　　They crossed in ships the sea,
They sought and found six feet of ground,
　　And there they died for me.

W.B. YEATS 1865–1939

A PRAYER FOR MY DAUGHTER

Once more the storm is howling, and half hid
Under this cradle-hood and coverlid
My child sleeps on. There is no obstacle
But Gregory's wood and one bare hill
Whereby the haystack- and roof-levelling wind,
Bred on the Atlantic, can be stayed;
And for an hour I have walked and prayed
Because of the great gloom that is in my mind.

I have walked and prayed for this young child an hour
And heard the sea-wind scream upon the tower,
And under the arches of the bridge, and scream
In the elms above the flooded stream;
Imagining in excited reverie
That the future years had come,
Dancing to a frenzied drum,
Out of the murderous innocence of the sea.

May she be granted beauty and yet not
Beauty to make a stranger's eye distraught,
Or hers before a looking-glass, for such,
Being made beautiful overmuch,
Consider beauty a sufficient end,
Lose natural kindness and maybe
The heart-revealing intimacy
That chooses right, and never find a friend.

Helen[5] being chosen found life flat and dull
And later had much trouble from a fool,
While that great Queen, that rose out of the spray,[6]
Being fatherless could have her way
Yet chose a bandy-leggèd smith for man.[7]
It's certain that fine women eat
A crazy salad with their meat
Whereby the Horn of Plenty is undone.

A PRAYER FOR MY SON

Bid a strong ghost stand at the head
That my Michael may sleep sound,
Nor cry, not turn in the bed
Till his morning meal come round;
And may departing twilight keep
All dread afar till morning's back.
That his mother may not lack
Her fill of sleep.

Bid the ghost have sword in fist:
Some there are, for I avow
Such devilish things exist,
Who have planned his murder, for they know
Of some most haughty deed or thought
That waits upon his future days,
And would through hatred of the bays
Bring that to nought.

Though You can fashion everything
From nothing every day, and teach
The morning stars to sing,
You have lacked articulate speech
To tell Your simplest want, and known,
Wailing upon a woman's knee,
All of that worst ignominy
Of flesh and bone;

And when through all the town there ran
The servants of Your enemy,
A woman and a man,
Unless the Holy Writings lie,
Hurried through the smooth and rough
And through the fertile and waste,
Protecting, till the danger past,
With human love.

STEPHEN CRANE 1871–1900

BEHOLD, THE GRAVE OF A WICKED MAN

Behold, the grave of a wicked man,
And near it, a stern spirit.
There came a drooping maid with violets,
But the spirit grasped her arm.
"No flowers for him," he said.
The maid wept:
"Ah, I loved him."
But the spirit, grim and frowning:
"No flowers for him."

Now, this is it –
If the spirit was just,
Why did the maid weep?

AMY LOWELL 1874–1925

A DECADE

When you came, you were like red wine and honey,
And the taste of you burnt my mouth with its sweetness.
Now you are like morning bread,
Smooth and pleasant.
I hardly taste you at all for I know your savour,
But I am completely nourished.

RUPERT BROOKE 1887–1915

THE SOLDIER

If I should die, think only this of me:
    That there's some corner of a foreign field
That is forever England. There shall be
    In that rich earth a richer dust concealed;
A dust whom England bore, shaped, made aware,
    Gave, once, her flowers to love, her ways to roam,
A body of England's, breathing English air,
    Washed by the rivers, blest by suns of home.
And think, this heart, all evil shed away,

A pulse in the Eternal mind, no less
    Gives somewhere back the thoughts by England given,
Her sights and sounds; dreams happy as her day;
And laughter, learnt of friends; and gentleness,
    In hearts at peace, under an English heaven.

GALWAY KINNELL 1927–

AFTER MAKING LOVE WE HEAR FOOTSTEPS

For I can snore like a bullhorn
or play loud music
or sit up talking with any reasonably sober Irishman
and Fergus will only sink deeper
into his dreamless sleep, which goes by all in one flash,
but let there be that heavy breathing
or a stifled come-cry anywhere in the house
and he will wrench himself awake
and make for it on the run—as now, we lie together,
after making love, quiet, touching along the length
    of our bodies,
familiar touch of the long-married,
and he appears—in his baseball pajamas, it happens,
the neck opening so small he has to screw them on—
and flops down between us and hugs us and snuggles
    himself to sleep,
his face gleaming with satisfaction at being this very child.

In the half darkness we look at each other
and smile
and touch arms across this little, startlingly muscled body—
this one whom habit of memory propels to the ground
    of his making,
sleeper only the mortal sounds can sing awake,
this blessing love gives again into our arms.

CHINMOY KUMAR GHOSE 1931–2007

ETERNAL HAPPINESS

Eternal happiness
Grows on
Life's service-tree.

JOYCE SNYDER 1945–

A PERFECT POEM

A perfect poem would be one
that sang my love to you
in melodies and harmonies
trilled in flawless pitch and tune.

A perfect poem would be one
that danced my eagerness for your love.
A graceful partner, I'd spin and twirl
right into the heart of you.

Oh, to paint a poem so fine
that colors broad and bright
blanket the canvas of you,
swirling, endlessly alive with love
and feeling and tone.

Alas, I have only words—
numb sentinels to my passion.
Like steadfast tin soldiers, they
yearn to bend in love,
but are held captive
by form.

BHIKSHUNI WEISBROT 1953–

AUTUMNAL REVIVAL

Six apples peeled, cored and diced.
I don't want culinary etiquette,
I want the juice, the tart sap,
to bake you the sweet warmth of this apple season
and remembrance of the autumnal sky—
lingering at the half-opened door,
arrested, beneath a strident star
savoring the woodsy air
before the shut-down of winter.

Rachel Jamison Webster 1974–

Late September

Gulls slide through the sky.

It's one of those days
I've tried to get out into my actual life.

Late September and I don't even need
art to heighten my seeing.

The low spotlight of the sun does it for me.

Each blade of grass sidling up to its black.

Trees lapped by shadow and the Great
Lake's frayed unending waterbreath

amid a yellowjacket hum
and the whirring spin of crickets singing
we are all just river pouring over
the wheel.

From here, I can see them at the park.

They are framed by the green ruffling
and all the times we will not be.

He leans against the slide reading a paperback.

She climbs the red step.

He lifts her into the cup of the swing,
and she throws her head back laughing.

I can't read their faces, only their forms.

They have the same saturation into body
that turns the grass to strips of light.

See, I am one of those who can't forget,
who loves the one burning branch turning the tree

to something various and mortal,
something true.

Who sees the world a long way off
even when it's close

as this girl I love now running up.

DANCE, BABY

Singing unpeals from the next
room and I am remembering now
her little body, her shoulders
dancing, how she bounced
them working on a turn.
Some people just have courage.
Already she is immortal, already
I hardly remember how she was
formed of me in my body.
What was beyond me
was within me in a way it had
always been and always will be.
Her bones like threads of light,
her flesh a pink cream thickening
into layers and drifts, her heart
her heart, the inner hiccup
of her kicking limbs.
From the other room
the voice swells louder, stronger.
How much time, I wonder,
does this singer have left?

Cycle 12: Relatedness to the Sacred

HEBREW BIBLE c. 900–200 BCE

PSALM 150

Praise YAH![1]
    Praise God in his sanctuary!
    Praise him in his heavens for
        his acts of power!
Praise him for his mighty acts!
    Praise him according to his
        excellent greatness!
Praise him with the sounding of
        the trumpet!
Praise him with harp and
        lyre!
Praise him with tambourine and
        dancing!
Praise him with stringed
        instruments and flute!
Praise him with loud cymbals!
    Praise him with resounding
        cymbals!
Let everything that has breath
        praise YAH!
    Praise YAH!

FARIDUDDIN 'ATTAR 1145–1221

HOW CAN SOBER REASON UNDERSTAND

How can sober Reason understand
The drunkenness of Love?

How can Reason solve
The mystery of Love?

Reason is like a drop
Removed from the ocean;
How can this drop understand
The meaning of Love?

Reason has put many a stitch on it,
But no robe could it sew
To fit the body of Love.

You may hate the two worlds
With all your soul,
Yet even then,
You'll feel the warmth of Love.

Since Love is the work of the heart
Open the eyes of your heart
And look at the friends,
How drunk they are with Love!

Each being in His love,
Breathes in His love.
If you are to be annihilated
Then lose yourself in Love!

As Being entered existence
And closed its eyes for a moment
It was overwhelmed
By the tumult of Love.

Since Attar's heart
Did a ray from this Sun gain,
He started his journey to roam
And arrived in the desert of Love.

—Trans. Mahmood Jamal

Sa'di of Shirazi c. 1184–1291

The Throne of the Heart

I sit on the throne of the heart;
That is the style of my poverty!
I am dust on my Beloved's path;

That is my elevated state!
No need to visit the mosque for me;
Your eyebrow is a prayer arch for me.
Sa'di, why this pilgrim's garb?
Why, indeed, this ritual of hajj?
Look at my Beloved's face;
That is the true worshipper's place!

JALÂL AL–DIN RUMI 1207–1273

ONCE MORE WE COME LIKE DUST ADANCE IN AIR

Once more we come like dust adance in air
    From beyond the skies of love, aturn
On the field of love like polo balls we roll
    skittering to the side, coming to the fore

Love reduces one to need—if that's your lot
    it suits you—not us, who come from the beyond
This gathering's in your honor and the guests
    have all arrived. But not for bread alone
    we come here; pour out the firewater!
As you course through our veins, made wretched by
    our wounds for you, thank God we come quick to life!
Shams of Truth this love of yours thirsts for my blood
    I head straight to it, blade and shroud in hand!
Tabriz aboil your salt alone can simmer!
    We—pride of all the earth in caring for you –
    have come to help you stir the age up.

—Trans. Franklin D. Lewis

HEART

Heart,
    sit at the foot of one who knows his heart's
    rest beneath the tree whose boughs bud fresh
Don't wander all around the market of perfumes
    sit in the stall of him who has a stash of sugar
You'll be fleeced by every seller –
    without a scale to take their measure
    you'll mistake the gilded slug for golden tender
They'll make you sit inside the shop
    sweetly promising "Just one moment, please"

Don't sit there waiting,
there's another door goes out the back
Don't wait with bowl in hand for every pot to boil
what stews in every pot is not the same.
Not every cane-cut pen drips with sugar
not every under has above
not every eye's possessed of vision
not every sea conceals a pearl

Sing your little heart out, nightingale
for your famed intoxicated lamentation
echoes and transmutes the stony hills and granite boulders
If your head cannot contain you—lose it
you can't pass through the needle's eye a knotty thread
The awakened heart's a lamp
cloak it from contrary airs beneath your mantle
for the windy air will do it harm.
Pass beyond the winds and reach the spring
become a secret confidant, welling with emotion
and then like a green tree you will swell with sap
and come to fruition as it courses through your heart

—Trans. Franklin D. Lewis

KABIR 1440–1518

IV

Do not go to the garden of flowers!
    O Friend! go not there;
In your body is the garden of flowers.
Take your seat on the thousand petals
    of the lotus, and there gaze on the
    Infinite Beauty.

—Trans. Rabindranath Tagore

XLVI

O SADHU! purify your body in
    the simple way.
As the seed is within the banyan tree,
    and within the seed are the flowers,
    the fruits, and the shade:
So the germ is within the body, and

within that germ is the body again.
The fire, the air, the water, the earth,
and the aether; you cannot have
these outside of Him.
O Kazi, O Pundit, consider it well:
what is there that is not in the
soul?
The water-filled pitcher is placed upon
water, it has water within and
without.
It should not be given a name, lest it
call forth the error of dualism.
Kabir says: "Listen to the Word, the
Truth, which is your essence. He
speaks the Word to Himself; and
He Himself is the Creator."

—Trans. Rabindranath Tagore

LVI

HE is the real Sadhu, who can re-
veal the form of the Formless to
the vision of these eyes:
Who teaches the simple way of attain-
ing Him, that is other than rites
or ceremonies:
Who does not make you close the doors,
and hold the breath, and renounce
the world:
Who makes you perceive the Supreme
Spirit wherever the mind attaches
itself:
Who teaches you to be still in the midst
of all your activities.
Ever immersed in bliss, having no fear
in his mind, he keeps the spirit of
union in the midst of all enjoy-
ments.

The infinite dwelling of the Infinite
Being is everywhere: in earth,
water, sky, and air:
Firm as the thunderbolt, the seat of
the seeker is established above the

void.
He who is within is without: I see
Him and none else.

—Trans. Rabindranath Tagore

LXX

HE who is meek and contented, he
who has an equal vision, whose
mind is filled with the fullness of
acceptance and of rest;
He who has seen Him and touched
Him, he is freed from all fear and
trouble.
To him the perpetual thought of God
is like sandal paste smeared on
the body, to him nothing else is
delight:
His work and his rest are filled with
music: he sheds abroad the radi-
ance of love.
Kabir says: "Touch His feet, who is
one and indivisible, immutable
and peaceful; who fills all vessels
to the brim with joy, and whose
form is love."

—Trans. Rabindranath Tagore

JUAN DE LA CRUZ 1542–1591

WITHOUT A PLACE AND WITH A PLACE

Without shelter and with shelter,
without light and living in the dark
I steadily become all consumed.

I

My soul is free from
all nourished things
and on itself is risen
and in a pleasant life
leaning only on it's God.

II

For this it now will be said
the thing that I cherish most
is that my soul now finds itself
without shelter and with shelter.

III

And although in dark I suffer
in this mortal life
my trouble is not so grown
because if light I lack
I have celestial life
because as love becomes more blind,
such is the life it gives
that it exhausts the soul
without light and in dark living.

IV

Love makes such an opus
since I've known it
that if there is good or bad in me
it gives all of it a flavor
and transforms the soul into itself
and, in this way, its delicious flame
that I am feeling in me
captures without leaving a thing,
I steadily become all consumed.

—Trans. Sandra Kunanele

George Herbert 1593–1633

Man

My God, I heard this day
That none doth build a stately habitation,
But he that means to dwell therein.
What house more stately hath there been,
Or can be, than is Man? To[2] whose creation
All things are in decay.

For Man is every thing,
And more: he is a tree, yet bears more fruit;

A beast, yet is or should be more:
Reason and speech we only bring.
Parrots may thank us, if they are not mute,
They go upon the score.

Man is all symmetry,
Full of proportions, one limb to another,
And all to all the world besides.
Each part may call the furthest, brother;
For head with foot hath private amity,[3]
And both with moons and tides.

Nothing hath got so far,
But man hath caught and kept it, as his prey.
His eyes dismount the highest star:
He is in little all the sphere.[4]
Herbs gladly cure our flesh, because that they
Find their acquaintance there.

For us the winds do blow,
The earth doth rest, heaven move, and fountains flow.
Nothing we see but means our good,
As our delight or as our treasure:
The whole is either our cupboard of food,
Or cabinet of pleasure.

The stars have us to bed;
Night draws the curtain, which the sun withdraws;
Music and light attend our head.
All things unto our flesh are kind[5]
In their descent and being; to our mind
In their ascent and cause.

Each thing is full of duty:
Waters united are our navigation:
Distinguished, our habitation;
Below, our drink; above, our meat;
Both are our cleanliness. Hath one such beauty?
Then how are all things neat?

More servants wait on Man
Than he'll take notice of: in every path
He treads down that which doth befriend him
When sickness makes him pale and wan.
O mighty love! Man is one world, and hath
Another to attend him.

Since then, my God, thou hast
So brave a palace built, O dwell in it,
    That it may swell with thee at last!
    Till then, afford us to so much wit,
That, as the world serves us, we may serve thee,
    And both thy servants be.

THOMAS TRAHERNE 1637–1674

LOVE

    O nectar! O delicious stream!
O ravishing and only pleasure! Where
    Shall such another theme
Inspire my tongue with joys or please mine ear!
    Abridgement of delights!
    And Queen of sights!
O mine of rarities! O Kingdom wide!
O more! O cause of all! O glorious Bride!
    O God! O Bride of God! O King!
    O soul and crown of everything!

    Did not I covet to behold
Some endless monarch, that did always live
    In palaces of gold,
Willing all kingdoms, realms, and crowns to give
    Unto my soul! Whose love
    A spring might prove
Of endless glories, honors, friendships, pleasures,
Joys, praises, beauties and celestial treasures!
    Lo, now I see there's such a King.
    The fountain-head of everything!

    Did my ambition ever dream
Of such a Lord, of such a love! Did I
    Expect so sweet a stream
As this at any time! Could any eye
    Believe it? Why all power
    Is used here;
Joys down from Heaven on my head do shower,
And Jove beyond the fiction doth appear
    Once more in golden rain to come
    To Danae's[6] pleasing fruitful womb.

His Ganymede![7] His life! His joy!
Or He comes down to me, or takes me up
   That I might be His boy,
And fill, and taste, and give, and drink the cup.
   But those (tho' great) are all
   Too short and small,
Too weak and feeble pictures to express
The true mysterious depths of Blessedness.
   I am His image, and His friend,
   His son, bride, glory, temple, end.

Joseph Addison 1672–1719

Ode

The spacious firmament on high,
With all the blue ethereal sky,
And spangled heav'ns, a shining frame,
Their great original proclaim:
Th' unwearied Sun, from day to day,
Does his Creator's power display,
And publishes to every land
The work of an Almighty Hand.
Soon as the evening shades prevail,
The Moon takes up the wondrous tale,
And nightly to the list'ning Earth
Repeats the story of her birth:
Whilst all the stars that round her burn,
And all the planets, in their turn,
Confirm the tidings as they roll,
And spread the truth from pole to pole.
What though, in solemn silence, all
Move round the dark terrestrial ball?
What though nor real voice nor sound
Amid their radiant orbs be found?
In Reason's ear they all rejoice,
And utter forth a glorious voice,
Forever singing, as they shine,
"The Hand that made us is Divine."

Ralph Waldo Emerson 1803–1882

Give All to Love

Give all to love;
Obey thy heart;
Friends, kindred, days,
Estate, good fame,
Plans, credit, and the muse;
Nothing refuse.

'Tis a brave master,
Let it have scope,
Follow it utterly,
Hope beyond hope;
High and more high,
It dives into noon,
With wing unspent,
Untold intent;
But it is a god,
Knows its own path,
And the outlets of the sky.
'Tis not for the mean,
It requireth courage stout,
Souls above doubt,
Valor unbending,
It will reward,
They shall return
More than they were,
And ever ascending.

Leave all for love;
Yet, hear me, yet,
One word more thy heart behoved,
One pulse more of firm endeavor,
Keep thee to-day,
To-morrow, forever,
Free as an Arab
Of thy beloved.

Cling with life to the maid;
But when the surprise,
Vague shadow of surmise,
Flits across her bosom young,
Of a joy apart from thee,

Free be she, fancy-free,
Do not thou detain her vesture's hem,
Nor the palest rose she flung
From her summer diadem.

Though thou loved her as thyself,
As a self of purer clay,
Though her parting dims the day,
Stealing grace from all alive,
Heartily know,
When half-gods go,
The gods arrive.

Emily Dickinson 1830–1886

Some Keep the Sabbath Going to Church

Some keep the Sabbath going to Church –
I keep it, staying at Home –
With a Bobolink for a Chorister –
And an Orchard, for a Dome –

Some keep the Sabbath in Surplice –
I just wear my Wings –
And instead of tolling the Bell, for Church,
Our little Sexton—sings.

God preaches, a noted Clergyman –
And the sermon is never long,
So instead of getting to Heaven, at last –
I'm going, all along.

Gerard Manley Hopkins 1844–1889

God's Grandeur

The world is charged with the grandeur of God.
    It will flame out, like shining from shook foil;
    It gathers to a greatness, like the ooze of oil
Crushed. Why do men then now not reck his rod?
Generations have trod, have trod, have trod;
    And all is seared with trade; bleared, smeared with toil;
    And wears man's smudge and shares man's smell: the soil

Is bare now, nor can foot feel, being shod.

And for all this, nature is never spent;
    There lives the dearest freshness deep down things;
And though the last lights off the black West went
    Oh, morning, at the brown brink eastward, springs—
Because the Holy Ghost over the bent
    World broods with warm breast and with ah! bright wings.

EDMUND GOSSE 1849–1928

THE TIDE OF LOVE

Love, flooding all the creeks of my dry soul,
    From which the warm tide ebbed when I was born,
Following the moon of destiny, doth roll
    His slow rich wave along the shore forlorn,
To make the ocean—God—and me, one whole.

So, shuddering in its ecstasy, it lies.
    And, freed from mire and tangle of the ebb.
Reflects the waxing and the waning skies,
    And bears upon its panting breast the web
Of night and her innumerable eyes.

Nor can conceive at all that it was blind.
    But trembling with the sharp approach of love.
That, strenuous, moves without one breath of wind,
    Gasps, as the wakening maid, on whom the Dove
With folded wings of deity declined.

She in the virgin sweetness of her dream
    Thought nothing strange to find her vision true;
And I thus bathed in living rapture deem
    No moveless drought my channel ever knew,
But rustled always with the murmuring stream.

RABINDRANATH TAGORE 1861–1941

59

Yes, I know, this is nothing but thy love, O beloved of my
heart—this golden light that dances upon the leaves, these
idle clouds sailing across the sky, this passing breeze leaving its

coolness upon my forehead.

The morning light has flooded my eyes—this is thy message to my heart. Thy face is bent from above, thy eyes look down on my eyes, and my heart has touched thy feet.

—from *Gitanjali*

72

He it is, the innermost one, who awakens my being with his deep hidden touches.

He it is who puts his enchantment upon these eyes and joyfully plays on the chords of my heart in varied cadence of pleasure and pain.

He it is who weaves the web of this maya[8] in evanescent hues of gold and silver, blue and green, and lets peep out through the folds his feet, at whose touch I forget myself.

Days come and ages pass, and it is ever he who moves my heart in many a name, in many a guise, in many a rapture of joy and of sorrow.

—from *Gitanjali*

BHIKSHUNI WEISBROT 1953–

THE NATURE OF LIGHT

The nature of light is
if you have worked hard
to aim your intentions towards it,
worked hard to recover your own
and over time committed—
a culmination of years of living hard and careless
then blessingfully rescued until goodness
was more than luck, more than habit,
more than yearning,
but the only place to live a life—
then light will claim you,
brazenly shine through
so that no longer is it imaginary
or wished for—
but absolutely you.

Cycle 13: Justice, Righteous Anger and Self-Determination

RICHARD LOVELACE 1618–1657

TO LUCASTA, GOING TO THE WARS

Tell me not, sweet, I am unkind,
    That from the nunnery
Of thy chaste breast and quiet mind
    To war and arms I fly.
True, a new mistress I chase,
    The first foe in the field;
And with a stronger faith embrace
    A sword, a horse, a shield.

Yet this inconstancy is such
    As you too shall adore;
I could not love thee, dear, so much,
Loved I not honor more.

ANONYMOUS NEGRO SPIRITUAL c. 1700S

GO DOWN, MOSES

Go down, Moses,
Way down in Egyptland
Tell old Pharaoh
To let my people go.

When Israel was in Egyptland
Let my people go
Oppressed so hard they could not stand
Let my people go.

Go down, Moses,
Way down in Egyptland
Tell old Pharaoh
"Let my people go."

"Thus saith the Lord," bold Moses said,
"Let my people go;
If not I'll smite your first-born dead
Let my people go!"

ANNA LAETITIA BARBAULD 1743–1825

THE RIGHTS OF WOMAN

Yes, injured Woman! rise, assert thy right!
Woman! too long degraded, scorned, oppressed;
O born to rule in partial[1] Law's despite,[2]
Resume thy native empire o'er the breast!

Go forth arrayed in panoply divine;
That angel pureness which admits no stain;
Go, bid proud Man his boasted rule resign,
And kiss the golden scepter of thy reign.

Go, gird thyself with grace; collect thy store
Of bright artillery glancing[3] from afar;
Soft melting tones thy thundering cannon's roar,
Blushes and fears thy magazine of war.

Thy rights are empire: urge no meaner[4] claim. –
Felt, not defined, and if debated, lost;
Like sacred mysteries, which withheld from fame,
Shunning discussion, are revered the most.

Try all that wit and art suggest to bend
Of thy imperial foe the stubborn knee;
Make treacherous Man thy subject, not they friend;
Thou mayst command, but never canst be free.

Awe the licentious, and restrain the rude;
Soften the sullen, clear the cloudy brow:
Be, more than princes' gifts, thy favors sued;–[5]
She hazards all, who will the least allow.

But hope not, courted idol of mankind,
On this proud eminence secure to stay;

Subduing and subdued, thou soon shalt find
thy coldness soften, and thy pride give way.

Then, then, abandon each ambitious thought;
Conquest or rule thy heart shall feebly move,
In Nature's school, by her soft maxims taught,
That separate rights are lost in mutual love.

George Gordon, Lord Byron 1788–1824

When a Man Hath No Freedom to Fight for at Home

When a man hath no freedom to fight for at home,
Let him combat for that of his neighbors;
Let him think of the glories of Greece and of Rome,
And get knock'd on the head for his labours.

To do good to mankind is the chivalrous plan,
And is always as nobly requited;
Then battle for freedom wherever you can,
And, if not shot or hang'd, you'll get knighted.

John Greenleaf Whittier 1807–1892

For Righteousness' Sake
Inscribed to Friends Under Arrest for
Treason Against the Slave Power

The age is dull and mean. Men creep,
Not walk; with blood too pale and tame
To pay the debt they owe to shame;
Buy cheap, sell dear; eat, drink, and sleep
Down-pillowed, deaf to moaning want;
Pay tithes for soul-insurance; keep
Six days to Mammon, one to Cant.[6]

In such a time, give thanks to God,
That somewhat of the holy rage
With which the prophets in their age
On all its decent seemings trod,
Has set your feet upon the lie,
That man and ox and soul and clod
Are market stock to sell and buy!

The hot words from your lips, my own,
To caution trained, might not repeat;
But if some tares among the wheat
Of generous thought and deed were sown,
No common wrong provoked your zeal;
The silken gauntlet that is thrown
In such a quarrel rings like steel.

The brave old strife the fathers saw
For Freedom calls for men again
Like those who battled not in vain
For England's Charter, Alfred's law;
And right of speech and trial just
Wage in your name their ancient war
With venal courts and perjured trust.

God's ways seem dark, but, soon or late,
They touch the shining hills of day;
The evil cannot brook delay,
The good can well afford to wait.
Give ermined[7] knaves their hour of crime;
Ye have the future grand and great,
The safe appeal of Truth to Time!

HENRY DAVID THOREAU 1817–1862

INDEPENDENCE

My life more civil is and free
Than any civil polity.

Ye princes keep your realms
And circumscribed power,
Not wide as are my dreams,
Nor rich as is this hour.

What can ye give which I have not?
What can ye take which I have got?
Can ye defend the dangerless?
Can ye inherit nakedness?

To all true wants time's ear is deaf,
Penurious states lend no relief
Out of their pelf—[8]

But a free soul—thank God—
Can help itself.

Be sure your fate
Doth keep apart its state—
Not linked with any band—
Even the nobles of the land

In tented fields with cloth of gold—
No place doth hold
But is more chivalrous than they are.
And sigheth for a nobler war.
A finer strain its trumpet rings—
A brighter gleam its armor flings.

The life that I aspire to live
No man proposeth me—
No trade upon the street
Wears its emblazonry.

FRANCES ELLEN WATKINS HARPER 1824–1911

BURY ME IN A FREE LAND

Make me a grave where'er you will,
In a lowly plain, or a lofty hill,
Make it among earth's humblest graves,
But not in a land where men are slaves.

I could not rest if around my grave
I heard the steps of a trembling slave:
His shadow above my silent tomb
Would make it a place of fearful gloom.

I could not rest if I heard the tread
Of a coffle gang to the shambles led,
And the mother's shriek of wild despair
Rise like a curse on the trembling air.

I could not sleep if I saw the lash
Drinking her blood at each fearful gash,
And I saw her babes torn from her breast,
Like trembling doves from their parent nest.

I'd shudder and start if I heard the bay
Of blood-hounds seizing their human prey,

And I heard the captive plead in vain
As they bound afresh his galling chain.

If I saw young girls from their mother's arms
Bartered and sold for their youthful charms,
My eye would flash with a mournful flame,
My death-paled cheek grow red with shame.

I would sleep, dear friends, where bloated might
Can rob no man of his dearest right;
My rest shall be calm in any grave
Where none can call his brother a slave.

I ask no monument, proud and high
To arrest the gaze of the passers-by;
All that my yearning spirit craves,
Is bury me not in a land of slaves.

WILLIAM ERNEST HENLEY 1849–1903

INVICTUS[9]

Out of the night that covers me,
   Black as the pit from pole to pole,
I thank whatever gods may be
   For my unconquerable soul.

In the fell clutch of circumstance
   I have not winced nor cried aloud:
Under the bludgeonings of chance
   My head is bloody, but unbow'd.

Beyond this place of wrath and tears
   Looms but the Horror of the shade,
And yet the menace of the years
   Finds and shall find me unafraid.

It matters not how strait the gate,
   How charged with punishments the scroll,
I am the master of my fate:
   I am the captain of my soul.

Ella Wheeler Wilcox 1850–1919

The Winds of Fate

One ship drives east and another drives west
With the selfsame winds that blow.
’Tis the set of the sails
And not of the gales
Which tells us the way to go.
Like the winds of the sea are the ways of fate,
As we voyage along through life;
’Tis the set of a soul
That decides its goal
And not the calm or the strife.

Paul Lawrence Dunbar 1872–1906

Sympathy

I know what the caged bird feels, alas!
    When the sun is bright on the upland slopes;
When the wind stirs soft through the springing grass,
And the river flows like a stream of glass;
    When the first bird sings and the first bud opes,
And the faint perfume from its chalice steals –
I know what the caged bird feels!

I know why the caged bird beats his wing
    Till its blood is red on the cruel bars;
For he must fly back to his perch and cling
When he fain would be on the bough a-swing;
    And a pain still throbs in the old, old scars
And they pulse again with a keener sting –
I know why he beats his wing!

I know why the caged bird sings, ah me,
    When his wing is bruised and his bosom sore, –
When he beats his bars and he would be free;
It is not a carol of joy or glee,
    But a prayer that he sends from his heart’s deep core,
But a plea, that upward to Heaven he flings –
I know why the caged bird sings!

JOHN MCCRAE 1872–1918

IN FLANDERS FIELDS

In Flanders fields the poppies blow
Between the crosses, row on row,
    That mark our place; and in the sky
    The larks, still bravely singing, fly
Scarce heard amid the guns below.

We are the Dead. Short days ago
We lived, felt dawn, saw sunset glow,
    Loved and were loved, and now we lie,
        In Flanders fields.

Take up our quarrel with the foe:
To you from failing hands we throw
    The torch; be yours to hold it high.
    If ye break faith with us who die
We shall not sleep, though poppies grow
    In Flanders fields.

FENTON JOHNSON 1888–1958

CHILDREN OF THE SUN

We are children of the sun,
    Rising sun!
Weaving Southern destiny,
Waiting for the mighty hour
When our Shiloh shall appear
With the flaming sword of right,
With the steel of brotherhood,
And emboss in crimson die
Liberty! Fraternity!

We are the star-dust folk,
    Striving folk!
Sorrow songs have lulled to rest;
Seething passions wrought through wrongs,
Led us where the moon rays dip
In the night of dull despair,
Showed us where the star gleams shine,
And the mystic symbols glow—

Liberty! Fraternity!
We have come through cloud and mist,
    Mighty men!
Dusk has kissed our sleep-born eyes,
Reared for us a mystic throne
In the splendor of the skies,
That shall always be for us,
Children of the Nazarene,
Children who shall ever sing
Liberty! Fraternity!

CLAUDE MCKAY 1889–1948

IF WE MUST DIE

If we must die, let it not be like hogs
Hunted and penned in an inglorious spot,
While round us bark the mad and hungry dogs,
Making their mock at our accursèd lot.
If we must die, O let us nobly die,
So that our precious blood may not be shed
In vain; then even the monsters we defy
Shall be constrained to honor us though dead!
O kinsmen! we must meet the common foe!
Though far outnumbered let us show us brave,
And for their thousand blows deal one deathblow!
What though before us lies the open grave?
Like men we'll face the murderous, cowardly pack,
Pressed to the wall, dying, but fighting back!

WILFRED OWEN 1893–1918

DULCE ET DECORUM EST

Bent double, like old beggars under sacks,
Knock-kneed, coughing like hags, we cursed through sludge,
Till on the haunting flares we turned our backs
And towards our distant rest began to trudge.
Men marched asleep. Many had lost their boots
But limped on, blood-shod. All went lame; all blind;
Drunk with fatigue; deaf even to the hoots
Of tired, outstripped Five-Nines that dropped behind.

Gas! Gas! Quick, boys! – An ecstasy of fumbling,
Fitting the clumsy helmets just in times;
But someone still was yelling out and stumbling,
And flound'ring like a man in fire or lime...
Dim, through the misty panes and thick green light,
As under a green sea, I saw him drowning.

In all my dreams, before my helpless sight,
He plunges at me, guttering, choking, drowning.

If in some smothering dreams you too could pace
Behind the wagon that we flung him in,
And watch the white eyes writing in his face,
His hanging face, like a devil's sick of sin;
If you could hear, at every jolt, the blood
come gargling from the froth-corrupted lungs,
Obscene as cancer, bitter as the cud
Of vile, incurable sores on innocent tongues, –
My friend, you would not tell with such high zest
To children ardent for some desperate glory,
The old Lie: Dulce et decorum est
Pro patria mori.[10]

ANTHEM FOR A DOOMED YOUTH

What passing-bells for these who die as cattle?
　—Only the monstrous anger of the guns.
　Only the stuttering rifles' rapid rattle
Can patter out their hasty orisons.
No mockeries now for them; no prayers nor bells;
　Nor any voice of mourning save the choirs,—
The shrill, demented choirs of wailing shells;
　And bugles calling for them from sad shires.

What candles may be held to speed them all?
　Not in the hands of boys, but in their eyes
Shall shine the holy glimmers of goodbyes.
　The pallor of girls' brows shall be their pall;
Their flowers the tenderness of patient minds,
And each slow dusk a drawing-down of blinds.

HAROLD NORSE 1916–2009

LET GO AND FEEL YOUR NAKEDNESS

Let go and feel your nakedness, tits ache to be bitten and sucked
Let go with pong of armpit and crotch, let go with hole a-tingle
Let go with tongue lapping hairy cunt, lick feet, kiss ass, suck cock and
 balls
Let the whole body go, let love come through, let freedom ring
Let go with moans and erogenous zones, let go with heart and soul
Let go the dead meat of convention, wake up the live meat of love

Let go with the senses, pull out the stops, forget false teachings and lies
Let go of inherited belief, let go of shame and blame in brief
Let go of forbidden energies, choked back in muscles and nerves
Let go of rigid rules and roles, let go of uptight poses
Let go of your puppet self, let go and renew your self and be free
Let go the dead meat of convention, wake up the live meat of love

Let go this moment, this hour, this day, tomorrow may be too late
Let go of guilt and frustration, let liberation and tolerance flow
Let go of phantom worries and fears, let go of hours and days and years
Let go of hate and rage and grief, let walls against ecstasy fall for relief
Let go of pride and greed, let go of missiles and might and creed
Let go the dead meat of convention, wake up the live meat of love

CHARLES BUKOWSKI 1920–1994

NO LEADERS, PLEASE

invent yourself and then reinvent yourself,
don't swim in the same slough.
invent yourself and then reinvent yourself
 and
stay out of the clutches of mediocrity.

invent yourself and then reinvent yourself,
change your tone and shape so often that they can
never
categorize you.

reinvigorate yourself and
accept what is
but only on the terms that you have invented
and reinvented.

be self-taught.
and reinvent your life because you must;
it is your life and
its history
and the present
belong only to
you.

DENISE LEVERTOV 1923–1997

VARIATION ON A THEME BY RILKE
(*The Book of Hours, Book 1, Poem 1, Stanza 1*)

A certain day became a presence to me;
there it was, confronting me—a sky, air, light:
a being. And before it started to descend
from the height of noon, it leaned over
and struck my shoulder as if with
the flat of a sword, granting me
honor and a task. The day's blow
rang out, metallic—or it was I, a bell awakened,
and what I heard was my whole self
saying and singing what it knew: *I can.*

JACK MICHELINE 1929–1998

POEM TO THE FREAKS

To lives as I have done is surely absurd
in cheap hotels and furnished rooms
To walk up side streets and down back alleys
talking to oneself
and screaming to the sky obscenities
That the arts is a rotten business indeed
That mediocrity and the rage of fashion rules
My poems and paintings piled on the floor
To be one with himself
A Saint
A Prince
To Persevere
Through storms and hard-ons
Through dusks and dawns

To kick death in the ass
To be passed over like a bad penny
A midget
An Ant
A roach
A freak
A Hot Piece
An Outlaw
Raise your cup and drink my friend
Drink for those who walk alone in the night
      To the crippled and the blind
      To the lost and the damned
      To the lone bird flying in the sky
Drink to wonder
Drink to me
Drink to pussy and dreams
Drink to madness and all the stars
I hear the birds singing

BRIAN THORNTON 1975–

ERBIL LIBRE
–ERBIL, IRAQ

Stand proud behind your shining sun,
and let your shadows claim your grains
in fields now filled with quiet guns.

The Euphrates carries across the plains,
its bends engorged and pressed to break
beneath the weight of sunken chains.

Forty years of spade and rake
now still above the hard pan drought
allow the weeds to overtake.

They punch the clay in fisted sprouts
and wrap the trunks of olive trees—
too dry, their withered twisted boughs.

They can't sustain the need of leaves
that, brittle, break when winter comes
with winds that spring from Saudi seas.

Stand proud behind your shining sun,

and let your shadows claim your grains
in fields now filled with quiet guns.

With Nawroz comes the mountain flames—
the trail-lit tribal tapestries,
that fear no tears or falling rain.

They blaze and raise the sophistries—
those calls to "keep the monkeys out,"
and "purify the histories."

Drunk on God, they stomp and shout,
"Let all here praise the Father's name,"
while dancing down the river's route.

Once the harvest has been reclaimed
and future yields are finally won,
the gowns can rid their reddened stains.

Stand proud behind your shining sun,
and let your shadows claim your grains
in fields now filled with quiet guns.

Cycle 14: Unity, Meaning, Serenity and Enchantment

JALÂL AL–DIN RUMI 1207–1273

BLISS

Bliss –
  the instant
    spent seated
      on the terrace,
        me next to you
          two forms and
          two faces
            with just one soul,
          me and you

The chatter of birds
the garden's murmur
  flowing
  like a fountain of youth
   as we stroll
  through roses,
        me and you

The stars of the firmament, bent low to look over us
Let's eclipse them, shine like the moon,
        me and you

       Me and you join,
       beyond Me
       beyond You
        in joy
happy, released from delire[1] and delusion
       Me and you, laughing like this,
reach dimensions where celestial birds suck sugary cubes

Magical! me and you, here,
      in our corner of earth,
            but wafting on airs of Iraq and Khorasan,
                  me and you
In one form here on earth
in other forms in paradise,
eternal, sunk in fields of sugar,
me and you

—Trans. Franklin D. Lewis

KABIR 1440–1518

XIV

The river and its waves are one
surf: where is the difference between the river and its waves?

When the wave rises,
it is the water;
and when it falls,
it is the same water again.

Tell me, Sir, where is the distinction?
Because it has been named as wave,
shall it no longer be considered as water?

Within the Supreme Brahma,
the worlds are being told like beads:
Look upon that rosary with the eyes of wisdom.

—Trans. Rabindranath Tagore

XXVIII

Before the Unconditioned, the
      Conditioned dances:
"Thou and I are one!" this trumpet
      proclaims.
The Guru comes, and bows down before
      the disciple:
This is the greatest of wonders.

—Trans. Rabindranath Tagore

Torquato Tasso 1544–1595

The Woods and the Rivers Fall Silent

The woods and the rivers fall silent,
And the sea without waves rests,
In the caverns, the winds have truce and peace,
And in the dark of night
The white moon forms noble silence;
And we keep hidden
The sweetness of love:
Love does not speak or breathe,
Let kisses be silent, and silent my sighs.

—Trans. Gabriella Basile

Henry Vaughan 1621–1695

Peace

My soul, there is a country
    Far beyond the stars,
Where stands a winged sentry
    All skillful in the wars;

There above the noise and danger,
    Sweet Peace sits crowned with smiles,
And One born in a manger
    Commands the beauteous files.

He is thy gracious Friend,
    And—O my Soul awake!—
Did in pure love descend
    To die here for thy sake.

If thou canst get but thither,
    There grows the flower of Peace,
The Rose that cannot wither,
    Thy fortress and thy ease.

Leave then thy foolish ranges,
    For none can thee secure
But One, who never changes,
    Thy God, thy life, thy cure.

WILLIAM WORDSWORTH 1770–1850

IT IS A BEAUTEOUS EVENING, CALM AND FREE

It is a beauteous Evening, calm and free,
The holy time is quiet as a Nun
Breathless with adoration; the broad sun
Is sinking down in its tranquility;
The gentleness of heavens broods o'er the Sea:
Listen! The mighty Being is awake,
And doth with his eternal motion make
A sound like thunder—everlastingly.
Dear Child! dear Girl! That walkest with me here,
If thou appear untouched by solemn thought,
Thy nature is not therefore less divine:
Thou liest in Abraham's bosom all the year,
And worship'st at the Temple's inner shrine,
God being with thee when we know it not.

UGO FOSCOLO 1778–1827

TO EVENING

Maybe because of the fatal quiet,
Your coming image is dear to me,
O evening! And when you are courted by the joyful
summer clouds and serene zephyrs,
And when from nervous restless air
You lead long darkness through the universe
Always you descend invoked,
and gently keep the secret roads of my heart.

You make me wander with my thoughts on the footsteps
That go to eternal nothingness; and meanwhile escape
This guilty time, and goes with it the crowds
Of cares that wave over and destroy itself and me.
And while I look at your peace, sleeps
That warrior spirit that inside roars.

—Trans. Gabriella Basile

John Greenleaf Whittier 1807–1892

What the Birds Said

The birds against the April wind
    Flew northward, singing as they flew;
They sang, "the land we leave behind
    Has swords for corn-blades, blood for dew."

"O wild-birds, flying from the South,
    What saw and heard ye, gazing down?"
"We saw the mortar's upturned mouth,
    The sickened camp, the blazing town!

"Beneath the bivouac's starry lamps,
    We saw your march-worn children die;
In shrouds of moss, in cypress swamps,
    We saw your dead uncoffined lie.

"We heard the starving prisoner's sighs,
    And saw, from line and trench, your sons
Follow our flight with home-sick eyes
    Beyond the battery's smoking guns."

"And heard and saw ye only wrong
    And pain," I cried, "O wing-worn flocks?"
"We heard," they sang, "the freedman's song,
    the crash of Slavery's broken locks!

"We saw from new, uprising States
    The treason-nursing mischief spurned,
As, crowding Freedom's ample gates,
    The long-estranged and lost returned.

"O'er dusky faces, seamed and old,
    And hands horn-hard with unpaid toil,
With hope in every rustling fold,
    We saw your star-dropt flag uncoil.

"And struggling up through sounds accursed,
    A grateful murmur clomb the air;
A whisper scarcely heard at first,
    It filled the listening heavens with prayer.

"And sweet and far, as from a star,
    Replied a voice which shall not cease,
Till, drowning all the noise of war,
    It sings the blessed song of peace!"

So to me, in a doubtful day
    Of chill and slowly greening spring,
Low stooping from the cloudy gray,
    The wild-birds sang or seemed to sing.

They vanished in the misty air,
    The song went with them in their flight;
But lo! they left the sunset fair,
    And in the evening there was light.

EMILY BRONTË 1818–1849

A DAYDREAM

On a sunny brae alone I lay
One summer afternoon;
It was the marriage-time of May,
With her young lover, June.

From her mother's heart seemed loath to part
That queen of bridal charms,
But her father smiled on the fairest child
He ever held in his arms.

The trees did wave their plumy crests,
The glad birds caroled clear;
And I, of all the wedding guests,
Was only sullen there!

There was not one, but wished to shun
My aspect void of cheer;
The very gray rocks, looking on,
Asked, "What do you here?"

And I could utter no reply;
In sooth, I did not know
Why I had brought a clouded eye
To greet the general glow.

So, resting on a heathy bank,
I took my heart to me;
And we together sadly sank
Into a reverie.

We thought, "When winter comes again,
Where will these bright things be?

All vanished, like a vision vain,
An unreal mockery!

"The birds that now so blithely sing,
Through deserts, frozen dry,
Poor spectres of the perished spring,
In famished troops will fly.

"And why should we be glad at all?
The leaf is hardly green,
Before a token of its fall
Is on the surface seen!"

Now, whether it were really so,
I never could be sure;
But as in fit of peevish woe,
I stretched me on the moor,

A thousand thousand gleaming fires
Seemed kindling in the air;
A thousand thousand silvery lyres
Resounded far and near:

Methought, the very breath I breathed
Was full of sparks divine,
And all my heather-couch was wreathed
By that celestial shine!

And, while the wide earth echoing rung
To that strange minstrelsy
The little glittering spirits sung,
Or seemed to sing, to me:

"O mortal! mortal! let them die;
Let time and tears destroy,
That we may overflow the sky
With universal joy!

"Let grief distract the sufferer's breast,
And night obscure his way;
They hasten him to endless rest,
And everlasting day.

"To thee the world is like a tomb,
A desert's naked shore;
To us, in unimagined bloom,
It brightens more and more!

"And, could we lift the veil, and give
One brief glimpse to thine eye,
Thou wouldst rejoice for those that live,
Because they live to die."

The music ceased; the noonday dream,
Like dream of night, withdrew;
But Fancy, still, will sometimes deem
Her fond creation true.

WALT WHITMAN 1819–1892

ON THE BEACH AT NIGHT ALONE

On the beach at night alone,
As the old mother sways her to and fro singing her husky song,
As I watch the bright stars shining, I think a thought of the
clef of the universes and of the future.
A vast similitude interlocks all,
All spheres, grown, ungrown, small, large, suns, moons,
planets,
All distances of place however wide,
All distances of time, all inanimate forms,
All souls, all living bodies though they be ever so different, or
in different worlds,
All gaseous, watery, vegetable, mineral processes, the fishes,
the brutes,
All nations, colors, barbarisms, civilizations, languages,
All identities that have existed or may exist on this globe, or
any globe,
All lives and deaths, all of the past, present, future,
This vast similitude spans them, and always has spann'd,
And shall forever span them and compactly hold and enclose
them.

A GLIMPSE

A glimpse, through an interstice caught,
Of a crowd of workmen and drivers in a bar-room, around
the stove, late of a winter night—and I unremarked,
seated in a corner,
Of a youth who loves me, and whom I love, silently
approaching, and seating himself near, that he may hold
me by the hand,

A long while, amid the noises of coming and going—of
    drinking and oath and smutty jest,
There we two, content, happy in being together, speaking
    little, perhaps not a word.

DANTE GABRIEL ROSSETTI 1828–1882

NUPTIAL SLEEP

At length their long kiss severed, with sweet smart:
And as the last slow sudden drops are shed
From sparkling eaves when all the storm has fled,
So singly flagged the pulses of each heart.
Their bosoms sundered, with the opening start
Of married flowers to either side outspread
From the knit stem; yet still their mouths, burnt red,
Fawned on each other where they lay apart.

Sleep sank them lower than the tide of dreams,
And their dreams watched them sink, and slid away.
Slowly their souls swam up again, through gleams
Of watered light and dull drowned waifs of day;
Till from some wonder of new woods and streams
He woke, and wondered more: for there she lay.

SILENT NOON

Your hands lie open in the long fresh grass,—
    The finger-points look through like rosy blooms:
    Your eyes smile peace. The pasture gleams and glooms
'Neath billowing skies that scatter and amass.
All round our nest, far as the eye can pass,
    Are golden kingcup-fields with silver edge
    Where the cow-parsley skirts the hawthorn hedge.
'Tis visible silence, still as the hourglass.

Deep in the sun-searched growths the dragon-fly
Hangs like a blue thread loosened from the sky:—
    So this winged hour is dropt to us from above.
Oh! clasp we to our hearts, for deathless dower,
This close-companioned inarticulate hour
    When twofold silence was the song of love.

EMILY DICKINSON 1830–1886

EXHILARATION IS THE BREEZE

Exhilaration is the Breeze
That lifts us from the Ground
And leaves us in another place
Whose statement is not found –

Returns us not, but after time
We soberly descend
A little newer for the term
Upon Enchanted Ground –

GERARD MANLEY HOPKINS 1844–1889

THE STARLIGHT NIGHT

Look at the stars! look, look up at the skies!
  O look at all the fire-folk sitting in the air!
  The bright boroughs, the circle-citadels there!
Down in dim woods the diamond delves! the elves'-eyes!
The grey lawns cold where gold, where quickgold lies!
  Wind-beat whitebeam! airy abeles set on a flare!
  Flake-doves sent floating forth at a farmyard scare!—
Ah well! it is all a purchase, all is a prize.
Buy then! bid then!—What?—Prayer, patience, aims, vows.
Look, look: a May-mess, like on orchard boughs!
  Look! March-bloom, like on mealed-with-yellow sallows!
These are indeed the barn; withindoors house
The shocks. This piece-bright paling shuts the spouse
  Christ home, Christ and his mother and all his hallows.

PAUL VERLAINE 1844–1896

LISTEN TO THE SONG SO SWEET

Listen to the song so sweet
Who only cries to please you.
She is discreet, she is nimble,
A shudder of water over moss!

The voice you had known (and loved?)
But now she is veiled

As a desolate widow,
Yet still proud, as she;

And in the long folds of her veil
Fluttering in the autumn breeze,
Conceals and reveals the heart that surprised
The truth like a star.

She said, the familiar voice,
That kindness is our life
That from the hate and envy
Nothing remains, when death came comes.

She also speaks of the glory
To be natural without further delay,
And the golden wedding and of the tender
Joy of a peace without victory.

Welcome the voice that persists
In her naïve epithalamium.
Come, nothing benefits a soul more
Than to make a soul less sad!

She is "in trouble" and "in passing"
The soul that suffers without wrath,
And as her moral is clear! ...
Listen to the very wise song.

—Trans. Kelly Johnson

RABINDRANATH TAGORE 1861–1941

78

When the creation was new and all the stars shone in their
first splendour, the gods held their assembly in the sky and
sang "Oh, the picture of perfection! the joy unalloyed!"

But one cried of a sudden—"It seems that somewhere
there is a break in the chain of light and one of the stars has
been lost."

The golden string of their harp snapped, their song
stopped, and they cried in dismay—"Yes, that lost star was
the best, she was the glory of all heavens!"

From that day the search is unceasing for her, and the cry
goes on from one to the other that in her the world has lost its
one joy!

Only in the deepest silence of night the stars smile and whisper among themselves—"Vain is this seeking! Unbroken perfection is over all!"

—from *Gitanjali*

W.B. YEATS 1865–1939

THE SONG OF WANDERING AENGUS

I went out to the hazel wood,
Because a fire was in my head,
And cut and peeled a hazel wand,
And hooked a berry to a thread;
And when white moths were on the wing,
And moth-like stars were flickering out,
I dropped the berry in a stream
And caught a little silver trout.

When I had laid it on the floor
I went to blow the fire aflame,
But something rustled on the floor,
And someone called me by my name;
It had become a glimmering girl
With apple blossom in her hair
Who called me by my name and ran
And faded through the brightening air.

Though I am old with wandering
Through hollow lands and hilly lands,
I will find out where she has gone,
And kiss her lips and take her hands;
And walk among long dappled grass,
And pluck till time and times are done
The silver apples of the moon,
The golden apples of the sun.

PAUL LAWRENCE DUNBAR 1872–1906

DAWN

An angel, robbed in spotless white,
Bent down and kissed the sleeping Night.

Night woke to blush; the sprite was gone.
Men saw the blush and called it Dawn.

James Joyce 1882–1941

III

At that hour when all things have repose,
    O lonely watcher of the skies,
    Do you hear the night wind and the sighs
Of harps playing unto Love to unclose
    The pale gates of sunrise?

When all things repose do you alone
    Awake to hear the sweet harps play
    To Love before him on his way,
And the night wind answering in antiphon[2]
    Till night is overgone?

Play on, invisible harps, unto Love,
    Whose way in heaven is aglow
    At that hour when soft lights come and go,
Soft sweet music in the air above
    And in the earth below.

Sara Teasdale 1884–1933

Peace

Peace flows into me
    As the tide to the pool by the shore;
    It is mine forevermore,
It will not ebb like the sea.
I am the pool of blue
    That worships the vivid sky;
    My hopes were heaven-high,
They are all fulfilled in you.
I am the pool of gold
    When sunset burns and dies—
    You are my deepening skies;
Give me your stars to hold.

STEPHEN SPENDER 1909–1995

VI

I am that witness through whom the whole
Knows it exists. Within the coils of blood,
Whispering under sleep, there moves the flood
Of stars, battles, dark and frozen pole.
All that I am I am not. The cold stone
Unfolds its angel for me. On my dreams ride
The racial legends. The stars outside
Glitter under my ribs. Being all, I am alone.
    I who say I call that eye I
Which is the mirror in which things see
Nothing except themselves. I die.
The things, the vision, still will be.
Upon this eye reflections of stars lie
And that which passes, passes away, is I.

BHIKSHUNI WEISBROT 1953–

MEDITATION

I am practicing being the horizon—
arms held wide side to side,
touching nothing.
This way the whole of me,
the beating heart of me, trusts.
I am practicing being perfect
and so still, even a slip of paper,
a single leaf windswept by autumn
makes a ruckus.

From a distance I assume I look
crucified or exhilarated,
but in fact I am neither.
I am as I have always wanted to be—
a single line stretched across the sky.

It has all come to this—
I am just above the dawn,
the barking dog so very far away.

JANE HIRSHFIELD   1953–

AGAINST CERTAINTY

There is something out in the dark that wants to correct us.
Each time I think "this," it answers "that."
Answers hard, in the heart-grammar's strictness.

If I then say "that," it too is taken away.

Between certainty and the real, an ancient enmity.
When the cat waits in the path-hedge,
no cell of her body is not waiting.
This is how she is able so completely to disappear.

I would like to enter the silence portion as she does.

To live amid the great vanishing as a cat must live,
one shadow fully at ease inside another.

SUSANNAH SPANTON   1959–

SOLITUDE

Singer of the light
Alone in thought
I reach into the day
Filled with knowing
Mindful to breathe deep

Take me to the water's edge to drink in the droplets of peace
The sound that fills my every sense
Like music of an opus
The crashing melody embraces who I am

Alone in awareness the honor to be present
I see too clear which fogs my vision
Thoughts of an ancient time
Remind me of the essence in the wind

RACHEL JAMISON WEBSTER 1974–

CREAM OF THE POUR IS THE CREAM OF SKIN THICKENING

I look out. Black leaves   color of dried blood
and my ulcerated tonsils flutter as I
breathe openmouthed.   Through the branches
there are branches.

Some remember their lives
of green   some hang languorous
sturdy with sap.

The question becomes how to live
the right life   filling with it
as a liquid converted from light
until it becomes the weight
that factors your place with gravity.

Until just walking to the car
with some coffee and a roll
you can sense   suddenly   purpose
in traffic and glances windswirls
coughing wrappers to the street

        and that branch quivering
as it touches another

which is also of course   itself.

Notes and Bibliography

Introduction Notes

1. Walt Whitman, *Leaves of Grass and Other Writings*, ed. Michael Moon (New York: Norton, 2002).

2. Byron, *Lord Byron: The Major Works*, ed. Jerome McGann (Oxford: Oxford University Press, 2008).

3. Adam Potkay, *The Story of Joy: From the Bible to Late Romanticism* (New York: Cambridge University Press, 2007), 226.

4. James Pawelski and D. J. Moores, eds., *The Eudaimonic Turn: Well-being in Literary Studies* (Madison, NJ: Fairleigh Dickinson University Press, 2012).

5. Darrin M. McMahon, *Happiness: A History* (New York: Grove Press, 2006).

6. Anti-essentialism is the prevalent idea that human identities are constructed not by some inherent essence determined by biology or genes but by language, culture, economics, and other cultural factors. Anti-essentialists often ignore, downplay, or elide the role of biology and genetics as determinants of human subjectivity. The relatively new field of literary Darwinism has arisen as a direct challenge to anti-essentialism.

7. Martha Nussbaum, "Social Justice and Universalism: In Defense of an Aristotelian Account of Human Functioning," *Modern Philology* 90 (1993): 55–57.

8. *Ibid.*, 58–59.

9. *Ibid.*, 57.

10. Sisela Bok, *Exploring Happiness: From Aristotle to Brain Science* (New Haven, CT: Yale University Press, 2010), 8.

11. Martin E. P. Seligman, Flourish: A Visionary New Understanding of Happiness and Well-being (New York: Free Press, 2012), 14.

12. Barbara Fredrickson, *Positivity* (New York: Three Rivers Press, 2009), 41.

13. Mihalyi Csikszentmihalyi, *Flow: The Psychology of Optimal Experience* (New York: Harper & Row, 1990), 49.

14. *Ibid.*, 50.

15. Seligman, *Flourish*, 17.

16. D. H. Lawrence, *Complete Poems*, eds. Vivian de Sola Pinto and Warren F. Roberts (New York: Penguin, 1994).

17. Christopher Peterson and Martin Seligman, *Character Strengths and Virtues: A Handbook and Classification* (New York: Oxford University Press, 2004).

18. Francis E. W. Harper, *Poems* (New York: Dodo, 2007).

19. *The Upanishads,* translated by Juan Mascaro (New York: Penguin Books, 1965), 140.

20. For a more complete discussion, see Antonio Damasio, *Looking for Spinoza: Joy, Sorrow, and the Feeling Brain* (New York: Houghton Mifflin, 2003), 60.

21. Jonathan Haidt, *The Happiness Hypothesis: Finding Modern Truth in Ancient Happiness* (New York: Basic Books, 2006).

22. For more in-depth study, see C.G. Jung, *The Collected Works.* 20 volumes, translated by R.F.C. Hull, edited by William McGuire. 2d. ed. (Princeton, NJ: Princeton University Press, Bollingen Series XX, 1983).

23. For a more practical discussion, see Robert Johnson, *Inner Work: Using Dreams and Active Imagination for Personal Growth* (San Francisco: Harper and Row, 1989).

24. William James, *Varieties of Religious Experience* (New York: Penguin, 1985).

25. Marghanita Laski, *Ecstasy in Secular and Religious Experiences* (Los Angeles: Tarcher, 1961).

26. See Abraham Maslow, *The Farther Reaches of Human Nature* (New York: Penguin, 1976); *Religions, Values and Peak Experiences* (New York: Penguin, 1970); *Toward a Psychology of Being* (New York: D. Van Nostrand, 1968).

27. Cited with her permission.

28. Maslow, *Farther Reaches*, 102.

29. Cited with his permission.

30. Jonathan Haidt. "Elevation and the Positive Psychology of Morality," in *Flourishing: Positive Psychology and the Life Well-Lived*, eds. Corey L. M. Keyes and Jonathan

Haidt (Washington, D.C.: American Psychological Association, 2003), 275–89.

31. D. J. Moores, ed., *Wild Poets of Ecstasy: An Anthology of Ecstatic Verse* (Nevada City, CA: Pelican Pond, 2011).

32. D. J. Moores, *The Ecstatic Poetic Tradition: A Study of the Ancients through Rumi, Wordsworth, Whitman, Dickinson, and Tagore* (Jefferson, NC: McFarland, 2014).

33. Cited in Allan Kellehear, *Experiences Near Death: Beyond Medicine and Religion* (New York: Oxford University Press, 1996), 62.

34. William Cowper, *The Complete Poetical Works of William Cowper* (Charleston, SC: Forgotten Books, 2012).

35. Thomas Lewis, Fari Amini, and Richard Lannon, *A General Theory of Love* (New York: Random House, 2000), 120.

36. Sigmund Freud, *Civilzation and Its Discontents*, trans. James Strachey (New York: Norton, 1989), 12–13.

37. Fredrickson, *Positivity*, 197.

38. Paul Ricoeur, *Freud and Philosophy: An Essay on Interpretation* (New Haven, CT: Yale University Press, 1970), 44.

39. See James Pawelski, *The Dynamic Individualism of William James* (Albany: State University of New York Press, 2007).

40. See Adam Potkay, *The Passion for Happiness: Samuel Johnson and David Hume* (Ithaca, NY: Cornell University Press, 2000); *Wordsworth's Ethics* (Baltimore: Johns Hopkins University Press, 2012).

41. The term *new formalism* was first used by Wolfson's critics, and, unfortunately, the label stuck.

42. See Susan Wolfson, *Formal Charges: The Shaping of Poetry in British Romanticism* (Stanford, CA: Stanford University Press, 1999).

43. See James Engell, *Forming the Critical Mind* (Cambridge, MA: Harvard University Press, 1989); *The Creative Imagination: Enlightenment to Romanticism* (Cambridge, MA: Harvard University Press, 1981).

44. See James Engell, *The Committed Word: Literature and Public Values* (University Park: Pennsylvania State University Press, 1999).

45. See D. J. Moores, *Mystical Discourse in Wordsworth and Whitman: A Transatlantic Bridge* (Dudley, MA: Peeters, 2006).

46. See D. J. Moores, *The Dark Enlightenment: Jung, Romanticism and the Repressed Other* (Madison, NJ: Fairleigh Dickinson University Press, 2010).

47. See D. J. Moores, ed., *Wild Poets of Ecstasy: An Anthology of Ecstatic Verse* (Nevada City, CA: Pelican Pond Press, 2011); D.J. Moores, *The Ecstatic Poetic Tradition: A Study of the Ancients through Rumi, Wordsworth, Whitman, Dickinson, and Tagore* (Jefferson, NC: McFarland, 2014).

48. See James Pawleski and D. J. Moores, eds., *The Eudaimonic Turn: Well-Being in Literary Studies* (Madison, NJ: Fairleigh Dickinson University Press, 2012).

49. Rita Felski, *Uses of Literature* (Oxford: Blackwell, 2008); "Suspicious Minds," *Poetics Today* 32:2 (2011): 217.

50. Heather Love, "Close but not Deep: Literary Ethics and the Descriptive Turn," *New Literary History* 41.2 (2010): 388.

51. Stephen Best and Sharon Marcus, "The Way We Read Now," *Representations* 108 (2009): 1–21.

52. Charles Altieri, *The Particulars of Rapture: An Aesthetics of the Affects* (Ithaca, NY: Cornell University Press, 2003).

53. Philip Fisher, *Wonder, the Rainbow, and the Aesthetics of Rare Experiences* (Cambridge, MA: Harvard University Press, 2003).

54. Vivasvan Soni, *Mourning Happiness* (Ithaca, NY: Cornell University Press, 2010).

55. M.M. Bakhtin and P.N. Medvedev, *The Formal Method in Literary Scholarship*, trans. A.J. Wehrle (Baltimore: Johns Hopkins University Press, 1978), 37, 38.

56. For a more complete discussion, see the following works: Janice Radway, *A Feeling for Books: The Book-of-the-Month Club, Literary Taste, and Middle-Class Desire* (Chapel Hill: University of North Carolina Press, 1997); Jane F. Thrailkill, *Affecting Fictions* (Cambridge, MA: Harvard University Press, 2007).

Cycle 3 Notes

1. Sâqi: one who pours the wine, usually an attractive, sometimes Christian young boy or girl, whose beauty the Sufi poets often extol in erotic imagery.

2. Katydid: male grasshopper that produces a characteristic song.

3. Daintree: a rainforest in Australia or a perhaps a tree in such a forest.

Cycle 4 Notes

1. heft: to lift something in order to estimate its weight.

2. Hecate: ancient Mediterranean goddess associated with witchcraft, herbology, and the moon.

3. Astarte: ancient Mediterranean and Near Eastern goddess associated with fertility, sexuality, and war.

Cycle 5 Notes

1. Tirzah: early capital of the Northern Kingdom.
2. circummortal: a word Herrick likely coined to designate that which wraps around something.
3. *Via Lactea*: Milky Way.
4. Ganges: famous, sacred river of India.
5. Humber: an estuary in Northeast England.
6. slow-chapt pow'r: the power of his slowly moving jaws.
7. 'Casta et Pudica': chaste and modest.
8. votaress: a female votary, or one who is bound by vows to live a religious life.

Cycle 6 Notes

1. Orinda: an appellation of Katherine Phillips, a celebrated seventeenth-century English poet and translator. Phillips blended metaphysical ideas with cavalier attitudes, attracting the praise of notable contemporaries such as Henry Vaughn.
2. Philomela: an Athenian princess who was brutally raped by her brother-in-law but later avenged and changed into a nightingale.
3. Parnassus: a mountain in central Greece near Delphi. The term has come to be associated with poets and poetry, and it can be used to designate a collection of poetry or a space in which poets write.
4. Maenad: a female follower of Dionysus, the god of ecstasy. Maenads are often depicted as being raving mad and sometimes violent.
5. Baiae's Bay: Underwater Roman ruins located at the northern end of the Gulf of Naples.
6. George Sand: the male pseudonym of the female French writer Lucile Aurore Dupin Dudevant.
7. Charon: the ferryman of classical mythology who ushered the souls of the dead across the river Styx in the underworld.
8. Petit-Poucet: a diminutive French fairy tale character who saves his brothers and himself from abandonment in the forest by leaving a trail of pebbles, which they follow home.
9. Ursa Major: the Great Bear constellation in the north containing the stars that form the Big Dipper.
10. "Steal away to Jesus": a Negro Spiritual song of unknown authorship. The other titles mentioned in the poem are also Negro Spirituals.
11. empyrean: relating to the heavens, the firmament.

12. Satyr: half-human/half-goat woodland deity found in the train of Dionysus.

Cycle 7 Notes

1. Tyrian hue: royal purple.
2. Nereid: sea-nymphs of Greek mythology.
3. Sophists: ancient Greek philosophers criticized for specious reasoning.
4. dell: small wooded valley.
5. phlegm: one of Hippocrates' four bodily humours, the balance of which was believed to control an individual's physical and emotional state. Phlegmatic people are relaxed and quiet.
6. Rhodora: North American shrub whose flowers bloom in the spring before its leaves.
7. hieing: hurrying.
8. rill: small rivulet or brook.
9. transept: any transverse part of the body of a church, usually crossing the nave, at right angles, at the entrance to the choir.
10. quire: a section of printed pages in proper sequence after folding.
11. Accouche! Accouchez!: inflections of the French word *accoucher*, which means to give birth.

Cycle 8 Notes

1. Pantisocracy: the term coined by Coleridge and Robert Southey to describe the egalitarian society they planned to build in America on the banks of the Susquehanna River.
2. Vita Nuova: new life.

Cycle 9 Notes

1. amaze: bewilder.
2. Ancient Greek honors bestowed on those who achieved excellence in the military (palm), civic service (oak), and poetry (bays).
3. here below: on earth.
4. white nor red: colors conventionally used by poets to signify beauty in the object of romantic love.
5. still: always.
6. curious: exquisite.
7. In the sixteenth century it was believed that the creatures of the ocean mirrored those on land in a one-for-one correspondence. The Neoplatonic suggestion here is that the mind contains correspondences to all things in the cosmos.
8. vest: garment, clothing.
9. whets: preens.

10. dial: presumably, the garden is manicured in the shape of a sun-dial.
11. appassionato: impassioned.
12. dingle: a deep narrow cliff between hills.

Cycle 10 Notes

1. Bacchic Song: Bacchus, the Greek name for Dionysus adopted by Romans. Ironically, this poem is addressed to Apollo, the god of reason, muted emotions, and poetry. In *The Birth of Tragedy* Nietzsche famously contrasted the Apolline with the Dionysiac.
2. sun: a reference to Apollo, the son of Zeus and Leto the swan, who is associated with the sun after the fall of Hyperion and the other Titans.
3. empyreal: relating to the heavens.
4. For auld lang syne: (Scottish) the days of long ago.
5. Danse Russe: French for Russian dance. Perhaps the poem is so titled because Russians are sometimes known for wildness in their (sometimes intoxicated) revelries.
6. Mariposa: (Spanish) butterfly.
7. petrels: any of numerous, tube-nosed seabirds of the families Procellariidae, Hydrobatidae, and Pelecanoididae.
8. bogart: hippie slang for not sharing marijuana, used commonly as a verb but also as a noun.
9. sepals: the specialized leaves forming the calyx, or green outer whorl, of a flower.
10. euonymous: a spindly tree, shrub, or vine native to eastern Asia; its wing-like branches have opposing leaves and bear green or purple flowers.
11. Balder: in Norse mythology, Balder, the second son of Odin, was well-loved for his graciousness and purity of character. The young god had a prophetic dream detailing his death, which prompted Loki, the mischief-maker, to craft a spear laced with magical herbs to assassinate Balder. Loki's sinister intentions came to fruition when Balder's blind brother, Höðr inadvertently killed the well-loved god with the spear.

Cycle 11 Notes

1. Al-Khidr and Elijah are mythological characters in Islam believed to have achieved physical immorality because of their noble deeds.
2. Jove: Jupiter, Zeus.
3. inmates: inhabitants.
4. "In all parts of the kingdom these films

are called *strangers* and supposed to portend the arrival of some absent friend." (Coleridge's note).
5. Helen: Helen of Troy, whose beautiful face is said to have launched the Trojan War.
6. Aphrodite.
7. Hephaestis, Aphrodite's husband. In multiple myths he is a lame-legged craftsman.

Cycle 12 Notes

1. Yah: A form of the Hebrew name, YHVH, or Yahweh (God).
2. To: that is, compared to.
3. private amity: friendship.
4. sphere: universe.
5. kind: kin.
6. Danae: Zeus impregnated Danae by transforming himself into a shower of golden rain, the result of which was the birth of Perseus.
7. Ganymede: a beautiful Trojan warrior whom Zeus lusted after and made his cup-bearer.
8. maya: Hindus believe the material world is an illusion, the realization of which leads to spiritual freedom, or *jivan mukti*.

Cycle 13 Notes

1. partial: biased.
2. despite: contempt.
3. glancing: gleaming.
4. meaner: humbler.
5. sued: sought.
6. Cant: personification of insincere or hypocritical language about high ideals or religious piety.
7. Ermine: a luxurious garment with a spotted pattern created from the white and black pelts of many small weasels. Because of the exorbitant cost of the tiny animals, ermine came to symbolize royalty.
8. pelf: wealth or riches regarded with contempt or acquired by condemnable means.
9. Invictus: Latin for unconquerable or undefeated.
10. Dulce et decorum est / Pro patria mori: (Latin) it is sweet and decorous to die for one's country.

Cycle 14 Notes

1. delire: delirium or madness.
2. antiphon: choral response.

Sources and Credits

Addison, Joseph. "Ode" from *Selections from the Writings of Joseph Addison*. New York: Ginn, 1917.

Aiken, Conrad. "Music I Heard with You" from *The New Poetry: An Anthology*. Ed. Harriet Monroe. New York Macmillan, 1917.

Angelou, Maya. "Woman Me" from *Oh Pray My Wings Are Gonna Fit Me Well*. Copyright 1975 by Maya Angelou. Used by permission of Random House, and imprint and division of Random House LLC, and Little, Brown. All rights reserved.

'Attar, Farduddin. "I Shall Be Drunk Tonight" and "How Can Sober Reason Understand" are from *Islamic Mystical Poetry: Sufi Verse from the Early Mystics to Rumi*. Edited by Mahmood Jamal. New York: Penguin Classics, 2009. Selections and introduction copyright Mahmood Jamal, 2009. Translations copyright Mahmood Jamal, 2009. Reproduced by permission of Penguin Books Ltd.

Balmont, C.D. "With My Aspiration I Caught...," "The Law of Life," and "The Sunbeam" are original translations (from Russian) by Tatsiana DeRosa.

Barbauld, Anna Laetitia. "The Rights of Woman" from *The Works of Anna Laetitia Barbauld*. New York: Longman, 1825.

Berry, Wendell. "I Go Among Trees and Sit Still." Copyright 1998 by Wendell Berry from *A Timbered Choir: The Sabbath Poems, 1979–1997*. Used by permission of Counterpoint.

Biely, Andrei. "On the Mountains" first appeared in *Urn* (1909) and is here translated from Russian by Tatsiana DeRosa.

Blake, William. "A Cradle Song," "The Echoing Green," "Eternity," "The Divine Image," and "Infant Joy" from *The Poetical Works of William Blake*. London: George Bell, 1890.

Bleecker, Ann Eliza. "On the Immensity of Creation" and "On the Religion of Nature" from *The Posthumous Works of Ann Eliza Bleecker, in Prose and Verse*. New York: T. and J. Swords, 1793.

Bradstreet, Anne. "Before the Birth of One of Her Children" and "To My Dear and Loving Husband" from *The Complete Works of Anne Bradstreet*. New York: Twayne, 1981.

Brontë, Anne. "In a Wood on A Windy Day" from *The Complete Poems of Anne Brontë*. London: Hodder and Stoughton, 1910 [University of Michigan Library, 1920].

Brontë, Charlotte. "Life" from *The Poems of Charlotte Brontë (Currer Bell)*. New York: White, Stokes, and Allen, 1883.

Brontë, Emily. "A Daydream" and "A Little While, A Little While" from *The Complete Poems of Emily Jane Brontë*. New York: Columbia University Press, 1995.

Brooke, Rupert. "The Soldier" from *Selected Poems: Rupert Brooke*. Sidgwick & Jackson, 1917.

Browning, Elizabeth Barrett. "VII," "X," "XXII," "To George Sand: A Desire," and "To Flush, My Dog" from *The Complete Poetical Works of Elizabeth Barrett Browning*. Boston: Houghton Mifflin,1900.

Browning, Robert. "Meeting at Night" from *Complete Works: Robert Browning*. New York: Kelmscott Society, 1898.

Bryosov, V. Y. "I" and "Pompeian Woman" are original translations (from Russian) by Tatsiana DeRosa.

Bukowski, Charles. "Mind and Heart" and "No Leaders, Please" from *Come On In!* San Francisco: HarperCollins, 2006. Copyright 2006 by Linda Lee Bukowski. Reprinted by permission of HarperCollins Publishers. "The Shower" from *Mockingbird Wish Me Luck*. San Francisco: HarperCollins, 1972. Copyright 1972 by Charles Bukowski. Reprinted by permission of HarperCollins Publishers.

Burns, Robert. "A Red, Red Rose" from *The Complete Poetical Works of Robert Burns*. New York: Appleton, 1844.

Byron. George Gordon (Lord Byron). "XIII," "LXXV," "LXXXVIII," "XCIII," and "When a Man Hath No Freedom to Fight for at Home" from *Byron's Poetry & Prose*. Ed. Alice Levine. New York: Norton, 2009.

Carew, Thomas. "Boldness in Love" and "Persuasions to Enjoy" from *The Poems of Thomas Carew*. New York: Scribner's, 1899.

Chinmoy, Kumar Ghose. "Obstructions loom large within and without" from *Compassion-Sea and Satisfaction-Waves*. Jamaica, NY: Agni Press, 1992. "The Answer" from *Ten Thousand Flower-Flames*. Jamaica, NY: Agni Press, 1981. "Start A New Beginning" from *You And I Are God*. Jamaica, NY: Agni Press,1973. "Not word, but work" from *The Garden of Love-Light*. Puerto Rico: Aum Press, 1973. "There Was A Time" from *My Flute*. Jamaica, NY: Agni Press, 1972. "Eternal Happiness" from *Seventy-Seven Thousand Service-Trees*. Jamaica, NY: Agni Press, 2006. "Aspiration" from *Seventy-Seven Thousand Service-Trees*. Jamaica, NY: Agni Press, 2004. All poems used with permission from the Sri Chinmoy Centre.

Clark, Kevin. "Sixties Noir" and "Le Secret—after Rodin" are from *Self-Portrait with Expletives*. Baton Rouge: Louisiana State

University Press, 2010. Used with the author's permission.

Clare, John. "Song: Love Lives Beyond the Tomb" from *Complete Works of John Clare*. Delphi Classics, 2013.

Coleridge, Samuel Taylor. "Frost at Midnight," "On Receiving a Letter Informing Me of the Birth of a Son," "Pantisocracy," "This Lime-Tree Bower My Prison," "To Nature," and "To a Friend Who Asked, How I Felt When the Nurse First Presented My Infant to Me" from *The Poetry of Samuel Taylor Coleridge*. New York: Scribner's, 1898.

Crane, Stephen. "Behold the Grave of a Wicked Man," "I Walked in a Desert," "The Impact of a Dollar upon the Heart," "A Man Saw a Ball of Gold in the Sky," and "Once There Came a Man" from *Stephen Crane: Complete Poems*. Library of America, 2011.

Cummings, E. E. "you shall above all things be glad and young" copyright 1938, © 1996, 1991 by the Trustees for the E.E. Cummings Trust; "let it go—the" copyright 1944, © 1972, 1991 by the Trustees for the E.E. Cummings Trust; "I thank you God for most this amazing" copyright 1950, © 1978, 1991 by the Trustees for the E.E. Cummings Trust, © 1979 by George James Firmage; "I love you much(most beautiful darling)" copyright 1958, 1986, 1991 by the Trustees for the E.E. Cummings Trust; from *E. E. Cummings: Complete Poems, 1904—1962* by E.E. Cummings, edited by George J. Firmage. New York: Liveright, 2013. Used by permission of Liveright Publishing Corporation.

Dante. "So Kind and Honest She Seems" is an original translation (from Italian) by Gabriella Basile.

Davis, Daniel Webster. "I Can Trust" from *'Weh down souf*. Cleveland: Helman-Taylor, 1897.

Dickinson, Emily. "The brain is wider than the sky," "Dare you see a soul at the white heat?" from *The Complete Poems of Emily Dickinson*. Ed. Martha Bianchi. Boston: Little, Brown, 1924.

_____. "Exhiliration Is the Breeze," "Exultation is the Going," "Hope is the thing with feathers," "Some Keep the Sabbath Going to Church," "Water, is taught by thirst," and "Wild Nights—Wild Nights!" from *The Complete Poems of Emily Dickinson*. Ed. Thomas Johnson. New York: Back Bay, 1976.

Donne, John. "Death Be Not Proud" from *The Complete Poems of John Donne*. Fuller Worthies, 1872.

Doolittle, Hilda. "Holy Satyr" and "Moonrise" from *H. D. Complete Poems: 1912–1944*. Ed. Louis L. Martz. New York: New Directions, 1986.

Dunbar, Paul Lawrence. "A Choice," "Dawn," "He Had His Dream," and "Sympathy" from *The Complete Poems of Paul Lawrence Dunbar*. Dodd & Mead, 1896.

Emerson, Ralph Waldo. "Bacchus," "Give All to Love," and "The Rhodora" from *The Works of Ralph Waldo Emerson: Poems*. Boston: Houghton Mifflin, 1895.

Field, Edward. "A Journey" from *After the Fall, Poems Old and New*. Pittsburgh: University of Pittsburgh Press, 2007. Copyright 2007 by Edward Field. Reprinted by permission of the University of Pittsburgh Press.

Foscolo, Ugo. "To Evening" is an original translation (from Italian) by Gabriella Basile.

Frost, Robert. "Pan with Us" and "The Tuft of Flowers" from *A Boy's Will*. New York: David Nutt, 1913.

Ginsberg, Allen. "Vision 1948" from *Collected Poems 1947–1980*. San Francisco: HarperCollins, 1984. Copyright 1948 by Allen Ginsberg. Copyright renewed. Reprinted by permission of HarperCollins Publishers / Copyright 2006 by Allen Ginsberg LLC, used throughout the United Kingdom and British Commonwealth by permission of The Wyle Agency LLC.

Giovanni, Nikki. "Winter Poem" from *My House*. San Francisco: HarperCollins, 2000. Copyright 1972 by Nikki Giovanni, renewed 2000 by Nikki Giovanni. Reprinted by permission of HarperCollins Publishers.

"Go Down, Moses" from www.negrospirituals.com.

Goethe, Johann Wolfgang von. All poems are original translations (from German) by Gert Niers.

Gosse, Edmund. "The Tide of Love" from *The Collected Poems of Edmund Gosse*. London: Heinemann, 1911.

Gray, Thomas. "Ode on the Death of a Favorite Cat" from *The Poetical Works of Thomas Gray*. London: George Bell, 1885.

Hardy, Thomas. "The Darkling Thrush" from *Selected Poems of Thomas Hardy*. London: Macmillan, 1916.

Harjo, Joy. "I Give You Back" from *She Had Some Horses*. New York: W.W. Norton & Company. Copyright 1983 by Joy Harjo. Used by permission of W.W. Norton & Company, Inc.

Harper, Frances E. W. "Bury Me in a Free Land" and "Learning to Read" from *Com-*

plete Poems of Frances E. W. Harper. New York: Oxford University Press, 1988.

Herbert, George. "Man" from *The Complete Works in Verse and Prose of George Herbert.* Ed. Alexander Grosart. Herbert Weir Smith. 1874.

Hebrew Bible. All selections are taken from http://www.publicdomainbibles.com/.

Henley, William Ernest. "Invictus" from *Poems by William Ernest Henley.* London: David Nutt, 1919.

Herrick, Robert. "To the Virgins, to Make Much of Time," "Upon Jack and Jill. Epigram," "Upon Julia's Breasts," and "Upon the Nipples of Julia's Breast" from *The Complete Poems of Robert Herrick.* London: Chatto and Windus, 1876.

Hirshfield, Jane. "Against Certainty" [11 l.] and "The Dead Do Not Want Us Dead" [8 l.] from *After: Poems by Jane Hirshfield.* San Francisco: HarperCollins, 2006. Copyright 2006 by Jane Hirshfield. Reprinted by permission of HarperCollins Publishers / Reproduced in the UK with permission of Bloodaxe Books on behalf of the author.

Hopkins, Gerard Manley. "Binsey Poplars," "God's Grandeur," "Spring," "Spring and Fall," "The Starlight Night," and "The Windhover" from *Poems from Gerard Manley Hopkins.* Ed. Robert Bridges. London: Humphrey Milford, 1918.

Horton, George Moses. "Imploring to Be Resigned at Death" from *African-American Poetry: An Anthology, 1773–1927.* Ed. Joan R. Sherman. Mineola, NY: Dover, 1997.

Housman, A. E. "XXXII," "XXXVIII," and "Lovliest of Trees" from *The Shropshire Lad.* London: Kegan, Trench, Trubner. 1896.

Hughes, Langston. "The Negro Speaks of Rivers" from *Crisis*: June 1921. "Mother to Son" and "Negro" from *Crisis*: December 1922.

Huxley, Aldous. "Scenes of the Mind" from *The Defeat of Youth and Other Poems.* Oxford: Blackwell, 1918.

Ivanov, Vyacheslav Ivanovich. "Alpine Horn" is an original translation (from Russian) by Tatsiana DeRosa.

Johnson, Fenton. "Children of the Sun" from *The Book of American Negro Poetry.* Ed. James Weldon Johnson. New York: Harcourt, 1922.

Johnson, James Weldon. "O Black and Unknown Bards" from *Fifty Years and Other Poems.* Boston: Cornhill, 1917.

Joseph, Allison. "Learning to Laugh" from *Passionate Hearts: The Poetry of Sexual Love.* Ed. Wendy Maltz. Novato: New World Library, 1996. Used with permission.

Joyce, James. "III," "X," and "XX" from *Chamber Music.* Dublin: Elkin Matthews, 1907.

Juan de la Cruz. "In Pursuit of an Amorous Encounter" and "Without a Place and with a Place" are original translations (from Spanish) by Sandra Kunanele.

Kabir. "IV," "XIV," "XVI," "XXVIII," "XLVI," "LVI," and "LXX," from *Songs of Kabir.* Trans. Rabindranth Tagore. 1915.

Kenny, Adele. "Like I Said," "Of Other," "Scenes of Mind," "Somehow the Angel," "Survivor," and "This Living" from *What Matters.* New York: Welcome Rain Publishers, 2011. Used with the permission of the author and the publisher.

Kinnell, Galway. "After Making Love We Hear Footsteps" from *Mortal Acts, Mortal Words.* New York: Houghton Mifflin, 2008. Copyright 1980, renewed 2008 by Galway Kinnell. Reprinted by permission of Houghton Mifflin Harcourt Publishing Company. All rights reserved.

Kunitz, Stanley. "Touch Me" from *The Collected Poems: Stanley Kunitz.* New York: W. W. Norton, 1995. Copyright 1995 by Stanley Kunitz. Used by permission of W.W. Norton & Company, Inc.

Laux, Dorianne. "The Orgasms of Organisms" from *Smoke.* Rochester, NY: BOA Editions, 2000. Copyright 2000 by Dorianne Laux; "The Thief" from *What We Carry.* Rochester, NY: BOA Editions, 1994. Copyright 1994 by Dorianne Laux. Both reprinted with the permission of The Permissions Company, Inc., on behalf of BOA Editions, Ltd., www.boaeditions.org.

Lawrence, D. H. "Glorie de Dijon" from *Look, We Have Come Through.* New York: Huebsch, 1917; "Mystery" from *Amores: Poems.* New York: Huebsch, 1916; "Piano" from *New Poems.* New York: Huebsch, 1920.

Leopardi, Giacomo. "Here the Waves Murmur" and "The Infinite" are original translations (from Italian) by Gabriella Basile.

Levertov, Denise. "Variation on a Theme by Rilke (The Book of Hours, Book I, Poem 1, Stanza 1)" from *Breathing the Water.* New York: New Directions, 1987. Copyright 1987 by Denise Levertov. Reprinted by permission of New Directions Publishing Corp.

Longfellow, Henry Wadsworth. "The Bridge" from *Poems by Henry Wadsworth Longfellow.* Boston: Houghton Mifflin, 1863.

Lovelace, Richard. "To Lucasta, Going to the Wars" from *Lucasta: The Poems of Richard Lovelace.* J. R. Smith, 1864.

Lowell, Amy. "A Decade" from *Picture of the Floating World.* New York: Macmillan, 1919.

Loy, Mina. "There is No Life or Death" from *Camera Work*, January 1914.

Marvell, Andrew. "The Garden" and "To His Coy Mistress" from *Andrew Marvell: Complete Poetry*. London: J. M. Dent, 1984.

McClellan, George Marion. "A September Night" from *African-American Poetry: An Anthology, 1773–1927*. Ed. Joan R. Sherman. Mineola, NY: Dover, 1997.

McCrae, John. "In Flanders Fields" from *In Flanders Fields, and Other Poems*. New York: Schirmer, 1918.

McKay, Claude. "America" and "If We Must Die" from *Claude McKay: Complete Poems*. Ed. William Maxwell. University of Illinois Press, 2004.

Micheline, Jack. "Poem to the Freaks." Reprinted with permission granted by the Jack Micheline Foundation.

Millay, Edna St. Vincent. "God's World" from *Renascence and Other Poems*. New York: Harper, 1917; "Mariposa" from *Second April*. New York: Mitchell Kennerly, 1921.

Moore, Thomas. "Believe me, If All Those Endearing Young Charms" from *The Poetical Works of Thomas Moore*. London: Spottiswoodes and Shaw, 1853.

Neruda, Pablo. "Caballos" from *Estravagario*; "Sonnet XII" from *Cien sonetos de amor*; "Oda a la pereza" from *Odas elementales*; "La palabra" from *Plenos poderes*. All poems are original translations (from Spanish) by Sandra Kunanele. Copyright Fundación Pablo Neruda, 2014. Permission is granted by Fundación Pablo Neruda through Angencia Literaria Carmen Balcells S. A.

Norse, Harold. "Let Go and Feel Your Nakedness" from *In the Hub of the Fiery Force*. Boston: Perseus, 2003. Copyright 2003. Reprinted by permission of Da Capo Press, a member of the Perseus Books Group.

Olds, Sharon. "Full Summer" from *Strike Sparks: Selected Poems, 1980–2002*. New York: Knopf/Random House, 2004. Copyright 2004 by Sharon Olds. Used by permission of Alfred A. Knopf, an imprint of the Knopf Doubleday Publishing Group, a division of Random House LLC. All rights reserved.

Owen, Wilfred. "Anthem for a Doomed Youth" and "Dulce Et Decorum Est" from *Poems by Wilfred Owen*. New York: Viking, 1921.

Penn, Emily Lewis. "Nachtmusik Sonnet"; "Stilettos." Used with permission.

"Poem to Ease Birth" from *Ancient Nahuatl Poetry*. Translation by Daniel G. Brinton. Philadelphia: D.G. Brinton, 1887.

Pushkin, Alexander. "Bacchic Song," "God, Don't Let Me Lose My Mind," "Oh, My Maiden Rose, I Am in Shackles," and "To …" are original translations by Tatsiana DeRosa.

Rich, Susanna. "Winter Trees"; "Laurels on the Appalachian Trail"; "Finding Raspberries by the Road"; "Walking Holly Down a Wooded Lane." Used with permission.

Rimbaud, Arthur. "My Bohemia" is an original translation (from French) by Kelly Johnson.

Robinson, Edwin Arlington. "Mr. Flood's Party" from *Collected Poems: Edwin Arlington Robinson*. New York: Macmillan, 1922.

Rossetti, Dante Gabriel. "Heart's Compass," "Love's Testament," "Nuptial Sleep," "A Sonnet," and "Silent Noon" from *Dante Gabriel Rossetti: Collected Poetry & Prose*. Ed. Jerome McGann. New Haven, CT: Yale University Press, 2003.

Rumi, Jalâl–Din. "With each new breath"; "Once More We Come Like Dust"; "Top of the morning"; "Heart"; "Bliss" from *Rumi: Past and Present*. Trans. Franklin Lewis. London: Oneworld Publications, 2007. Used with permission.

Sa'di. "The Throne of the Heart" from *Islamic Mystical Poetry: Sufi Verse from the Early Mystics to Rumi*. Edited by Mahmood Jamal. New York: Penguin Classics, 2009. Selections and introduction copyright Mahmood Jamal, 2009. Translations copyright Mahmood Jamal, 2009. Reproduced by permission of Penguin Books Ltd.

Sassoon, Sigfried. "Everyone Sang" from *War Poems*. Heinemann, 1919.

Shah, Baba Bulleh. "He Who Is Stricken by Love" from *Islamic Mystical Poetry: Sufi Verse from the Early Mystics to Rumi*. Edited by Mahmood Jamal. New York: Penguin Classics, 2009. Selections and introduction copyright Mahmood Jamal, 2009. Translations copyright Mahmood Jamal, 2009. Reproduced by permission of Penguin Books Ltd.

Shelley, Percy Bysshe. "Ode to the West Wind," "To Constantia," and "To a Skylark" from *The Poetical Works of Percy Bysshe Shelley*. 3 vols. London: Gibbings, 1894.

Snyder, Joyce. "Change"; "Balance"; "I Came Here to Fly"; "Action"; "A Perfect Poem." Used with permission.

Spanton, Susannah. "Moments." Used with permission.

Spender, Stephen. "VI"; "I Think Continually of Those Who Were Truly Great" from *New Collected Poems: Stephen Spender*.

Faber & Faber, 2004. Copyright 2004 by Stephen Spender. Reprinted by kind permission of the Estate of Stephen Spender.

Stickney, Trumbull. "Live Blindly" from *The Poems of Trumbull Stickney*. Boston: Houghton Mifflin, 1905.

Tagore, Rabindranath. "20," "31," "57," "59," "72," "78," and "95" from *Gitanjali: Song Offerings*. New York: Macmillan, 1914.

Tasso, Torquato. "The Woods and the Rivers Fall Silent" is an original translation (from Italian) by Gabriella Basile.

Teasdale, Sara. "The Answer" from *Rivers to the Sea*. New York: Macmillan, 1915; "Peace" from *Love Songs*. New York: Macmillan, 1917.

Tennyson, Lord Alfred. "Come Down, O Maid, from Yonder Mountain Height" from *Tennyson's Complete Poems*. London: Donohue, Henneberry,1800.

Thomas, Dylan. "Fern Hill" from *The Poems of Dylan Thomas*. New York: New Directions, 1939. Copyright 1945 by The Trustees for the Copyrights of Dylan Thomas; "The Force That Through the Green Fuse Drives the Flower" from *The Poems of Dylan Thomas*. New York: New Directions, 1939. Copyright 1939 by New Directions Publishing Corp. Both poems reprinted with permission from David Higham Associates and New Directions Publishing Corp.

Thomson, James. "The Bridge" from *The Oxford Book of Victorian Verse*. Oxford: n.p. 1922.

Thoreau, Henry David. "Independence" and "Nature" from *The Writings of Henry David Thoreau*. Boston: Houghton Mifflin, 1906.

Thornton, Brian. "Erbil Libre—Erbil, Iraq" and "The Paradox of Peripheral Vision." Used with permission.

Traherne, Thomas. "love," "The Rapture," "To the Same Purpose," and "Wonder" from *The Poetical Works of Thomas Traherne*. London: Dobell, 1903.

Turell, Jane Colman. "To My Muse..." from *The American Female Poets*. Ed. Caroline May. Lindsay & Blakiston, 1854.

Vaughan, Henry. "Peace" and "The Morning Watch" from *The Poems of Henry Vaughan, Silurist*. New York: Scribner's, 1896.

Verlaine, Paul. "Listen to the Song So Sweet" is an original translation (from French) by Kelly Johnson.

Webster, Rachael Jamison. "Through Hooded Clouds Untranslatable, Once"; "Late September" "Kauai"; and "Cream of the Pour is the Cream of Skin Thickening" from *September*. Evanston, IL: TriQuarterly Books/Northwestern University Press, 2013. Copyright 2013 by Rachel Jamison Webster. All rights reserved. Used with permission. "Dance, Baby"; and "Neruda" used with permission.

Weeks, Daniel. "A Tenderness Has Come"; "He Lay Down in Green Timothy"; and "Long Branch" used with permission.

Weisbrot, Bhikshuni. "Daintree"; "Spring Again" from *A Sense of Place*. Treadwell, NY: Bright Hill Press, 2007; "Autumnal Revival"; "Meditation"; "The Nature of Light"; "I Just Want to Be Happy"; "Safety Harbor"; and "The Play" used with permission.

Wetta, J. C. Augustine. "Running down Straight Street" used with permission.

Whitman, Walt. "The Base of All Metaphysics," "Beautiful Women," "A Clear Midnight," "A Glimpse," "I Am He That Aches with Love," "I Sing the Body Electric," "Laws for Creations," "Me Imperturbe," "Miracles," "Mother and Babe," "O Me! O Life!" "On the Beach at Night Alone," "One Hour to Madness and Joy," "One's-Self I Sing," "Over the Carnage Rose Prophetic a Voice," "Roots and Leaves Themselves Alone," "A Song of the Rolling Earth," "Sparkles from the Wheel," "That Music Always Round Me," "That Shadow My Likeness," "There Was a Child Went Forth," "To a Common Prostitute," "To One Shortly to Die," "To You [13]," "To You [175]," "We Two Boys Together Clinging," "We Two, How Long We Were Fool'd," "When I Heard the Learn'd Astronomer," and "When I Read the Book" from *Leaves of Grass*. David McKay, 1894.

Whittier, John Greenleaf. "For Righteousness' Sake," "The Worship of Nature," and "What The Birds Said" from *The Poetical Works of John Greenleaf Whittier, Complete*. London: Warwick House, 1874.

Wilcox, Ella Wheeler. "The Winds of Fate" from *World Voices*. New York: Hearst's International Library Company, 1916.

Wilde, Oscar. "In the Gold Room: A Harmony" and "Vita Nuovo" from *The Poems and Fairy Tales of Oscar Wilde*. New York: Modern Library, 1896.

Williams, William Carlos. "Danse Russe," "Dawn," and "Love Song" from *A Book of Poems: Al Que Quiere!* Boston: Four Seas, 1917.

Wordsworth, William. "Composed upon Westminster Bridge," "Expostulation and Reply," "I wandered lonely as a cloud," "It Is a Beauteous Evening, Calm and Free," "Lines Composed a Few miles above Tintern Abbey, on Revisiting the Banks of the Wye during a Tour," "My Heart Leaps Up," "Ode: Intimations of Immortality from

Recollections of Early Childhood," "Simon Lee, the Old Huntsman," and "The Tables Turned" from *The Complete Poetical Works of William Wordsworth*. New York: Thomas Crowell, 1892.

Yeats, W. B. "The Fiddler of Dooney," "The Lake Isle of Innisfree," "A Prayer for My Daughter," "A Prayer for My Son," and "The Song of Wandering Aengus" from *The Collected Poems of W. B. Yeats*. Wordsworth Poetry Library, 1994.

Yunus, Emre. "The Fleeting Life" is an original translation (from Turkish) by Melda Yildiz.

Index of First Lines

289

Index of Poets